ELMER ELLIS

Elmer Ellis, President of the University of Missouri

Elmer Ellis

Teacher
Scholar
and
Administrator

———————

UNIVERSITY OF MISSOURI PRESS

COLUMBIA

UNIVERSITY OF MISSOURI PRESS   •   COLUMBIA

Printed and Bound in the United States of America.

Preface

THIS book has been designed to present the personal, academic, and administrative career of our friend and teacher, Elmer Ellis. Part one contains three essays written by former students or colleagues. These include a short biographical sketch, a discussion of his teaching and writing, and an examination of his administrative career. In the second part, selections from some of Ellis' best writings are reprinted. Between 1946 and 1960 Elmer Ellis made a number of important addresses on different aspects of American education. Several of these speeches are included in part three.

On this, his sixtieth birthday, we are proud to recognize his outstanding achievements in, and contributions to, higher education in America. Moreover, we are deeply appreciative of his original and continued personal and professional interest in all of us. We hope that in some small way this volume will show our high esteem for him and his work.

Former students provided the publication cost and gave the manuscript to the University of Missouri Press which was established by President Ellis. Proceeds from the sale of this volume will be used to advance the publishing program of the Press.

July 27, 1961

Committee of Former Students

HOMER CLEVENGER
LOUIS G. GEIGER
WILLIAM A. SETTLE, JR., *Chairman*
GILBERT C. FITE, *Editor*

Table of Contents

THE CAREER OF ELMER ELLIS

A Biographical Portrait 1

Teacher and Scholar 33

Administrator 57

SELECTIONS FROM PUBLISHED WRITINGS

Selections from *Henry Moore Teller: Defender of the West* . . . 83

Selections from *Mr. Dooley's America:*
The Life of Finley Peter Dunne 139

"The Dilemma of the Social Studies Teacher" 159

Illustrations . . . . facing page 166

"Public Opinion and the Income Tax, 1860-1900" 173

"The Profession of Historian" 191

SELECTED SPEECHES, 1946-1960

The Social Studies Teacher and the World Crisis 215

The College of Liberal Arts 225

The Needs of Higher Education in Missouri 237

Responsibility for the Superior Student 245

The Role of Higher Education in Meeting the Teacher Shortage . 251

The Responsibility of the Educated 261

The State University 271

Remarks at the Dedication of the Harry S. Truman Library . . . 277

Crescendo in Higher Education 281

The Support of Higher Education in Missouri 291

THE
CAREER
OF
ELMER
ELLIS

1

A Biographical Portrait

S TUDENTS hurrying across the Red Campus of the University
of Missouri on their way to early morning classes are likely to
receive a friendly greeting from President Elmer Ellis, who is
walking at a leisurely pace the block from his home to his office
in Jesse Hall. Those who know the President most intimately
attribute his early morning calm to his habit of rising early and
thinking through the course of his activities for the day. Having
done so, he approaches his work with orderliness and certainty.
A retentive memory, the habit of facing issues before they reach
a stage of crisis, and a prodigious capacity for work promise well
for each day that lies ahead of him. As to his worries and personal
problems, he seldom speaks of them, even to his closest associates,
apparently because to him they are a natural and inevitable part
of life.

President Ellis is a graying man of average height and weight who dresses conservatively. Of all his physical characteristics, his eyes most accurately reflect his character. Ordinarily they express his basically friendly and sympathetic nature, but they can on occasion indicate withdrawal of interest in an idea or program being urged upon him, and when necessary they express a firm resolve. Observing him at age fifty-seven, a journalist reported:

> he is a patient, rather precise man with alert blue eyes and an easy manner. . . . Ellis is not a college president with an automatic handshake and a toothy smile who is likely to lead a pep rally cheer; neither is he a suave, fashion-plate type who would be expected to overwhelm alumni and others with immense charm. He is an earnest, plain-spoken man who appears before legislative committees, talks impressively and usually gets results.[1]

A deep respect and affection for all human personality has led the Ellises to take a personal interest in the lives and careers of students and associates. Students have been attracted to Ellis because they respect his ability and scholarly achievements, but that respect has generally ripened into a deep devotion. The Ellises have invited graduate students and their families into their home; they keep track of them when they leave the campus; and they take pleasure in their achievements. Few advisors of graduate students know so intimately the personal histories of their proteges as do the Ellises. Yet they have advised and consoled these students without demanding compliance with their own wishes. Even now, with the heavier duties of the presidency, the Ellises enjoy entertaining former students who visit Columbia. They have extended this same warmth and sympathy to colleagues and associates. By visits, letters, and with other evidences of their concern, the Ellises reach out to associates and friends in need of kindly attention.

Energetic and ambitious by nature, Ellis enjoys responsibility.

---

[1] James W. Scott in the *Kansas City Times*, September 5, 1958.

Although he has had moments of reluctance before relinquishing a current post to assume still more responsibility, he has never complained of the sacrifices which added responsibility has entailed. Instead, he has thoroughly enjoyed grappling with new problems and seeing projects with which he is connected move ahead. Moreover, he has confidence in himself in spite of his naturally easy manner.

During the course of his career, President Ellis has won the respect and admiration of many people. When the Board of Curators began looking for a successor to President Frederick A. Middlebush, a Columbia, Missouri, businessman wrote an unsolicited letter recommending Ellis for the post. Said he, "I have known the man for twenty to twenty-five years. I have never heard an uncomplimentary remark made about him—an enviable record for any man." Many others have commented to the same effect, judgments based on their observations of his character and actions. He has never been a candidate for a job in which another person is being removed against his will; his appointments have been to positions opened by voluntary retirement, death, or by expansion. Intrigue is abhorrent to him. He dislikes factions and cliques, and dislikes most of all those people who place an immoderate value on their services to others. He never gossips about another person, and those who carry malicious stories to him become uncomfortable in telling them. He respects the ability of others, is genuinely sincere in praising their achievements, and willingly helps them without calculating the possible advantages to himself in doing so. As a result, colleagues and associates are inclined to give him a full measure of devotion.

If Ellis has any fears about his own personality, they perhaps stem from his abhorrence of the possibility of his becoming a "stuffed shirt." As a university president, he has to preside at many formal ceremonies and occasionally to listen to unusually fulsome praise from a toastmaster. On one occasion, after sitting through such an ordeal, he remarked to a colleague that he felt

like an old railroad conductor who said to a prudish lady trying
to be sure that her ankles were covered when she mounted the
train steps, "Lady, move along; ankles ain't no treat to my eyes."

Still another factor in Ellis' acquisition of a wide circle of
friends and admirers has been his great range of interests. He is at
home with people from almost any occupation or state in life.
Businessmen like and respect him because he recognizes their
problems and is a good businessman in his own right. He makes
good financial investments and shops carefully and wisely when
buying for himself. Growing up in a small town, he knows something of the farmer's problems and of those of the wage earner.
Travel, wide reading, and experience in the academic world make
the Ellises delightful and understanding companions in university
circles.

In spite of his deep and liberal convictions, Ellis will probably
never be known as a crusader. Fundamentally, he believes in
working to achieve the possible. If that seems faint praise, it
must be remembered that he interprets the possible far more
courageously than most people would do. He has far more liking
for doers than for exhorters. He hates exploitation in any form,
and seeks to the best of his ability to widen the field of opportunity for all. Though his gift for conciliation may seem to overshadow his talent for advancing worthwhile goals, real progress
usually results from his position on issues. Few people have ever
seen him lose his temper. He welcomes advice, attempts to
carry through programs that have possibilities, and seldom dis-
misses an importunate adviser with a curt "No!" He will debate
a point to a reasonable degree, express his views, and then lapse
into silence. An occasional visitor to his office may leave thinking
that he has argued the President into acquiescence, but the temporary glow of triumph quickly gives way to the realization that
Ellis has said no.

For years his friends have tried to persuade him to take up a
hobby—golf, fishing, anything that will break his constant pace of

work. Fundamentally, however, his interest in people and in work constitutes his hobby. In the evening he enjoys dinner and a cocktail with other people, reading, and listening to good music. He has collections of old textbooks, of books in the field of American humor, and of musical records. Gilbert and Sullivan operas are his favorites among the latter. All such activities are hobbies to him; he seems incapable of compartmentalizing his life into separate categories such as hobbies, exercise, work, and so on. Work and play are intermingled in his busy world.

As a sixth child in a family of eleven children on the North Dakota frontier, Ellis grew up in a family that had no time to fret about the egos of the various members of the clan. At his birth on July 27, 1901, near Anamoose in McHenry County, North Dakota, his parents christened him Elmer, not bothering to supply him with a middle name. On at least one occasion as a youngster he seems to have felt neglected in that respect. One of his boyhood chums bore the elegant name of Clarence, which Ellis liked so much that he asked an understanding older friend to enter his name on some official roll as "Elmer Clarence Ellis." For a day or so he enjoyed the possession of a really distinguished middle name, only to have his pleasure marred by one of the temporary quarrels with his chum which characterize the course of childhood friendship. Before the tiff had healed Ellis asked his obliging older friend to shorten his name once again to Elmer Ellis, which has proved eminently satisfactory to him over the years. When he came to the University of Missouri campus to be interviewed as a prospective member of the staff, Professor Jonas Viles, then chairman of the history department, remarked to Ellis that he personally had never cared for the name Elmer. To which Ellis replied that Jonas had never been a favorite name of his. Perhaps a frank exchange of opinion served to inaugurate the working relationship between the two men which developed rapidly, for both of them were proud of the names they bore.

Ellis comes from American pioneer stock. His paternal grandfather, Levi Ellis, born in Maine, and his grandmother, Susan Young, born in New Hampshire, migrated in 1856 to Minnesota and settled on a farm in Winona County. After a few years the Levi Ellis family moved to Detroit Lakes in the same state, where their son, Thomas Clarkson Ellis, Elmer's father, was born on May 25, 1864. When the Soo Line Railway opened, land became available for homesteading in the Dakotas, so the Levi Ellis family, including married sons and daughters, moved to the vicinity of Valley City, North Dakota, to take advantage of better opportunities to acquire land.[2]

The Ellises were only one of the many family groups who helped create the boom period which existed in the Dakota region in the early 1880's. From the establishing of the first land office in Dakota Territory until June 30, 1880, a period of eighteen years, the number of pre-emptions and claims filed was only 44,122; but from the taking of the census of 1880 to December 31, 1881, less than nineteen months, 16,718 claims were entered. Population increased from 135,177 in 1880 to about 330,000 in 1883. Rising real estate prices in other states and a cycle of increased rainfall locally made Dakota land more attractive. Introduction of hard spring wheat and the roller-milling process seemed to promise increased prosperity for Dakota settlers. Railroad extensions into Dakota Territory, accompanied by the usual railroad, private, and governmental promotion of colonization, increased the appeal of this new frontier to farmers. It was a day of magnificent promise. The optimism which pervaded the Dakota region at the time when the Levi Ellis family entered it is admirably described in Bryce's famous *The American Commonwealth*.

A letter written by Elmer Ellis' mother late in life to her son Wilfred told much of the early difficulties and activities of the family. Her maiden name was Lillie Butterfield. She was born

---

[2]Letter from Mrs. N. M. Krick, Minot, North Dakota, January 27, 1950, who has furnished much information.

in Houston County, Minnesota, near the town of Hokah, on November 18, 1870, the daughter of Ira and Marietta Sheldon Butterfield. While still a young girl she moved with her parents to a farm near Valley City, North Dakota. She attended schools in Valley City, and later became a teacher at Fort Ransom. On April 21, 1891, she married Thomas Clarkson Ellis in Valley City, and the young couple returned to the vicinity of Detroit Lakes, Minnesota, where their first children were born. In 1898, however, they moved to a homestead between Anamoose and Drake in McHenry County, North Dakota. Mrs. Ellis remembered vividly the pioneering years spent by her and her husband in Minnesota and North Dakota:

My dear Children,

It is just wonderful to think you will have a home of your own and I am sure you will enjoy it but you will enjoy the building and planning as much as any part and it makes me think of Tom and I when we built a house at Aubudon [Minnesota]. We went to work in a saw mill when Earl was a baby a year old that January. And Dan ran the engine and Mr. Hunt was the father of the man that had the saw mill and we cooked for the men till they sawed up lumber enough and built a house for us to live in. We had 2 rooms downstairs and a pantry and then all one room for the men to sleep in upstairs. My but it did seem nice—2 thicknesses of boards just green lumber, with paper between, but it was nice and clean and smelled so like the woods. I had canned and made all the pickles I could so we had lots of good things to eat and Chas. and Earl was all the entertainers we needed. The men were so anxious for Earl to walk every day they would stand him against the wall and coax him to try and everyone urging him to try. I remember lots of happy times we had that winter. Grandpa and Mother drove up once to see us and we went down to see Minnie as Mother thought she was not going to live she was so sick. This was the winter before RG was born and my but she was ill but all at once it was gone and she was soon up and about again. Then we took our pay in lumber and the next year, we had to wait over a year and let the lumber dry, we built our first new house and you and Brownie will never be prouder of

your home than we were of that one. The frame was all hard wood
and we had earned it by good hard work. Dad had got out the logs
the year before. He and Wilber Hunt had cut the timber on an Island
and hauled it across the ice to the place where they were to have the
mill. So it really was 2 years work getting ready to build and that
house still stands just as we built it north of Audubon, Minn. We
had 3 rooms and a pantry downstairs and 2 bedrooms upstairs. And
Martha was born in the old house and you were born the 2nd year
in the new house. When I think we didn't build the year we planned
but had to wait over as the crop wasn't so good and Martha was born
in the old log house. And then the next year we built and lived in
a year before it was plastered and then you were born the next
October and the house was not all finished but it did seem good to
have so much room. And my kitchen floor was white birch and what
a time I had to keep that clean for there was never any varnish on
it. And how I did hate to move to North Dakota and leave it. But
it seemed we never were able to only pay the interest and taxes and
it looked like we could never pay off the mortgage. And I guess Dad
got the western fever as a lot of the men did. Uncle George and
Uncle Everett and John and Andrew Abelein left the fall you and
Chas. Wright were born and filed on their farms near Anamoose.
And Tom went out the next summer in June after his crop was in
and filed on his. The men from McHugh all had their shanties and
were getting started. Uncle Jim and Goodlaxen filed that year too.
And my there was nothing like the new country. Well that fall we
planned on moving in the spring. Tom got out posts and timber for
a barn and had a lot of lumber sawed that was to make our North
Dakota home and how he worked. I was alone so much he was
always hauling hay and grain and getting something we would need
in our new home. We got groceries and flour enough by trading to
last a long time. Then in March I left, as soon as things were packed
ready to ship. I went to Valley City and stayed at Mothers till he got
the barn up. You know how lovely it was to visit with 4 children.
We drove to Detroit and had you four oldest pictures taken. The
first good ones we ever had and Chas. and Earl had their first ready
made clothes. We stayed at the Wilkins home. They were old
neighbors that had moved to Detroit, after he was elected County
Judge of Becker Co. And he was County Judge till he died, a very
well read "Old Soldier" and a good Judge. They were lovely neighbors. Only he was not her first love. Her sweetheart had been killed

in the Civil war and Mr. Wilkins had brought her his last messages and wanted her to let him take his friends place. A wonderful couple with the love left out but they had 11 children and got so used to a baby that when there wasn't any at their house they took a little orphan and raised her and it was her that helped the mother in her old age. But the youngest daughter had been her father's clerk for many years before he died. So they were more than sisters and always wonderful friends. The Wilkin's oldest daughter and Marshall Murry had gone out and filed on claims near Anamoose just before the men from McHugh and that started the rest. A Murry girl, Burta, and the oldest Cravath boy had gone out long before the Railroad and had a ranch near Anamoose and it was them that got the others started as soon as the Railroad went through. And how we all did enjoy the new country and the storms. Well the 3rd of April 1899 I got a letter from Tom saying if I could live in one end of the barn to come on. So I was soon on my way with 4 children and Aunt Lydia went along and Tom located her on a homestead that lies right west of the Tinker place. She stayed a month then went back to V.C. and earned enough money to pay for lumber for her shantie on her claim. Then came back in time to help with the threshing and to take care of me when Grace was born. Our crop was so good that fall what we had and we had corn raised right on the sod just chopped in with an axe and all kinds of vines. Pumpkins were wonderful as we had no frost till October 16 and everything was ripe before it came. When I left Mothers to take the train an old friend Mrs. Ella Erickson came to the train to see me and I invited her to come on up and get a farm for her boys. And sure enough we had not been there many days when she arrived. And came out for us to help her get a farm and Tom took time off and hunted her a claim. And there was a land office in Anamoose so she didn't have to go to Towner to file as the others had had to do. Tom when he filed rode a horse, loaned him by Fred Cravath, to Towner to file on his Claim and he was pretty stiff as he rode the 40 miles back the next day. What good times we had in the Barn. There was a floor where the beds was but the stove and table and cupboards were right on the ground and the board partition between us and the horses had cracks in and we could hear them eating and everything sounded so plain in the night. We lived there till some time in August when we got the house built. I made butter set the milk in pans on the table at night with a sheet draped over it then skimmed it in the morning and used the same pans to set again but had to put it in the cupboard during the day but would have to skim at night again. I always churned early in the morning so my butter would come nice and hard and then we could sell it for 15 and 20 cents a pound but bought the nails shingles and paper for our house with it and we were sure glad to get into the house with a new baby coming and winter too. There was lots to do. Well Aunt Lydia came back in time to help with the threshers and be on hand to take care of the baby. But Mrs. Erickson while she was there in May decided Anamoose needed a hotel so in August the hotel was started. Mrs. Sikes, Mrs. Ericksons mother, had decided to go into the hotel business. This was Anamooses first hotel and it burned down some time after 1906. The hotel became the center of all social things as soon at it was up. Before it was finished Mrs. Erickson and her two boys came back to see that things were the way she wanted them to be and as she couldn't stay at the hotel she came to our house and so I had her and the boys which made a house full at the time Grace was born but she sure was good help. And the hotel was ready to go into by October so they went to town and got busy with their work. And the first school was held that winter in . . . the hotel and Everett Ellis taught. Charles stayed at the hotel with the boys through the school week then the three boys would come out to our house Friday night and I would have them till Monday morning and we called it even on the board. Grandpa had written and wanted Earl in the fall they were so lonesome with all the boys away. And a neighbor Maynard Wilkins came out and got him a Claim east of Anamoose and he took Earl back to Grandpas so I lost him for many years as they seemed to think Earl belonged to them but when he was ready to start school he came home and started at Anamoose but that was after the 1st school house was built. And I can just see Earl yet the first day he came home from school he was so proud. Said he had the nicest Teacher and she was not as tall as I was and she was so pretty. He had started alone as Chas. had to herd the cattle and didn't start the first week. This first teacher, I don't remember her name, married a Mr. Redding who was our Sunday School Superintendent for a long time. Our first Sunday School and church was also in the Hotel. Had it in the office and this was the time I met the Armstrongs who were old ranchers. And in 1901 our Church was organized. Held services upstairs over the Printing office and in the school house afterward. Till our Church was built. Tom had been the Treasurer of the Church till he decided it was too much for him and he resigned. Then they elected me and Tom went on doing the work only it was my name went on the deed when the Church was built. And this is what I remember about Anamoose for we moved to Town from the farm when Elmer was less than a year old. Dad got so nervous and I decided he just couldn't work that hard any more and we traded the farm for the store in Anamoose. Well Grace and Elmer were both born out on the farm without any frills. We moved to Anamoose in the spring of 1902 and then to Towner in 1905.

Thomas Clarkson Ellis seems to have been an energetic person with a zest for life and a genuine interest in people. When he moved his family to the outskirts of the small prairie village of Anamoose and took over the store for which he had traded his farm, he acquired an occupation better suited to his temperament than farming and also less exacting physically. He loved sports and participated actively in local community affairs. He served for many years as an elder in the Presbyterian Church, and was a Mason and a member of the Modern Woodmen of America. In 1905 he and his brother Everett bought a hardware store in the county seat at Towner, which they operated until 1909. Following that, Ellis owned a store at Maxbass, where the family lived for a short time before returning to Towner. In 1914 Ellis was elected county judge of McHenry County, a position that except for one term he held continuously until his death in 1927. During this interval, 1920-1922, the family resided at Velva, North Dakota. Thus, except for short periods at Maxbass and Velva, the Ellises lived in Towner after moving there in 1905, and there the children grew up.

A family of eleven children consumed most of Mrs. Ellis' time during their early years. Both parents imbued the children with the idea that they must have an education. Moreover, although the Ellises lived comfortably, the children realized that they would have to depend to a considerable extent on their own efforts to make their way in the world. A woman of great physical energy, Mrs. Ellis seems to have given her children a feeling of being greatly loved, while at the same time making them aware of the need for relying upon their own resources. Perhaps the parents succeeded so well in such efforts because their love of people extended beyond the confines of their own large brood, which encouraged the children to look beyond their own immediate desires to the welfare of others. For many years Mrs. Ellis was active in the work of the Presbyterian Church, the Women's Relief Corps, and the Eastern Star. When Judge Ellis died in 1927, the County Commissioners selected her to complete her husband's term of office, an unusual appointment at that period. She continued to live in Towner until 1935, when ill health forced her to leave there and live with her children.

Elmer Ellis came naturally to his liking for people from the example set by both of his parents. He seems to have admired his father greatly and exchanged letters with him regularly. Those who knew his mother in later years have commented on how much the outlook of the parents seems to have shaped their children. In a large, busy, and optimistic family, the children learned self-reliance, consideration for others, and the futility of self-importance.

Although it served as the county seat, Towner had considerably less than a thousand population during Ellis' boyhood years. Situated in the heart of a farming and ranching area, it had the usual grain elevators, grocery, drygoods, and hardware stores that characterized such communities. A good many citizens found employment at the local courthouse, but there was no manufacturing and little economic specialization. Nevertheless, there was a hotel, a dentist, doctors, and drugstores.

As a boy, Elmer Ellis worked after school and on weekends at various jobs in Towner. For a considerable period of time he helped wait on customers in one of the local stores, made deliveries of groceries, tested cream, and did many other chores connected with the operation of a grocery business in a small community. During one summer vacation he followed the harvest as a hand.

Towner had a graded elementary school system and a four-year high school, the different classes averaging around twenty students each. Although many students dropped out without completing their education, the Ellises had instructed their children too thoroughly on the value of learning for any of them to miss the opportunities available. Mrs. Harriet (Edgerly) Elliott served as principal and teacher in the Towner High School from the fall of 1915 to the spring of 1918, at the time when Elmer was in attendance there. On a return visit to Towner in the spring of 1958, she visited the old high school building, now altered and enlarged for use as a grade school, and with one of Elmer's former classmates reminisced about early days. Mrs. Elliott remembers her three years in Towner as the most satisfying in her teaching career, primarily because of the quality of the student body. She recalls that the students had considerable conviction as to the value of education and did not pretend a sophistication which might have blurred their vision. She and some of Ellis' classmates of those years recall his great interest in reading, and, with the benefit of hindsight, think that he must have been absorbed most of all in historical literature.

As a youngster in Towner, Ellis belonged to a Boy Scout troop whose interest centered in a camp on the nearby Mouse River. This camp provided facilities for swimming in summer and skating in winter. The Towner High School played baseball, and Ellis served as catcher on the team. He also played regularly on the basketball team which won the district championship in 1920. Since his expression in the picture taken of that team is quite determined, he obviously could be as intent on winning an athletic contest as in reading a history book, and quite as proud of his accomplishments on the playing field as in the classroom.

In his junior year he began to court Ruth Clapper, an attractive auburn-haired girl. She was sixteen and a senior; Elmer, seventeen and a junior. Ruth Clapper was born in Callaway County, Missouri, and was one of the five children of Mr. and Mrs. Lee Clapper. In the early 1900's, the Clappers moved to North Dakota to take charge of a farm implement agency. Lee Clapper served as deputy sheriff of McHenry County, North Dakota, for two years, during which time the family lived in Towner and Ruth completed the first two grades. After his term of office, the Clappers moved to a farm near Deering, North Dakota, where Ruth attended a rural school. For high school she returned to Towner, staying during the school year with the Horace Bagley family, who were friends and neighbors of the Ellises. Elmer had already read the novels of Sir Walter Scott from Mr. Bagley's well-stocked personal library, and he had still other books to complete, but his major interest seems to have shifted in the direction of Ruth Clapper.

Both young people wanted a college education, however, and any thought of marriage had to be delayed. Ruth attended Stephens College in Columbia, Missouri, during Elmer's freshman year at Fargo College, but they kept in touch by correspondence. During the next several years Elmer put himself through college by his own efforts, received his M.A. degree from the University of North Dakota, and obtained his first college teaching job; Ruth taught the intermediate grades in a consolidated school in North Dakota for three years. On August 14, 1925, the two young people were married. In personality and interests the Ellises are very much alike, and Ruth Clapper Ellis has contributed greatly to her husband's success.

Ellis might have started his college work at the Normal School in Minot but two of his older brothers had previously gone to Fargo College in Fargo, North Dakota, and the College offered him a scholarship. At the time, Fargo was a hustling little city of something over twenty thousand people and served as the chief distribution center for a large trade territory to the northwest. In addition to commercial activity that surpassed the efforts of many another community of similar size, it served as the home of the North Dakota Agricultural College as well as that of Fargo College.

Fargo College had a small endowment, but depended primarily upon tuition for support. When Ellis went there, the school was already in financial difficulties and had to cease operations the following year. It was strictly a liberal arts college offering only the bachelor's degree, although one could qualify for a B. S. No graduate work was offered. Not counting local students who were taking music at the conservatory, the College had two to three hundred students, most of whom came from eastern North Dakota and western Minnesota. There were probably not over a dozen full-time members on the faculty, most of whom held M.A. degrees. The librarian was a New England "gentleman of the old school" who had taught Latin and Greek until demand for such courses lessened. The dean of the institution had been a Rhodes Scholar. The College prided itself on high academic standards and was proud of its traditions.

Its physical plant consisted of three buildings. The main structure housed the administrative offices, some classrooms, and dormitory facilities on its third floor for out-of-town girls. The science building was a three-story structure and had fairly adequate equipment. There was also a modern library building, with classroom space for the humanities and social sciences in which Ellis was most interested.

C. M. Correll, who later joined the faculty of Kansas State University at Manhattan, Kansas, taught all the history and political science courses during the year that Ellis attended the College. As Correll later commented, each member of the faculty tended to occupy a "settee in place of a chair" because of the range of subject matter that he had to teach. Correll remembers Ellis as a good student, but claims no marked influence of the College on him during his brief stay there:

I don't know that one can claim that the year at Fargo College played any big part in the education of Ellis. It furnished the opportunity for him to make the transition from the home high school to a college environment away from home, and possibly a small college was a better place for making that transition than a large institution would have been.[3]

A Fargo newspaper of the period carried a picture of the school's football team, of which Ellis was a member, and he thus gained direct experience in the field of college athletics. Tradition has it that Ellis played in the first football game that he ever saw, and that the team lost!

The "Roaring Twenties" failed to give the American farmer and farm communities the same prosperity that seemed to characterize the large urban centers. Even if Fargo College had been able to struggle on for another year, Ellis still would have needed to take time out to earn money to continue his education. After his freshman year in college he was on his own.

From September of 1921 to May of 1922, he served as principal and teacher in the three-teacher Sherman District School near Antler, North Dakota. Wilmar Peterson, who was president of the Sherman School Board in 1959, has furnished an account of Ellis' work at that school:

This information was given to me by Mr. A. W. Nelson, a pioneer of our community. He was a member of the Sherman School Board at the time Mr. Ellis taught here and he is serving as treasurer of the school district at the present time. . . .

Sherman school is located about ten miles south of the Canadian border, Antler being the nearest town. Mr. Ellis taught a nine-month term in our school from Sept., 1921, until May of 1922. His salary was $175.00 per month. We had three teachers that term, with an enrollment of sixty-five pupils. Mr. Ellis was principal, teaching algebra, Grammar, History, and Science. The salaries of the other two teachers were $125.00 each per month. They taught the first

---

[3]Letter from C. M. Correll, Manhattan, Kansas, January 5, 1959.

eight grades. Mr. Ellis also did the janitor work which was a furnace heated by coal so he had the pleasure of shoveling the coal and ashes. We now heat the school with gas.

Our school, built in 1915, is a one-story frame building 48 by 48 feet and has two large classrooms, full basement with coal bin, boiler room, storeroom and recreation room.

Our district consists of a square township of thirty-six sections, with school in center of township. Some of the children would travel up to six miles to school. Some went by horse and buggy and some would ride horseback as had a barn in the schoolyard at that time. They drove with cars when the weather permitted. The patrons were all farmers. Covered rigs were used in the winter time.

Mr. Ellis lived in the teacherage in the schoolyard, a four-room house, heat and rent free. An elderly lady (relative) kept house for him at least part of the time. He was a very industrious young man and attended to everything as a perfect gentleman and was very much liked by young and old. He had no specific duties as coach but always took time to play with the children, being it baseball, running races or any other kind of game.

With Mr. Ellis at the helm we had a very good Christmas program. In the spring we had what is called Playday when neighboring schools got together and competed for prizes in various athletic activities. Sherman school came out on top and everyone had a good time.

With all his work and duties at the school Mr. Ellis done a lot of studying even though sometimes it meant only five hours of sleep.

When Mr. Ellis was here we had no electricity in the farm homes as we do now, but the school had what was known as a Delco lighting plant.[4]

Such a picture seems far removed from what Americans like to call the "Roaring Twenties." Only when the "booze" runners thundered down the highway out of Canada did Ellis and his students glimpse at firsthand incidents that typified so much of the national life. Otherwise, Sherman School District seemed closely allied to the best of the frontier past and to be preparing for the best of the future.

---

[4]Letter from Wilmar Peterson, Antler, North Dakota, January, 1959. Ellis took some correspondence courses from the University of North Dakota during the year.

The year at Sherman gave Ellis his first administrative experience, and he obviously did well at it. He came to know still better the problems of primary and early secondary education, and he managed to find time to extend his own knowledge. Moreover, he saved enough money to permit him to move on to the University of North Dakota at Grand Forks the next fall to continue work on his bachelor's degree.

Ellis was twenty years old when he entered the University as a sophomore in the fall of 1922. Whereas Fargo had been nearly defunct, the University at Grand Forks was entering a period of rapid physical growth. Enrollment had passed the thousand mark for the first time in the fall of 1919. By 1925, when Ellis left the University with his M.A., it had increased by another five hundred. University appropriations also rose sharply after World War I, from $675,000 for the biennium of 1919-1921 to $1,160,000 for 1921-1923.

The increased enrollments and appropriations resulted in a revived building program, expansion of the faculty and the curriculum, and some shifts in organization. The faculty grew from about 70 in 1917-1918 to 120 in 1924-1925. Several new departments were added and most of the old ones were expanded. The departments of history and sociology were separated, for example, and the history faculty grew from two full-time members in 1917 to four in 1921. Moreover, the organization of the institution was pushed several steps further toward the status and maturity implied by the name "University." The School of Education and the College of Liberal Arts were clearly differentiated for the first time in 1919, and various departments specifically assigned to one or the other.

A particularly significant step was a modest expansion of the graduate program and an effort to organize a graduate school. Advanced work had actually been instituted a few years before World War I and put under the general supervision of a standing faculty committee. The new president, Thomas F. Kane, appointed in 1919, wanted to enlarge this program, and in 1922 he attempted to have the "graduate department" elevated to the status of a school supervised by its own dean. Although the Board refused to approve the suggestion, largely because the president had acted without formally consulting his faculty, he nevertheless persisted in his efforts to expand the advanced program. One aspect of this expansion was a modest improvement in the library which, although it continued to be inadequate for the support of graduate work, was throughout the 1920's under the direction of a succession of unusually able librarians, every one of whom moved up in his profession when he left North Dakota. In many respects, therefore, the 1920's were an optimistic time at the University.

On the other hand, the University was having some severe difficulties. The post-war economic slump had just begun in 1921, and it struck particularly hard in North Dakota, where the economy depended almost wholly upon agriculture. The depression affected the University in the form of sharp cutbacks in legislative appropriations in 1923 and 1925. More serious, although probably unnoticed by all but the most sensitive students, factionalism centering around President Kane rapidly developed among the faculty. Whatever the merits of the quarrel, it was nonetheless true that, with few exceptions, the anti-Kane party included the ablest and the most independent-minded figures on the campus.

Among the president's leading critics were the men to whom Ellis would look most as his mentors and favorite teachers. They were Orin G. Libby (Professor of History), William G. Bek (Professor of German and Dean of Freshmen), John M. Gillette (Professor of Sociology), Joseph Kennedy (Professor of Philosophy and Dean of the School of Education), and Ezra T. Towne (Professor of Economics and Political Science).

How much Ellis knew about the controversy involving Kane and about the opinions of the men he admired is difficult to say, but it is not likely that anyone as observant as he could spend three years on the campus without becoming aware of the situation. Perhaps he came to realize the petty nature of faculty gossip and faculty jealousy, as well as the necessity of taking a stand on basic issues, once a conflict has been aroused; certainly the situation at the University of North Dakota was an excellent laboratory course in the personal and academic problems of a university. Perhaps most of all he came to realize the need for meeting problems before they reach a critical stage, thereby saving needless wear and tear on faculty and institution alike.

Ellis' financial problems and his scholastic interests left him with little time to engage in the lighter aspects of campus life. His name almost never appeared in campus publications. The *Daily Student* did report that he had been elected president of the La Follette-for-President Club in 1924, but someone else was elected to the post a week later. Ellis' picture appeared only once in the college annual, and only then when he was a graduate student. The only organization that he seems to have joined was Phi Beta Kappa, and he apparently participated once in oratory, though he won no prize. In fact, he never lived on the campus (except for one summer session when he roomed in Budge Hall) or even near it, but took rooms downtown, a mile or more from the campus, and commuted daily to his classes by streetcar. His associates were drawn mostly from the Budge Hall Dormitory crowd, but he probably spent little time with them. In order to continue directly toward his degree, he worked a good many hours weekly at the University Library to supplement the savings that he had brought with him for his education.

The man who influenced Ellis most perhaps was Orin G. Libby. Of extraordinary energy, possessing an almost fiercely held standard of moral and scholarly integrity, Libby was a demanding teacher, the sort whom lazy students avoid. Libby was unpopular with administrators, and, for that matter, with more than a few of his faculty colleagues. Trained at Wisconsin, he had been the first Ph.D. advisee of Frederick Jackson Turner. After coming to North Dakota in 1902, Libby had turned from early national history to early exploration and plains history, and by 1921, when Ellis came to the University, he was in firm possession of the accolade "father of history in North Dakota." Libby's prestige was more than local; he was one of the founders and early presidents of the Mississippi Valley Historical Association.

Standing second only to Libby in Ellis' regard was Joseph P. Kennedy, Dean of the School of Education and Professor of Philosophy. Kindly and gentle in demeanor, beloved by students, not particularly interested in formal scholarship, Kennedy was superficially very unlike Libby. Yet in his own way he was likewise a man of moral courage and intellectual independence. He was a Roman Catholic, but an ardent disciple of John Dewey and the pragmatists, and an open critic of parochial education. More than once he engaged in sharp public controversy with his church over his views. Almost entirely self-taught in the field of philosophy, Kennedy was an inspirational teacher. Ellis was to remember Kennedy as one of the truly influential teachers of his college days.

Gillette, Towne, and Bek were all highly respected on the campus both for their characters and for their scholarly abilities. By 1921 Gillette possessed a nationwide reputation as "father of rural sociology," was publishing regularly in his field, and was well along toward the day when he would be honored with the presidency of the American Sociological Society. Towne, with whom Ellis took a graduate minor in economics and political science, held a doctorate from the University of Halle, and had written several solid studies in his field. Bek, a professor of German, was a humanist, more of a historian of German America than a language drill-master or linguist. Although German was outside the realm of Ellis' main interests, he found Bek to be the kind of scholar and personality toward whom he gravitated almost automatically, and he took more than the minimum language requirements for the A.B. degree.

Ellis concentrated on history and education as an undergraduate, obviously with the intention of preparing to teach in the public schools. For his M.A. degree, which he received at the end of the summer session of 1925, Ellis offered a major in history and a minor in political science.

Ellis actually took a considerable part of his graduate work in semi-absentia, being employed full-time during the winter of 1924-1925 as teacher of ninth-grade civics and algebra in the high school of East Grand Forks. At the time, the school had an enrollment of about two hundred students in the combined junior-senior division, and thus Ellis could concentrate on teaching fewer subjects than had been the case at Sherman. His salary for the year was fifteen hundred dollars. Although working on his M.A. degree at the same time, he seems not to have slighted his teaching duties. At least, one of his former students, now secretary to the superintendent at East Grand Forks, remembers Ellis as "the only teacher I ever had who could make me understand mathematics."

Immediately upon completing his M.A., Ellis became a member of the Department of Social Science at the State Teachers College in Mayville, North Dakota. From 1925 to 1928 (including two or three summer sessions), the Ellises lived and worked at Mayville, a community of twelve to thirteen hundred people located in what is considered to be the best farming area in the state of North Dakota, the famous Red River Valley of the North.

Mr. Erich Selke, a colleague of Ellis at Mayville and later a member of the faculty of the University of North Dakota, reports:

> The college at that time had an enrollment of about 400 and a faculty of approximately 30. . . . The college was small but had and still has an excellent reputation for the type of student that it produces. It was considered to have the most progressive and energetic faculty in the state, barring no institutions, and those who were

students at that time have become leaders in education and other circles not only in the state but elsewhere. Needless to say the faculty were of very high caliber. As I recall, several became presidents of institutions, others deans and professors in schools throughout the nation.[5]

The college offered one- and two-year diplomas, as well as the bachelor's degree. The one-year diploma qualified those planning to teach in one-room rural institutions; the two-year diploma was tailored to the needs of teachers in elementary schools. The student body came largely from the immediate vicinity, with a considerable number from western Minnesota which lay only twenty-five miles to the east.

During his three years at Mayville, Ellis taught American history, general history, civics, political science, and a methods course in history. He also served on the Convocation Committee and the Curriculum Committee of the College. Faculty members of the school at that time were not ranked from assistant to full professors, all members of the teaching faculty apparently having the same official standing[6].

Ellis' career at the Mayville College impressed others in much the same way that his previous and later activities would be judged by contemporary observers. As Selke recalls:

Dr. Ellis was well liked by the staff, the student body and the town's people. Elmer was a serious-minded, studious young man who devoted much of his time to the preparation of his work. This helped to make him an inspired teacher. . . . He had a good sense of humor and his hearty laugh was contagious. He was stable and energetic. His interests were varied and so he was interested in all school activities as well as community affairs. He contributed to magazines and was a co-author of a geography textbook dealing with

[5]Letter from Erich Selke, Grand Forks, North Dakota, February 11, 1959.

[6]Letter from Prof. Waldron R. Reese (currently Chairman of Department of Social Science of State Teachers College in Mayville), Mayville, North Dakota, February 3, 1959.

North Dakota. Perhaps I should call it a workbook.[7] Dr. Ellis did considerable public speaking, speaking before community groups, teachers' conventions and also high school graduation exercises.

By the spring of 1928, the Ellises had saved sufficient money to see Elmer through to the doctorate if he could obtain an assistantship or fellowship. He thought of going to one of the large eastern graduate schools, but finally decided on the University of Iowa. Perhaps Dr. H. D. Welte, who has been president of Connecticut College for Women at New London, Connecticut, for many years, most influenced Ellis' choice of Iowa. A colleague of Ellis at the State College in Mayville, Welte had virtually completed work on his own doctorate in education at Iowa before the Ellises moved there in the fall of 1928. Welte returned to Mayville in the spring of 1928 to teach during the summer session. Finding Ellis still undecided as to where he would go, Welte arranged for an interview with Professor W. T. Root, then Chairman of the Department of History at Iowa, which resulted in Ellis' receiving a part-time teaching assistantship in American history for the fall semester. Moreover, Professor Louis Pelzer, with whom Ellis was to do his doctoral dissertation, had a special interest in the history of the Great Plains, the field in which Ellis preferred to concentrate his research efforts. The Ellises also had friends in Iowa City from their earlier days. And so they moved to the University of Iowa.

Ellis seems to have worked so intensively for the next two years that his friends and associates during that period remember only that he was "friendly" and "busy." The Ellises took an apartment at 1025 East Washington Street, where Professor George R. Davies and his wife also lived. Davies and Ellis had been friends in North Dakota, where a mutual interest in mapping areas according to voting and other criteria had drawn them together. Now Professor Emeritus of Commerce at the University of Iowa, Professor Davies recalls that the Davies and the Ellises visited

---

[7]*Directed Study Workbook in Our State* (North Dakota).

constantly, but on the informal basis common among faculty and graduate students immersed in their intensive studies. On Christmas Day of 1930, the Davies had the Ellises over to their apartment for dinner, a welcome interlude since, as Professor Davies remembers, "both Elmer and I were pretty busy."[8]

Although Ellis did some teaching in the University High School, as well as in the history department, he completed his doctorate in the minimum time of two years and with virtually a straight A record. In addition, he found time to publish one historical article and to review books for periodicals and newspapers. In all this, his wife took an active part as typist, note-taker, critic, and fellow worker. Thus, by May 22, 1930, Ellis was ready for his final examination for the doctorate in history, the program for which is reproduced here in full to indicate more specifically the direction of his work:

FINAL EXAMINATION
of
ELMER ELLIS
B.A., UNIVERSITY OF NORTH DAKOTA, 1924
M.A., UNIVERSITY OF NORTH DAKOTA, 1925
FOR THE DEGREE
OF DOCTOR OF PHILOSOPHY

Thursday, May 22, 1930, at 3:00 P.M.
Board Room, Old Capitol

Committee in Charge:
    Professor Pelzer
    Professor Root
    Associate Professor Andrews
    Professor Plum
    Professor Shambaugh
    Professor Raiford
    Professor Davies

---

[8]Letter from Professor George R. Davies of Iowa City, Iowa, December 18, 1958.

Major Subject: American History
> History of the West (Pelzer)
> Colonial History (Root)
> American Constitutional History (Libby)
> Contemporary American History (Libby)

Minor Subject: Modern European History
> Modern European History (Andrews)
> Modern England (Plum)
> Nationalism and Imperialism (Dodson)

Minor Subject: Political Science
> Constitutional Law (Shambaugh)
> Modern Governments (Shambaugh)
> American Political Parties (Porter)
> American Political Ideas (Briggs)

PUBLICATIONS

"Recollections of a Bad Lands Rancher," *North Dakota Historical Quarterly,* October, 1926.

"Why Not Apprentice Voters?" *Historical Outlook,* November, 1928.

"The Failure of Minor Parties," *Current History Magazine,* April, 1930.

Book reviews in the *Current History Magazine, Historical Outlook, New Republic, New York Times Book Review, North Dakota Historical Quarterly,* and *Quarterly Journal of the University of North Dakota.*

BIOGRAPHY

Born: July 27, 1901.

Secondary Education: Towner High School, North Dakota.

Undergraduate: Fargo College and University of North Dakota.

Graduate Student: University of North Dakota, 1924-1925; University of Iowa, 1928-1930.

Professor: North Dakota State Teachers College, 1925-1928.

Lecturer: University of Iowa, 1929-1930.

Member: American Historical Association, Mississippi Valley Historical Association, National Council for the Social Studies, North Dakota Historical Association.

His graduate work completed, Ellis had a difficult decision to make. The University of North Dakota invited him to join its faculty, an appealing offer because of his friendships there and his loyalty to the school. Although he seriously considered returning to his alma mater, he decided otherwise after the president of that institution reluctantly advised him to take an assistant professorship at the University of Missouri which promised greater opportunity for advancement.

The Missouri appointment might well have made any candidate pause, for it involved the difficult assignment of teaching in two administrative divisions, the School of Education (now a college) and the College of Arts and Science. Although Ellis joined the Missouri faculty as Assistant Professor of History, and was assigned to the College of Arts and Science, he also had to teach methods courses in social science in the School of Education and supervise graduate theses of students combining training in both subject matter and professional courses in education. Although the deans of the two divisions at the University of Missouri agreed on the wisdom of employing a professor who would teach in both fields, and the history department welcomed his appointment, Ellis faced a difficult task in cutting across conventional academic lines.

Nevertheless, he rapidly demonstrated that one could teach successfully in two divisions. High school teachers working towards the Master's degree at the University of Missouri found his methods courses highly useful in their subject-matter fields, and many of them did their graduate work under his supervision. He took part in state teachers conventions, helped revise the state course of study, and worked closely with the National Council for Social Studies. He edited one of the yearbooks published by that organization and was elected its national president. He also served as chairman of the junior college inspection committee of the University of Missouri, which advised such institutions on matters of accreditation and standards. Annual visits to junior colleges and attendance at teachers conventions gave him a wide acquaintance among teachers in the state.

In the same period, his course Recent United States History developed an outstanding reputation on the campus. Because of its scholarly approach to twentieth century history, it soon became a requirement of students in journalism and education, and a favorite subject with those enrolled in the College of Arts and Science. His advanced course, Social Forces in American History, also attracted a growing number of students. Graduate students in the field of history found him a stimulating scholar, and he directed a growing number of doctoral dissertations until increasing administrative duties made it impossible for him to give time to graduate students. His research activities as a Guggenheim Fellow and his growing reputation as a scholar will be discussed elsewhere in this volume.

Ellis made friends rapidly throughout the various divisions of the University. His wide-ranging interests and service on various University committees brought him into contact with men whose teaching fields were far removed from his own specialties. During the summers of 1936, 1939, and 1941, he served as Acting Dean of the Graduate School, and more and more he found himself being appointed to special committees to resolve problems affecting University affairs.

His scholarly publications and appointments to various posts in the Mississippi Valley Historical Association during the same period brought him to the attention of scholars and administrators elsewhere. During the summer of 1937 he served as Visiting Professor of History at Ohio State University. Shortly thereafter he received an offer to join the history faculty of another institution, but the University of Missouri increased his salary and urged him to remain in Columbia. Within a very few years, however, another university offered him an appointment to its most distinguished, and endowed, chair of history. No historian could take such an offer lightly, and Ellis felt that he should accept the opportunity. In keeping with his efforts to retain outstanding members of the faculty, President Frederick A. Middlebush readily approved adjustments in salary and teaching load for Ellis that demonstrated Missouri's desire to have him remain. Fortunately, Ellis did not make his decision strictly on the grounds of financial advantage. He and Mrs. Ellis liked Missouri and the opportunities for service which it provided. Since the University obviously wanted them to stay, and backed its sentiments with as attractive an offer as its resources justified, the Ellises decided to remain in Columbia.

During World War II, when there was decreased enrollment at the University of Missouri, Ellis was away from the campus. In 1943 he was commissioned a captain in the United States Army and served until 1945, being discharged with the rank of Major. During that time he served in the Historical Branch, War Department General Staff. His duties were those of a military government officer and later of an historian, in which capacity he compiled histories of Pacific campaigns. While in military service, he was stationed for a time at Schofield Barracks in Hawaii and later at the Pentagon in Washington.

In 1945 Ellis came back to Missouri University as Vice-President in Charge of Extra-Divisional Educational Activities. In this position he had charge of divisions at the University such as the library, student health, and physical education. In 1946 he became Dean of the College of Arts and Science, a post which he held until he became President of the University on April 16, 1955.

When he took over his post-war administrative duties, Ellis had hoped to continue to teach at least one class. Nor did he give up hope of continuing to write and publish in the historical field. Constant pressure of immediate administrative problems decreed otherwise, however, and so he found it necessary to concentrate his energies on administration. His administrative work is discussed elsewhere in this volume.

In 1943 Ellis acquired a grant from the Rockefeller Foundation to establish the Western Historical Manuscripts Collection as a part of the University of Missouri Library. The grant carried the Collection through its formative years, and it is today supported wholly by the University. Over one million manuscript items have been deposited in the Collection, including the papers of governors, senators, businessmen, and others prominent in the public and business life of the United States. Ellis has also filled various posts in connection with the State Historical Society of Missouri, and is currently a member of its executive committee. Thus, although pressure of duties has prevented him from continuing to publish in the historical field, he has contributed greatly to the work of others by helping to improve the resources available to them at the University of Missouri.

Nor did he lose interest in teaching. As Dean of the College of Arts and Science, he concentrated on hiring the best qualified people to replace retiring faculty members. He insisted that they must be excellent teachers and potentially productive scholars. As an administrator, he has never lost sight of the fact that an institution can be no better than the quality of its staff. Moreover, his staff knows that he thinks constantly in terms of the classroom and the laboratory as the heart of the University. It was largely through his efforts that the University in 1949 received a fifty-thousand-dollar grant from the Carnegie Foundation for the Advancement of Teaching. This grant financed a five-year program of study for improvement of teaching in colleges and universities throughout Missouri.

In 1951-1952 he took leave of absence to accept a Fulbright Grant as Visiting Lecturer at the University of Amsterdam in Holland. During that period, he also served on the faculty of the Salzburg Seminar of American Studies. But this could only be an interlude in the administrative career to which he was now committed.

On September 10, 1954, he became Acting President of the

University of Missouri upon retirement of President Frederick
A. Middlebush. During the next few months some two hundred
individuals were considered for the presidency, but it was no
surprise to those who had known Ellis over the years that he became the new President of the University on April 16, 1955. It
would have been hard to find a man with a greater range of administrative experience; it would have been impossible to find one
who was more loyal or more devoted to the welfare of the
University of Missouri.

In addition to his duties on the campus in Columbia and
at Rolla, Missouri, he has served on many boards and commis-
sions. He has been a member and for a time chairman of the
History Advisory Committee of the United States Army; a trustee
of the Midwest Research Institute of Kansas City, Missouri; a
member of the Board of Directors of the Social Science Research
Council; a member and for a time chairman of the Commission
on Instruction and Evaluation of the American Council on Education; a member of the Board of Regents of the American Foundation for Greece; a member of the Finance Committee of the
North Central Association of Colleges and Secondary Schools;
a member of the Board of Foreign Scholarships, United States
Department of State; President of the Board of Directors of the
Harry S. Truman Library Institute for National and International Affairs; and a member of the President's Board, William
Rockhill Nelson Trust, Kansas City, Missouri.

He has been honored with honorary degrees—by the University
of North Dakota in 1946; by Central College of Fayette, Missouri, in 1955; by Drury College of Springfield, Missouri, in
1956; and by Washington University of St. Louis in 1960.

In addition to his administrative duties on the campus, President and Mrs. Ellis have visited alumni groups at widely scattered points in the United States and in foreign countries. At
such meetings and in his heavy speaking schedule to a great
variety of organizations and institutions, the President has stressed

the importance of making the University of Missouri a truly great educational center. His achievements as President are discussed elsewhere in this volume. If past events are sound bases for judging the future, these achievements foretell still greater progress for the university in the remaining years of his presidency.

2

Teacher and Scholar

ELMER ELLIS has proved his abilities in nearly every role offered in the academic world—as a teacher, as a scholar, as a liberal arts college dean, and as a university president. His versatility, which carried him out of the ranks of teachers and scholars at a comparatively early age, has meant that he must remain a historian of much promise rather than one with a full career. Louis Martin Sears's comment on Woodrow Wilson comes to mind: "As a historian, one may conclude that greatness lay within his grasp but that he never fully seized it. His nature was too rich to be so circumscribed." Moreover, it is not easy for any former student to write of Ellis impersonally. As Henry S. Commager wrote of Henry Adams, "what he was is more important than what he wrote." Ellis' former students remember his kindliness, his consideration, his unfailing good temper and easy humor, and his genuine modesty about his achievements.

33

Most of the testimony about Ellis the teacher that has been re-corded comes of course from his graduate students, and it would be easy to ignore his relations with undergraduates. He was never one who merely tolerated the teaching of undergraduates as an unavoidable chore which stood between him and the library and graduate students. Ellis liked the younger students and he taught them well, and they liked him. His classes were always large even though he was reputed to be demanding. He despised histrionics, or "colorful" behavior, but he taught with vigor and resourceful-ness. An important aspect of his lectures, especially in the Recent United States course, was the wide range of knowledge from which they were drawn. As to their content, Ellis left the con-nected narrative and the chronological framework to the textbook, and concentrated on analysis, hypotheses, and the creation of a sense of contact with living men and their problems. His lectures were closely organized, frequently illustrated with graphs, car-toons, and contemporary commentary, a favorite source for the latter being the "Mr. Dooley" columns by Finley Peter Dunne. Ellis could slip into the vernacular when it suited his purpose, and his humor had a broad rural touch, but there was an almost prudish avoidance of the off-color and profane, a reflection per-haps of a proper upbringing in North Dakota.

In his two main courses, Recent United States and Foundations of Twentieth Century America, there was more emphasis on politics and social and cultural developments than on diplomacy and foreign affairs. It is doubtful whether his students were as aware of his emphases as they were of the general excellence of the lectures and the appropriateness of the accompanying reading requirements. A significant aspect of these courses, especially the Recent United States, was Ellis' rationale for them. He attempted to present them in a form suitable both for the senior history major and for the upper classman who was taking them as elec-tives or to meet a history requirement of another college—both the schools of journalism and education sent many students to

Ellis. He viewed his course as an exercise in "general social science" for those not majoring in history, and a "unifying experience" for those who already had a substantial understanding of sociology, economics, and government. Recognizing the difficulty of presenting a balanced picture of a period close to the present, he believed that courses in recent history had the advantage of "motivation of present urgency," that their being close to everyday experience provided an opportunity of presenting the picture of society in the whole. "Any profitable study of an historical period," he once wrote, "is a course in all the social sciences, as it must show a system functioning in all its significant aspects."

In an article published by the magazine *Social Education* in 1943, Ellis expanded these views. Although his remarks were concerned primarily with justifying the presence of the Recent United States course in the college curriculum, the broader issue of why history should be taught at all was also raised. Ellis had few doubts of the practical value of history for the ordinary citizen. He suggested that the course limited in time or area was best for the beginning or one-course student because it did not suffer from the deadening repetitiousness of the general survey courses, particularly that in American History, which covered much of the same material that the average college student had already covered two or three times in elementary and high school. On the more positive side he saw a number of other advantages in the Recent United States course for the non-history major. It offered the facts and ideas essential to the understanding of the present and of the immediate future, including such matters as changes in the American position in the world economy, trends in the growth and distribution of population, and the ebb and flow of political change. The course would provide the opportunity to integrate the social science knowledge already possessed by the student. The "one ideal source of unifying experience," he wrote, is a history course which attempts to fit basic social science concepts into the framework of a functioning society, but this aim is thwarted by "slavery to the survey course with its necessary concentration upon very few aspects of society." The course in recent United States history, or for that matter any history course covering a short period, improved upon the specialized courses by "giving an opportunity to compare and contrast a going social system of a particular date with the same system at a different date." Ellis expected that one of the most important results of his own course would be a sharpened interest in public affairs and improved reading habits. He believed that assigned reading for history courses should include material from newspapers and magazines, and sound semi-popular works such as Frederick Lewis Allen's *Only Yesterday*. His encouragement of "basically important experiences" made Ellis' courses popular. Some of the immediate values to the journalism students were apparent in the frequency with which his Recent United States lectures made their way, often without due acknowledgment, into the editorial columns of the University daily, *The Columbia Missourian*.

The similarities between Ellis' views and those of James Harvey Robinson's New History are not hard to see. Just how much Ellis owed directly to Robinson is difficult to measure, but most young historians of the 1920's and 1930's were influenced to some degree, and in Ellis' case his first distinguished teacher, Orin G. Libby, was a Robinson admirer.

Effective though he was with undergraduates, Ellis' talents as a teacher and scholar, as well as the full impact of his personality, were most apparent in his relations with graduate students—in the seminar or readings course, or as the adviser on a thesis or dissertation. His seminar students usually found that this serene and kindly man was working them extremely hard, yet they were never quite sure how this had been managed. Without analyzing their motivations they were conscious that they wanted to please him, to win the word or two indicating that they had done well. His command of his own special field, the post-Civil War era, and other fields as well, always impressed them; he seemed to have read most of the literature, to have explored the sources, and to remember even minor details with perfect accuracy. Never ill-humored or even mildly caustic, Ellis was firm and uncompromising when occasion demanded. He had the knack of interjecting a gentle, almost innocent question which exposed yet did not unnecessarily embarrass the careless or lazy researcher, or the author of hasty conclusions. The effectiveness of the method is evident in the frequency with which his advanced students recall such apparently unforgettable rebukes.

The quality of Ellis' teaching and his reputation were of course extremely important to graduate students, but these qualities do not explain the considerable affection that has accompanied the respect in which they have held him. Students liked the man himself. His warmth, good temper, and easy manner put the most timid at ease. And this was managed even though Ellis has always been a very busy man, a "real dynamo" one of his students has called him. But his is busyness without the harried confusion exemplified by the desk piled high with a mass of misplaced papers. Somehow every student who went to see him, even at the most inopportune moments when he was dean of a large college, found him able to turn from his work, to answer a question or two or to chat idly for a moment. At the same time all but the most insensitive would quickly realize that this man's time ought not be wasted and would soon take themselves off. On other occasions Ellis would find time to take the new Ph.D. candidate to lunch to talk about his program or to confer over the most recent chapter of his thesis. At departmental parties where faculty and graduate students got together, usually at Christmas and again in the spring or summer, Ellis never failed to seem otherwise than thoroughly relaxed; he talked easily with students about their homes, reminisced about his own experiences as a young ranch hand or as a rural school teacher in North Dakota. He wore his professorial status and his academic reputation lightly, and when conversation switched to history or more serious current affairs he refrained from expressing himself so dogmatically as to discourage students from expressing their own views. Yet somehow the professor-student relationship remained well defined. Although Ellis and his colleagues managed to establish something of that "community of scholars" atmosphere of which Woodrow Wilson spoke so often when he was professor and president at Princeton, there was none of the first-name "palship" at Missouri that has been affected at some institutions.

Perhaps the single quality most marked in Ellis' character is generosity. This spirit appeared in his sympathetic patience with the insecure beginner in graduate study. Ellis put him at his ease and helped him recover at least some of his self-confidence. Such students might fail—a good many did of course—but rarely would one of them suggest that Ellis and not his own deficiencies were to blame. The quality of generosity was reflected in the restraint of his criticism of a poor performance and his quick word of commendation for a good one, in his searching yet sympathetic conduct of a doctoral examination, and in the energy of his assistance to the fledgling Ph.D. seeking his first teaching post. The quality was apparent in his refusal to monopolize his students, to surround himself with a corps of disciples. Students who came to him were encouraged to "shop around" among his colleagues before settling on a dissertation topic, and colleagues' advisees were treated with the same cordial courtesy and interest that he accorded his own. More than one promising student owed his good luck in finding the part-time employment which enabled him to continue at the university to the unobtrusive intercession of Ellis, and one discovered only by accident years after the event that Ellis had made the largest contribution to a fund raised for him when he had been injured in an automobile accident and confronted with a hospital bill he simply could not meet.

An important phase of Ellis' teaching days at the University of Missouri was his work with the training of social studies teachers for the public schools. His appointment to the University of Missouri faculty in 1930 was to fill the newly created position of assistant professor of history in the College of Arts and Science, with part of his time to be given over to the supervision of the social studies teachers' training in the Laboratory School of the School of Education. Throughout the 1930's he taught the courses in "methods," both on the undergraduate and graduate levels. This was work for which he was well qualified by training, experience, and sympathetic understanding. After a year at Fargo College, he had taught in a rural school. At the University of North Dakota, which he entered in 1922, he took enough courses in education to qualify for a high school teaching certificate. The first year following his graduation (A.B., 1924), during which he also completed work for the M.A. degree in history, he taught social studies and mathematics in the East Grand Forks, Minnesota, high school, and from 1925 to 1928 he taught social studies in the little state teachers college at Mayville, North Dakota.

Ellis brought energy and imagination to the training of high school teachers, and in the first decade of his career at the University of Missouri his success in this field was a major element in his rising professional reputation. By the end of the 1930's he was playing a leading role in shaping the social studies curriculum for the Missouri public schools and was active in the Teachers Section of the Mississippi Valley Historical Association. In 1937 he was president of the National Council for the Social Studies.

Ellis has therefore expressed his views more frequently than most academic scholars on the problem of relating professional scholarship to the task of teaching in the public schools. In his first article in a National Council for the Social Studies publication (1931 *Yearbook*, "Recent Books for Teachers of History"), Ellis wrote that he considered an informed, objective approach to public issues the main objective of social studies teaching in the schools. "Public opinion," he observed, "is the chief product of citizenship training, and only as the forces that mold it are understood will civic education be fully effective." Writing at a time when the issue of propaganda versus information was not yet fully visible to everyone, Ellis saw history and the social sciences as the main bulwark against the barrage of misinformation and interested argument by press and radio to which the ordinary citizen was subjected every hour of the day. This theme recurred often in Ellis' public statements, and was increasingly relevant in the 1930's when the anti-democratic dictators of Europe seemed the "wave of the future" to many. Alarmed Americans, observing the success of propaganda and indoctrination elsewhere, were calling upon teachers, particularly in the social studies, to use their special knowledge and skills and the privileged platform they occupied to counter-indoctrinate for democracy. Many people, including representatives of the teaching profession, saw no other alternative. They contended that the democracies stood a good chance of falling before their unscrupulous rivals unless they used strong measures themselves. This was a harder argument to meet than the familiar one that social studies teachers must teach reverence for free enterprise and should raise no embarrassing questions about false advertising, maldistribution of wealth, and the like. Ellis did not deny the urgency of the problem. Yet he saw that to stoop to the dictators' methods would be a denial of the fundamental principles underlying all scholarship and learning, that is, that the truth must be searched out and taught, that no true progress is possible on the basis of false premises.

Ellis took the reconciliation of indoctrination with scholarship as the subject for his presidential address, "The Dilemma of the Social Studies Teacher," before the annual meeting of the National Council for the Social Studies at St. Louis in November, 1937.[1]

His views, necessarily expressed in somewhat general terms to suit the requirements of a public address, were further defined in the *Seventh Yearbook* (1937) of the National Council, which

---

[1]This address is included on pages 159-171.

Ellis edited. Entitled *Education against Propaganda*: *Developing Skills in the Use of the Sources of Information about Public Affairs*, the volume's contributors included such recognized scholars as Harold Lasswell of the University of Chicago and Howard K. Beale then of the University of North Carolina. Ellis observed in his introduction that it had become well-nigh impossible for the ordinary citizen to make rational decisions on public issues because of the arguments from special pleaders and advertising pitchmen which assailed him on every hand. The schools must cope with this problem, he wrote, by offering specific training to make students aware of the element of persuasion, not only in the frank advertisement, but also in the ostensibly objective analysis of public issues provided by private interests, and even in the measured tones of the news commentator. The first eight articles of the *Yearbook* sought to define certain basic concepts; others outlined specific educational programs, beginning with a unit worked out for Grade VII at the University of Missouri Laboratory School.

How to achieve the broad aims Ellis prescribed was too large a problem of course to be solved by the mere insertion of a unit on indoctrination into the public school curriculum. Speaking on a panel before a meeting of the National Council in 1938 on the subject of "American History in the Junior and Senior High School," Ellis observed that American history suffered severely in prestige and presentation—and hence in effectiveness—because it was taught without regard to any clearly conceived objective or in any orderly manner. He pointed out that the course appeared four times in the educational life of the person who attended college—at about the ages of ten, thirteen, sixteen, and nineteen. The great evil in these cycles, he said, is "undifferentiated repetition" of what is basically the same survey course. Could anyone expect even the most skillful teacher to keep alive any "real sense of discovery" through three repetitions? "Sheer disgust," he warned, "with the lack of citizenship values resulting from this repetition is back of most of the current tendency to substitute non-historical courses, both the useful innovations and the more numerous ones of questionable value." Why not reduce the four cycles to two and beyond that make some attempt to differentiate between the courses? He suggested four possible solutions: (1) a progressive chronological approach, with the first course devoted to colonial history, and the last a treatment of the United States in the context of world history; (2) a topical emphasis, beginning with social history in the first course, following with economic development, and so on; (3) an alternation of the chronological and topical approaches, with two years of each. The latter plan, which he believed to be the most usable, would not eliminate repetition entirely, but it would provide some of the variation that was lacking in the old method.

Ellis' views were subjected to a practical test in 1939 when he and W. Francis English,[2] a high school principal at Carrollton, Missouri, played the major roles in reconstructing the Missouri "state course of study" for social studies. The broad outlines of their program appeared as one of sixteen articles in the first of a new series of National Council for the Social Studies bulletins on curriculum.[3] Reasoning that students must know the backgrounds of institutions before they undertook to deal with contemporary problems, they made history the center of their program. They also offered a solution to the problem of repetition. The first course, in Grade IV, was "Ways of Living in the Past," or "organized historical studies" of social life. For Grade V they prescribed "Ways of Living Today," composed primarily of geographical units on Latin America, Asia, and Africa; for Grade VI,

---

[2]English later completed work for the doctorate in history under Ellis' direction. He joined the history faculty at the University of Missouri in 1930, and in 1954 he succeeded Ellis as dean of the College of Arts and Science when Ellis became acting president of the University.

[3]James A. Michener (ed.), *The Future of the Social Studies: Proposals for an Experimental Social-Studies Curriculum*, Curriculum Series, Number One (The National Council for the Social Studies, Cambridge, Massachusetts, 1939). A number of the articles outlined suggestions for social studies curricula, but Ellis' and English's was the only one which actually described a program in process of adoption by a state.

"Ways of Living in Europe, Yesterday and Today," history and geography; Grades VII and VIII, "Ways of Living in America, Yesterday and Today," the course for Grade VII being a survey of American history in its geographical setting from 1492 to 1840, with emphasis on the origin and development of institutions, and for Grade VIII, American history from 1840 to the present, with some attention to local and regional developments; Grade IX, "World Economic Geography"; Grade X, "The Evolution of our Civilization," that is, World History; Grades XI and XII, "Modern Institutions, Social Trends, and Problems," with one semester devoted to American political institutions and processes, one to American social institutions and problems, a third to American economic institutions, and the fourth to international relations and problems. In the last two years, they said, "a real effort should be made . . . to organize the pupil's knowledge of society into the patterns of accepted scholarship." The Ellis-English course of study, officially accepted for the Missouri schools and published in 1940, has been continued with few fundamental changes to this writing.

Ellis' work with the Missouri public schools and the National Council for the Social Studies was only one facet of the activity of an extremely busy young professor. He taught nine years, from 1930 to 1939, without a leave. This meant carrying a full teaching schedule, including the direction of numerous M.A. theses and several doctoral dissertations, during the regular terms and most of the summers. In the summers of 1936 and 1939 he was acting dean of the graduate school, a mark of recognition from his University and an indication of future assignments in administration.

At the same time Ellis was becoming known as a rising young historical scholar and attracting the notice of other institutions. In the summer of 1937 he taught at Ohio State University, and he received several offers of professorships from institutions somewhat larger and better known than the University of Missouri. His thorough knowledge of the fields in which he supervised graduate students was testimony on his own campus that he was keeping pace not only with published literature but that he was pursuing investigations of his own. During these years Ellis expanded his doctoral dissertation, "The Public Career of Henry Moore Teller," wrote a short study of the income tax movement after the Civil War, and completed research for a biography of Finley Peter Dunne, the Chicago newspaperman who had won fame as the creator of Mr. Dooley, the saloon-keeper of Archey Road. Ellis was also appearing regularly on the programs of the Mississippi Valley Historical Association (he read papers on the Silver Republicans of the 1890's and the income tax movement), and contributing to its journal numerous book reviews and both the aforementioned papers as articles. In 1934, when the Mississippi Valley Historical Association met at Columbia, Missouri, to honor its president for that year, Jonas Viles, then chairman of the Missouri department of history, Ellis was active in arranging the program, and in 1935 he served as program chairman for the annual meeting of the association.

In 1938, Alfred Knopf of New York published a collection of Dooley essays, *Mr. Dooley at His Best*, which Ellis edited. A year later a Guggenheim fellowship provided Ellis with time to complete his biography of Dunne, published by Knopf in 1941 under the title *Mr. Dooley's America: A Life of Finley Peter Dunne*. Before he left the Missouri campus in the fall of 1939 for his year's leave, he completed the enlargement and revision of his doctoral dissertation, which would also be published in 1941. All of which leads one to speculate on how much Ellis might have published had not the "teacher and scholar" phase of his career been interrupted by military service in 1943 and by his shift to administration after the war—vice president of the University, 1945-1946, dean of the College of Arts and Science from 1946 to 1955, and president of the University in 1955.

Even so, the momentum of the busy 1930's as well as his own reluctance to abandon entirely this phase of his career carried

Ellis some distance further along the path of teaching and scholarship. His army career, begun in military government, soon shifted to a history section in the Pentagon. From 1945 to 1954 he continued to do some teaching—an occasional lecture course, his seminar (held in the evenings in the dean's office), and the advisement of doctoral candidates and supervision of their dissertations. In fact he directed more dissertations while he was dean than he had in the 1930's; one was still in progress when he moved up to the presidency, and he had some small part in its final supervision. Moreover, he served as president of the Mississippi Valley Historical Association in 1950-1951, ending his term with an address, "The Profession of Historian," and in 1951-1952 he was Fulbright lecturer in American Civilization at the University of Amsterdam.

It would be inaccurate to suggest, however, that Ellis had affected to despise administrative work as a distasteful duty which he could not escape. One of his closest friends has observed that he has frankly enjoyed the full round of university activities, that perhaps one of the reasons for his remaining at the University of Missouri was that it provided more opportunities for his varied talents and interests than did the other institutions which sought his services. Ellis, however, had become a historian by deliberate choice, and he had received his training from men devoted to the profession; one does not easily give up the interests and habits of twenty years.

Ellis had made his decision to be a historian in the early 1920's. The milieu in which he grew to manhood, his educational background, and the scholarly fashions of the 1920's must certainly have influenced the course his historical interests would take. Ellis was fifteen years old when the "political prairie fire" of Arthur C. Townley's Nonpartisan League seized control of the North Dakota state government in 1916. In the next half dozen years or so, as Ellis progressed through high school and college, North Dakota was the scene of violent political controversy centering around the League, the United States' entry into World War I, and the "red scare." While he was an undergraduate at the University of North Dakota, the first League governor, Lynn Frazier, was removed from office in a recall election, only to be elected to the Senate a year later.[4]

At the University, Ellis came under the influence of Orin G. Libby. The assessment of one man's influence upon another is a hazardous business, but Ellis himself has acknowledged his debt to Libby, whose framed photograph hangs on the wall of the president's office at the University of Missouri. No two men could be more unlike in personality. Libby was a difficult colleague, coldly critical and inclined to controversy. But these characteristics were tempered by an uncompromising idealism, liberal political views, and sympathy for the wronged. Libby, as well as several of the others who were Ellis' teachers at North Dakota, was in sympathy with the program of the Nonpartisan League if not entirely with its leadership and methods; in fact, while Ellis was at the University, Libby was in difficulties with its administration, partly because of his political position.

Few men are more devoted to a profession than Libby was to his. Students may have found him difficult to love, but discerning ones learned to respect him for his standards of scholarship and teaching, his high principles, and his prodigious industry. Professional historians elsewhere knew and respected him. As Frederick Jackson Turner's first Ph.D. advisee, Libby had written one of those rare doctoral dissertations which are real milestones in the history of a discipline. It was published in 1894, under the title, *The Geographical Distribution of the Vote of the Thirteen States on the Federal Constitution, 1787-1788.* A seminal work which anticipated and influenced Charles A. Beard's better known studies of the economic origins of the Constitution and

---

[4] The League had elected its first Senator, Edwin F. Ladd, in 1920. When he died in 1925, the year Ellis received his M.A. degree at the University of North Dakota, he was succeeded by Gerald P. Nye. Conservative Republicans in the Senate very nearly succeeded in preventing his being seated.

Jeffersonian democracy, it is still referred to by scholars. Although Libby never entirely abandoned his original interests, he was shifting to studies of the West before he left Wisconsin for North Dakota in 1902. Libby's "A Study of the Greenback Movement, 1876-1884" was published in 1899 in the *Transactions of the Wisconsin Academy of Science, Arts, and Letters*. In North Dakota he turned increasingly to studies of exploration and early settlement in the northern plains and to the early history of his adopted state, North Dakota, which had achieved statehood only thirteen years before his arrival.

Under the circumstances Ellis' topic for his M.A. thesis, "Minor Parties from the Civil War to 1900," was a natural choice, and one that his adviser fully approved. Libby felt that the post-Civil War era, "the most important of all" in his view, had been too long neglected by historians. The selection was especially significant, for Ellis had more or less marked out at this early stage in his development the area of his professional specialization. Although the completed study produced no new information or interpretations, one can not read through it and examine the bibliography without sensing that Ellis had approached his subject with enthusiasm, that it had meant more to him than a routine hurdle preceding an M.A. degree. A lengthy discussion and analysis of the "geography of insurgent parties" and the "geography of free silver" within the general summary reflected Libby's predilections. The degree was duly awarded at the end of the summer session in 1925.

For the next three years Ellis taught history and social science at the State Teachers College at Mayville, North Dakota. In 1928 he moved on to the University of Iowa to begin study for the doctorate. Here he came under the influence of another historian of the West, Louis Pelzer, who was an old acquaintance of Libby. The two historians had played leading roles in the founding of the Mississippi Valley Historical Association in 1907, and both were prominent in its affairs for many years:

Libby was president in 1909-1910 and a frequent contributor to its journal; Pelzer was a member of the executive committee, president, and editor of the journal. Pelzer's primary interest was social history, particularly of the Midwest. His *Marches of the Dragoons in the Mississippi Valley* and his biographies of Augustus Caesar Dodge and Henry Dodge had earned him a solid reputation by the 1920's, although his most widely known work, *The Cattlemen's Frontier*, was still to come when Ellis first met him. The young man from North Dakota found a kindred spirit in the kindly, dryly humorous professor at Iowa. In his own way Pelzer was as painstaking a scholar and as demanding a teacher as Libby, and he had the added quality of warmth which Libby lacked. Pelzer, like Ellis, came from a rural background, and he too appreciated the earthy humor of farmers and Westerners as well as their problems and grievances.

The subject Ellis chose for his dissertation was a study of the public career of Henry Moore Teller, Senator from Colorado and the leading exponent in his time of free coinage of silver. There was much to recommend the choice. Teller's career and the free silver issue together spanned the entire period from the Civil War until well into the twentieth century. In addition, consideration of the money question would ensure the dissertation's being broadened to include economic problems as well as political activities. And, from the standpoint of academic opportunism, the study was timely, because agrarian movements, particularly the Farmers' Alliances and the People's Party, were enjoying a considerable vogue in historical journals during the late 1920's and early 1930's. At the time, Ellis was probably no more aware of this purely professional consideration than most graduate students when they choose a dissertation subject, but the timing actually did work in his favor. Two years after he received the Ph.D., his first article, one drawn from the dissertation and entitled "The Silver Republicans in the Election of 1896," appeared in the *Mississippi Valley Historical Review*. In 1939 Ellis presented another phase of the Teller biography as a paper, "The Origin and Meaning of the Teller (or Fourth) Resolution," read before a session of the Mississippi Valley Historical Association at its annual meeting in Memphis. Another article published in the *Mississippi Valley Historical Review* in 1940, "Public Opinion and the Income Tax, 1860-1900," had been developed in the course of research preparatory to the publication of an expanded version of his dissertation. This appeared in 1941 as *Henry Moore Teller: Defender of the West* (Caxton Printers, Caldwell, Idaho).

Henry Moore Teller of Colorado was the sort of public figure who invites rescue from oblivion. Lacking the color which catches the eye of the press or the people, the Tellers of American public life are frequently passed over for such men as Ignatius Donnelly, Ben Tillman, Roscoe Conkling, and James G. Blaine. Yet time and reflection may, and often do, demonstrate that the Tellers are those who in the end actually influenced the course of events in their time and who have left a mark of solid achievement, while all that remains of the Conklings and Blaines are vague memories of their posturings and empty rhetoric.

The Ellis biography was a contribution to the history of the post-Civil War era because in several respects it supplemented the standard works on agrarian-Western reform movements. Ellis' book contained the first full account of the Silver Republicans, a group which had received little more than cursory attention in previous studies. John D. Hicks's highly regarded *The Populist Revolt*, published ten years before the Teller, had given surprisingly little space to their role in the party battles of the 1880's and the 1890's, and Hicks treated the silver issue largely in terms of its part in confusing the forces of reform and ruining the prospects of the People's Party in 1894-1896. The only mention of Teller in *The Populist Revolt* is in connection with a brief discussion of the Silverites' bolt of the Republican convention of 1896. Moreover, working from the vantage point of a study of the career of a respected and influential United States Senator,

Ellis added the dimension of national perspective to the standard accounts of the agrarian-Western reform movements. Hicks, for example, had considered the Farmers' Alliance and the People's Party almost entirely from the standpoint of their grass-roots manifestations.

But the book is more than a footnote to the work of others. Ellis himself saw it as an historical analysis of the role of the West in national affairs during a critical transition period. Teller's sobriquet, "Defender of the West," was conferred, not because he surpassed all rivals in the role of errand boy for Western special interests, but because of his success in elevating Western grievances and complaints to the level of national concerns. Ellis' book drives home the point that Western views were no more sectional and self-centered than those accepted as sound guides to national policy by Eastern-urban-industrial spokesmen in Washington, and that Westerners' and Southerners' exasperation with phony arguments disguising Eastern self-interest was a major cause of the revolution in domestic national policies ushered in by the twentieth century. Few scholarly books on the post-Civil War era make so convincing a case for Western complaints, are documented so thoroughly by reason and fact, or reveal so plainly the self-interest and narrow sectionalism of those who defended a deflationary policy and a banking and money system controlled by private interests.

Among Teller's chief virtues were his judicious calm, and his reliance upon cold fact and reasoned argument, in an era when the intemperate charge was the common currency of public debate. The Ellis book is suited to its subject. The tone is good-tempered, tolerant, and above all, judicious. Although he is a Westerner writing on a Western subject, Ellis reveals none of the sectional prejudices that have afflicted some historians when they have written about the region of their origins. There are few signs in his work, for example, of the kind of bias for the West that Edward Channing exhibited for New England. Ellis is no colorless chronicler, however. He is sympathetic to his section and he admires his subject, but the problems of the West are weighed in the balance of the national interest, and the actions of Teller judged by the standard of public service, not only to his section for the moment, but to the nation in the years to come. Ellis' own standard of statesmanship appears in his description of Teller: Possessing "the common touch that distinguishes a real statesman in a democracy," his youthful idealism surviving "the warm competition of business, law, and politics," he was "one of the small group of political leaders of whom it can be said that political experience made him increasingly sensitive to the needs of the under-privileged."

Ellis' second book—actually the first to be published—was *Mr. Dooley's America: A Life of Finley Peter Dunne*. The subject was one to which he was drawn almost unconsciously over the years. As a boy, still too young to grasp their full implications, Ellis had chuckled over the Dooley sallies; the Irish dialect had its own particular appeal around Towner, North Dakota, where the local Norwegians' misadventures with English were a favorite source of amusement for their Yankee neighbors. Years later, when Ellis was writing his doctoral dissertation, he learned to look for Mr. Dooley's flashes of insight to bring life to the dead past, and after he began teaching at the University of Missouri he adopted the practice of using Dooley commentary in his lectures. Admiration for Dooley led to interest in his creator, Finley Peter Dunne.

Mr. Dooley's America was reviewed enthusiastically when it appeared; praised as one of the important biographies of 1941, its reviewers included Franklin P. Adams in the Sunday *New York Herald-Tribune*, John Chamberlain in the *Times*, and William Allen White in the *Saturday Review of Literature*. Historians were no less kind than the newspapermen. There was not a little nostalgia in many of the reviews, for most of the reviewers either knew Dunne personally or remembered Mr. Dooley as a pleasant and regular part of their lives. (Dunne had died only five years before his biography appeared, although the Dooley articles disappeared in the early 1920's.) The reviewers recognized the solid qualities of the book in such terms as "a real contribution to American social history," "particularly significant to the historian since it recounts many important political events," "a political history of the United States from 1893 to Dunne's death in 1936," and "a picture of America and American life and politics." William Allen White called it "a G-string obbligato of American history from McKinley and Byran to Wilson."

All were correct in a sense, but it is a special kind of America which passes in review: the posers, the humbugs, the egotists, and pretence in every form. "Imperialism, militarism, smug corruption in government and business, pretentious nonsense in religion and education, the protective tariff, fake reformers, self-deified aristocrats, and dishonest journalists," all these and more were objects of the perceptive ridicule of the saloon-keeper of Archey Road. As one reviewer observed: "Dunne was at his best when his Mr. Dooley was debunking the demagogues and stuffed shirts of politics and finance, espousing the fight of the underprivileged and the wronged, or acting as a censor of the morals of his time. He was at his best when he drew liberally on his Irish Catholic background and the wisdom of his people."

What endeared Mr. Dooley to Americans in the decade and a half before World War I, and to Dunne's biographer of the 1930's, was the "kindest tolerance and good nature as well as candor" that he brought to bear upon his targets. As Ellis wrote, his was a Thackerayan "realism that went beneath pretence and humbug but which did not eliminate the elements of human sympathy and decency." Moreover, Dunne played no favorites. The self-important reformer, particularly one who used reform to further his private political ambitions, was as open a target as the recipients of his bitterest gibes, Charles T. Yerkes and George S. Pullman. Himself something of an anarchist with no great faith in human institutions, Dunne ridiculed the Chicago anarchists of his day and the socialists for their "dull oratory and fuzzy ideas of political strategy."

The influence of Mr. Dooley's commentary upon his America is impossible to measure, but Ellis concluded that the national tone could hardly escape being improved to a degree by exposure to the regular diet of common sense that Dunne purveyed in the guise of a fictitious saloon-keeper whom his readers had come to regard as a living personage. For example, Ellis believes that Dooley's classic, much-quoted remark that "th' Supreme Coort follows th' iliction returns," rescued Americans from "the probability of making the court a symbol too sacred to be the subject of discussion or change. . . ."

In writing on Dunne-Dooley and handling his subject as he did, Ellis reveals something of himself. His evident delight in Dooley and his approval of his view of life are apparent on every page. Like Dooley, Ellis is impatient of cant, of pose, of self-importance; he is intolerant of wrong and is sympathetic to the underdog and the wronged. Like Dooley, Ellis likes mankind, but he does not expect more of him than he is capable of. The calm tolerance, the good sense, the faint cynicism of Mr. Dooley are also a part of Elmer Ellis. So it happened that the thoroughly urban and elegant Finley Peter Dunne—or perhaps it was after all the more earthy Mr. Dooley—found his ideal biographer in a young man not too many years removed from the North Dakota prairies.

Completed when Ellis was only forty years old, the Dunne and Teller biographies were his last historical publications, except for some addresses and the writing he did while he was a historian for the Army. It remains therefore to conclude this commentary on Ellis' work as historian and scholar with some remarks about Ellis' views on history in general.

Probably the most marked characteristics of Ellis' work are balance and judiciousness. He is good-humored and tolerant, even when writing of the tempestuous times and ill-humored men that figure so prominently in the Teller biography. Ellis does not disguise his sympathies, yet he is singularly free from personal crotchets or pet theories. To him the historian's first task is to find out, to interpret, and to reveal. In his presidential address before the Mississippi Valley Historical Association in 1951 he observed that unremitting research was an essential of first-class college teaching: "The validity of the generalizations to which [the historian] leads students will be just as sound as his research, and nothing else will make it better." Content to leave philosophizing and elaborate hypotheses to others, Ellis would diligently search out the facts related to any subject he investigated, establish their relationships, interpret their meaning, and attempt to place his subject in its proper relation to its own time and to the larger stream of human events. He insisted on no rigid system of methodology, but viewed this as a flexible matter subject to adaptation to the worker and to the nature of his subject and material. Historians, he frequently remarked, would improve their understanding and interpretations as much or more by using the knowledge and techniques developed by the specialized social scientists, as by endlessly specializing and periodizing their own studies or by refining their methods so as to be able to discover the last insignificant minutiae of the past. He constantly encouraged his students to take work in such fields as economics and political science, and his own writing, although usually cast in a political framework for the sake of familiarity and clarity, is particularly rich in its economic and social considerations.

Much as he himself loves his discipline, Ellis is not a "history for its own sake" historian. He is firmly convinced that history has its own practical values. The specialized social scientist can test his theories by studying the past, where cause and effect are most clearly related. In the broader sense, knowledge of the past informs the present, although the past may have no specifically or presently applicable lessons. The beginning of wise policy in the present and for the future, he believes, is accurate knowledge about and a clear understanding of what has happened before. Everyman's need for a knowledge of history gives the historian a major role in maintaining the health of the nation: upon him rests the responsibility of informing the citizenry.

Although Ellis would be the last to look upon himself as some variety of historical philosopher, the fact that he wrote biographical studies of crusaders for the public good implies a theory of the springs of human events. Ellis believes that it is men that count, and that moral men with a conscience and a sense of justice and sympathy for the underdog count the most. In short, Ellis sees man as no helpless victim of great impersonal forces leading him through an inevitable course of events to an inevitable and inglorious end. His is a humane rather than a religious or mechanistic approach, an essentially optimistic, liberal-progressive view of the past.

3

Administrator

THE TECHNIQUE of college and university administration
has been discussed by a number of men who have known the
work from experience, most recently in the book by Harold W.
Stoke, *The American College President* (1959). Inevitably, most
of this literature is biographical rather than analytical in character.
It is possible that some day college and university administration
will be reduced to a set of principles and procedures similar to
that which has been developed for business administration. But
those who know the college and university intimately are likely
to believe that many of the essential characteristics will always
defy analysis. College administration is still a highly personal
thing. That is why, when an institution chooses a businessman or
other non-academic person for the top position in a university, it
is generally assumed that somewhere, just below the top perhaps,

there is an administrator of academic experience who is really making the wheels turn. It is hard to believe that the administrator without academic experience can actually make the academic enterprise move properly. This idea could be wrong, but it is a common notion.

When a man of academic training and experience becomes president of a fairly large university, his first concern must be for the business structure of the institution. This is true because, as a rule, this is the side of the institution's affairs in which his own experience is most limited. Even if his experience has been in the areas closely allied to business, or if he is an academic man coming from the ranks of the faculty, he will lack experience in the management of university business enterprises. It is the business office of the university which is, by ordinary faculty members, known the least and criticised the most. Inevitably, the large structure of business organization required to operate a big university has aroused the suspicion and even the hostility of the academic staff. Many of the rules which a professor encounters have to do with expenditure of money, accounting for expenditures, travel vouchers, purchase orders, and rules concerning the use and care of the physical plant. Very simply, the academic point of view is that all this machinery should exist only to assist in getting done the job of teaching and research. The professor constantly sees tendencies which indicate to him that business operations, not education, have become the primary function of the institution. A new president who knows these things will not have the alternative of reducing the business operations below the point necessary to carry out essential procedures. Moreover, many of the members of the governing board, at least when newly appointed, will be, or appear to be, more interested in business details than in any other matters. The good academic administrator knows that, so far as faculty opinion is concerned, his *attitude* and *approach* to business affairs are much more important than the business structure itself.

In 1955 when Elmer Ellis became president of the University of Missouri, he inherited a university business structure that had definite characteristics. It was highly centralized, and efficient, and was served by several younger men of great ability. The head of the whole centralized business operation had served the institution for forty years and had constructed around himself an organization of a type similar to those built by Morey at Illinois and Middlebrook at Minnesota. These men, in their tight centralization of business affairs, served their institutions well by obliterating all traces of petty, unsupervised business operations in the hands of departments and agencies of the university. To the greatest extent possible, they drove home to all the idea that there should be no personal or departmental perquisites, and that all the facilities of the university belonged to the institution, not to certain parts or segments of it. They did a good job. The days when professors sold coal or fence-posts to the university were left far behind. Even they, however, were never quite able to get the principle accepted that a class in History or English might be held in a building constructed primarily for Law or Medicine.

The new President, after a careful study of the business organization and with the retirement of the Vice-President in charge of business operations, Leslie Cowan, established a Comptroller and a Business Manager, each directly responsible to him. The Comptroller became an important budget officer as well as head of the whole internal audit and accounting system. The Business Manager, as one of his first tasks, revised and centralized the purchasing system of the university, establishing under his office in addition to the purchasing department, departments for maintenance of the physical plant and for new construction. The Comptroller and the Business Manager were already staff members of the university, two young men of great ability.

As might have been expected, with the strong centralization of business affairs for many years, some activities had become the function of the business office which, in the opinion of the faculty, belonged in the hands of academic personnel. Gradually, and after due consideration, these activities were removed from the supervision of the business office. An example is the establishment of the Office of Aids and Awards. Student financial aids had grown up gradually over the years, with scholarships administered by a committee, and loans and student labor handled largely in the business office. These functions were combined so that scholarship funds, loans, and jobs could be used to take care of many cases of need under the supervison of a Director of Aids and Awards, a teacher with academic training.

The most evident and most dramatic achievement of the administration of President Ellis thus far has been in the expansion of the physical plant. His predecessor, President Frederick A. Middlebush, had been able in the last eight years of his administration to construct a number of new buildings. The Union Building was paid for by money appropriated for student feeding and housing, and by revenue bonds, while a number of units for married students was financed entirely by bonds. Houses for faculty members were erected, using sections brought from an army base. A smaller number of faculty and student housing units was built at the School of Mines at Rolla. The largest building project in many decades was carried out in President Middlebush's administration—construction of the Medical School and Hospital at Columbia.

When President Ellis assumed office, it was quite clear that the university must expand its physical plant. The University of Missouri had constructed few buildings during the two decades before World War II, as had been done at several large middlewestern universities. No large expansion had been carried out since the buildings around Francis Quadrangle had been erected in 1895. President Ellis recommended that, since state revenues could not provide adequate funds, a state bond issue be authorized to expand the existing facilities of state institutions. Appointed by the Governor as chairman of a committee to lay before the people the need for a state bond issue of $75,000,000, he drew upon the support of eminent citizens all over the state, and the issue was authorized at a statewide election. To be liquidated within a maximum period of twenty-five years, the issue was to provide building funds for all state institutions. Almost one-third of the total amount was allotted to the University of Missouri at Columbia and Rolla by the General Assembly. This was a real test of the skill and ability of a new university president. His boyhood in North Dakota, residence in Iowa and Missouri, and his deep historical study of the western plains states had enabled Ellis to present this issue to the people in terms they could understand. It was generally acknowledged that his leadership was a crucial factor in the success of the campaign.

With funds allotted from this bond issue, there has been constructed in Columbia a new building for Business and Public Administration; one for Fine Arts, including a little theater; dormitories; and additions for Agriculture, Electrical Engineering, Home Economics, and Law. In process (1960) is a large addition doubling the size of the Library, a building for Veterinary Medicine, new greenhouses, a classroom building, a building for Industrial Education, and an addition for Journalism. The contract has been let for an atomic reactor to be paid for in part by federal funds, and approval has been given for a federal loan making the enlargement of the student union possible. Also authorized are items for repairs and remodeling, an addition to the power plant, and a building for a fire station and fire training. At the School of Mines, structures have been authorized for Engineering laboratories, Civil Engineering and Mechanics, a classroom building, additions to the power plant, dormitories, and remodeling. In addition to these expansions, revenue bonds for additional dormitories at Columbia and Rolla have raised the total amount spent or to be spent during this brief period to $36,000,000—a truly gigantic undertaking. Nevertheless, when the bond issue funds were allotted, the President warned the General Assembly that this expansion would take care only of present needs and that within ten years he expected to ask for a similar sum to provide expansion necessary for larger enrollments. The university president must not only help to get the money, he must see that its expenditure within the institution is carried out in the best way to promote the mission assigned to the institution. Accordingly, Ellis appointed a Campus Planning Committee which constantly studies and makes recommendations concerning the future physical expansion of the University. Furthermore, in the design of new buildings, he has insisted that the plans and programs of departments as well as the latest knowledge of architects be taken into account.

It is quite clear that, in the final analysis, the president of a university cannot be evaluated as an administrator by the size of the physical plant, the number of students and faculty, or the amount of money in the total annual operating budget. The final test must be found in the way he makes use of the funds he gets in order to carry on and advance the cause of teaching, research, and educational service to the people of his generation. No public enterprise of this type ever has enough money to do everything that seems to be worth doing at the time. The president must, in terms of long-range goals and basic values, make decisions every day as to whether this or that, not both, should be done. From this point of view, the presidents of universities, whether large or small in size, may be evaluated and compared. So it must be in this realm of genuine educational achievement that the president, as well as his academic staff, must be weighed and measured.

President Ellis inherited from his predecessor, Frederick A. Middlebush, a sound academic institution. Ellis had played an important part in planning and building the University's program. In the period before World War II, the administration had leaned heavily on him for advice and leadership. He had been called upon to help with the important surveys conducted by the Board of Visitors, and he prepared the report of this body at one time. As a member of the Library Committee he had worked toward improving the administration of the library, helped plan and carry into execution a sound program of purchases of scholarly materials, and had secured the grant for establishing the Western Historical Manuscripts Collection in 1943. He kept in close touch with the public schools and the junior colleges, and he had the respect and confidence of the public school leaders.

When the veterans of World War II began to return in 1945, the university administration faced a herculean task in providing facilities, materials, and staff for them. It was quite clear that another top level administrator was needed to assume responsibilities in supervising many of the administrative units that were not attached to a college or school, and to take on the added responsibilities of being the strong right arm of the President in many matters that needed attention and careful planning.

In late 1944 the Board of Curators created the position of Vice-President in charge of Extra-Divisional Activities and asked the Army to release Captain Ellis as early as possible for this assignment. He returned to the campus in March, 1945, and plunged into this task. He assumed the administrative responsibilities for directing such services as the library, the admissions office, the health services, the R.O.T.C., the Extension Division, and the Department of Physical Education.

Within the year, however, Dean W. C. Curtis of the College of Arts and Science announced that he wanted to be relieved of the deanship. Dr. Curtis had become acting dean in 1939, dean in 1940, and had guided the College through the hectic years of the pre-war and World War II period. In 1945 expansion of the staff was necessary because a number of the younger men were not returning, several of the elderly professors were ready for retirement, and the teaching duties of the College were exceedingly heavy. It was clear that the faculty of the College of Arts and Science needed a young, resourceful dean who knew the faculty and who was acquainted with the College. Ellis was clearly the choice of the faculty. It was with some reluctance that President Middlebush recommended his appointment as Dean just as Ellis was getting the program of the vice-presidency under way. Ellis became Dean of the Faculty on February 1, 1946.

The task that he assumed was a difficult one. There were several departments that had become progressively weaker during the decade before the war. This was due to a number of things. During the thirties recruitment had been difficult because of a shortage of funds. Age had taken its toll in those years. Some departments had been content with one or two strong men and had filled their teaching ranks with less effective staff members. Two departments, previously strong ones, were torn with dissension. Some of the very best young men who had gone into the service went elsewhere or remained in government employment. The budget was never adequate for the task at hand.

Ellis was concerned with improving the faculty by filling positions with top scholars who were good teachers and who were ready to work hard at both teaching and scholarly tasks. He was concerned about the quality of teaching and was insistent that the departmental chairmen and senior staff members take the leadership in improving instruction. A committee was appointed to undertake the job of improving instruction among young staff members in the art of college teaching. As a result, the Carnegie Corporation granted the University $50,000 for a five-year program in the improvement of college teaching.

The choice of staff members, always a difficult one in any University, was pushed with vigor and good results. The curriculum committee was asked to take leadership in the study and appraisal of the general education courses. A number of departments were given new chairmen who were willing to take leadership in developing good teaching and encouraging research.

In no way did Ellis' leadership emphasize revolution and

radical reorganization. The College had always had great strength, and the institution was encouraged to grow in confidence and vigor. Those who were teachers and scholars were rewarded. The Dean followed the open-door policy in all matters. Faculty members knew that their ideas would be considered and acted upon with vigor if they were sound and attainable. Policy remained firmly in the faculty's hands, but the leadership was in the hands of an intelligent, sympathetic, and vigorous dean.

Ellis was particularly concerned about student welfare and services. Because many veterans had had poor academic backgrounds, he took the lead in helping to adjust subject matter to their capabilities. Several remedial courses were instituted, but they were for the purpose of getting students to where they could stand on their own academic feet; Dean Ellis would not support a watered-down curriculum in upper class courses. A reading clinic and a language laboratory were provided. Better student services were made available in the College's office.

The faculty supported with enthusiasm Ellis' vigorous and democratic leadership. It was recognized as a strong leadership and not one that lagged behind faculty thinking. If a proposition was not supported, Ellis made clear why he withheld his approval. All matters were thrashed out, and many times a faculty man came away from a conference with the Dean marveling at how much the Dean knew about his specialty and about the problems surrounding it.

Overall, Ellis' record as dean was outstanding. He built a strong faculty and rewarded good teaching and research. He knew what good teaching and research were because he had made an outstanding record in both fields as a member of the Department of History. He had held a Guggenheim Fellowship, and his use of a Carnegie Grant for the improvement of instruction had made a noticeable impact on the quality of college teaching in the state. Thus, in 1955, Ellis brought to the office of President a high concern for the teacher as a person and as a professional man and he believed that academic achievement could be and must be evaluated without deception or sentiment. These qualities and experiences, more than any others, have enabled him to become the president as the faculty member sees and knows him.

There are two kinds of staff members in a college or university, the academic and the non-academic. It may be a peculiarity of academic people, but it is certain that no university president has the option of taking care of one group at the expense of the other. If the faculty were the unfavored group, it would rebel. If it were favored, it would resent the abandonment of human values indicated in policies unfavorable to the other group. For, above all, faculty people, as a rule, care about people and are concerned that none be mistreated or be the object of discrimination.

Shortly after he took office, President Ellis began negotiations to bring staff members under the provisions of the state workman's compensation law. This move meant most to non-academic staff members but it was widely approved by the faculty. A few years later, he approved the establishment, in the office of the comptroller, of a personnel officer for the non-academic staff. This was good business for the university but it was also good for the staff members themselves.

The whole matter of so-called "fringe benefits" was in a confused and unsatisfactory state when Ellis became president. This was due not to any fault of the former president but was the result of a series of unforeseen events. The university, in the 1920's, had instituted a system of group insurance, but the plan had failed for various reasons and had been abandoned within a few years. Hence, there was no provision for group insurance or for group health benefits, except the plan of Group Hospital Service, Inc. of St. Louis which enrolled members on a voluntary basis. This helped many staff members a great deal but it had no provisions to cover the major medical catastrophe which is such a nightmare to a man on a moderate salary.

There was no institutional retirement program. About 1940, the University had instituted a retirement plan whereby the institution matched, later more than matched, the contribution of the individual. This plan was compulsory for academic staff members and was taken in the form of an annuity contract which became the property of the individual. Then in the early 1950's, when Social Security was extended to teachers, the law provided that individuals in public institutions with such plans were not eligible. The governing board abandoned the annuity in order that staff members might come under Social Security, which, in 1954, was the only retirement benefit provided. A few older members in the College of Arts and Science were eligible for Carnegie Pensions, but these had been stabilized at a low rate. Moreover, staff members in other divisions and younger staff members had no pensions at all.

The retirement plan and the plan for medical benefits that were finally adopted had been checked with the faculty many times. The plans were drafted by the Committee on University Policy and were the result of the long and devoted labor of several members of the faculty. The retirement plan was somewhat controversial in that it departed from the widely accepted idea of a completely funded plan with benefits fixed at the time of adoption. Less controversial, since more and more institutions were coming to adopt it, was the provision for no contribution from the faculty member at all. The Committee, after long study, concluded that, whether in line with current business thinking or not, there were two basic principles necessary for a sound retirement policy.

1. The retirement benefit should not be fixed as to amount but should be calculated on the basis of salary scale so that the retirement stipend would be as nearly in line with monetary buying power as was possible. The Committee had known of cases in which a retirement planned

in 1933 for $150.00 a month had been received in 1955 when that monthly sum was quite inadequate.

2. The plan should be, largely, unfunded. The Committee believed it to be illogical and unsound for a state institution, depending upon tax funds, to set aside a large sum to be held into the distant future from which relatively low income would be derived. It also considered it unsound for the faculty member to pay a portion of an already modest salary into such a fund. This plan, as approved, provided for a modest fund purely for the purpose of easing unusual retirement demands in making the operating budget.

The retirement plan was under consideration for several years, and a man less patient than the President would probably have been discouraged long before it was adopted. Before its final acceptance the General Assembly adopted a new retirement plan for employees of the state, all of whom would be covered unless certified by the department as coming under some other plan. This system is a contributory one and does not provide as large benefits as the one adopted by the University. Not only were all the academic staff members covered by the University plan, but also clerical, supervisory, and other non-academic staff members who received more than a certain annual salary. It was not intended that either plan would cover part-time employees.

The medical benefits and group insurance plan has been adopted more recently and is still in an unfinished state. Two plans for medical benefits were offered, one providing for immediate or first-dollar coverage for staff members on lower salaries; the other providing for the faculty a plan to cover medical catastrophes resulting in such large costs that payment would be virtually ruinous. A small group life insurance feature was included and this part will probably be extended. The whole structure, moreover, may be modified many times in the future to meet the needs of staff members.

Faculty members worked hard on these plans, but they worked with a leader who was honest and intelligent and who held as his basic tenet the belief that people are important and that it is matter of great moment what happens to them. This spirit, more than all the fringe benefits and monetary rewards, has done a tremendous job toward motivating the whole University. Other men, frequently, have the same beliefs, but the President shows clearly in what he says and does that this is his guiding principle and he intends to act upon it.

The President also insists upon having an academic achievement of highest quality. He has made it clear over and over again that he wants excellence from staff members and students as well. Even though at times the judgment may fall heavily upon him, no academic man worthy of his position has any sympathy for any other approach than this. Many staff members would agree that what such a person needs in order to do his best is not just the time and facilities necessary, but he also needs an atmosphere, a spirit of respect for learning and the academic life. The spirit, given a man of great ability, will often produce startling results with inferior facilities. Most academic persons would probably agree that it is within this framework of academic achievement and stimulation that the matter of academic salary scale deserves discussion.

The University of Missouri had been able to maintain its academic salary levels somewhat above those of the universities situated to the west and south but generally somewhat below those of universities to the north and east. Salary scales at Missouri were not in a wretched position when Ellis became president, but scales were rising so rapidly elsewhere that it was a tremendous task to hold Missouri's relative position. Moreover, as the President told the General Assembly, salaries at Missouri should be comparable to those at the great institutions to the north and east.

Only three such institutions were really comparable—Wisconsin, Minnesota, and Illinois, because only in these, and in Nebraska to the west, had the Land-Grant establishment been combined physically with the state university. Moreover, only in Wisconsin and Minnesota was the situation entirely comparable, since only these had a medical school on the same university campus. Even here, the locations at Minnesota were not entirely comparable. The physical dispersion of the highest educational facility may and does become important when considered with respect to the share of state revenues that should be allotted for this purpose.

Of the five states mentioned, Wisconsin, Minnesota, Illinois, Nebraska, and Missouri, only Illinois had a greater population and higher income than Missouri, but in both Wisconsin and Minnesota a greater share of the state income had been given to higher education than had been done in Missouri. In contending that Missouri should find its place among the leading state universities, the President based his contention on facts well known within the University. Contrary to the opinion of some people, the top academic men do not move from one place to another just because of a few hundred or even a thousand dollars higher salary per year. Such men usually have ties of family, sentiment, recreation, and strong friendships. They set a high value upon the spirit of an institution and upon the academic quality of the colleagues with whom they are associated. During the twenty-five years from 1905 to 1930, when the University of Missouri lost many able men to other institutions, most of them had gone to a comparatively small number of universities. Of twenty-two men who left after their reputations were already made, not young men who left and later made a name for themselves, four went to Cornell, three each to Harvard and the University of California, two each to Yale, Illinois, and Minnesota, and one each to

Princeton, Chicago, Ohio State, Washington, Stanford, and Duke. One, the well-known Thorstein Veblen, went to the New York City School for Social Research.

The outstanding men who leave a good university do so, not at a lower salary to be sure, but primarily because of facilities for further work. And of all these facilities, none are so important as the laboratory and library. Laboratories, except for the great machines in use today such as wind-tunnels and atomic reactors, can be readily provided to meet specific needs. But a library of high quality for research is the work of many generations. The new agriculture laboratory was built before Ellis became president but there has been added during his administration new research facilities for electrical engineering and psychology, some medical laboratories, new laboratories at Rolla, and considerable additions in many other fields. But the great achievement, that which more than any other determines the academic quality of the institution, is the expansion of the University Library. Not only is the collection being improved and increased at a rapid rate, but the holdings are being systematically studied and evaluated in order that all funds be used to build the right kind of library for a university. So soundly is the basic collection built at the present time that, with the incomparable holdings of the library of the State Historical Society of Missouri housed in the same building, the University Library, if it continues to grow at its present rate, will be one of the finest university libraries in the Middle West. This policy of building the library is not the result of accident but has been foreseen and provided for by the President himself.

During his administration and with his encouragement, the faculties have tried to improve instruction by committee studies, careful sectioning, revising the grading system, and in other ways. On recommendation of a committee, the President provided funds for a language laboratory and a closed circuit television station where experimentation with these new teaching techniques could be carried on.

Ellis' leadership has also been felt in the field of research. During his administration, the regulations concerning control and ownership of patents, work begun under President Middlebush, has been largely completed. The knotty problem of extra compensation to staff members for research and outside consultation has been continually wrestled with but not yet solved. All institutions are struggling with this problem but none has yet found an entirely satisfactory solution of it. Great strides have been taken in research in agriculture, with new experimental fields and stations established in various parts of the state. New research agencies have been set up in the field of Business and Public Administration; the Bureaus of Government Research and of Business Research. In 1958 the University reached a goal which Ellis had looked forward to for many years—the establishment of the University of Missouri Press.

President Ellis has also supported every movement to increase the service programs for residents of the state. Increasing salaries in the Agricultural Extension Service has been a major problem, while in the other extension fields, new programs are constantly undertaken which require financial support. Among these have been the program in community development and conferences in various fields. The general extension service, now called the Division of Continuing Education, has been made a department supported by the general maintenance budget and is no longer classified as an extramural activity. On July 1, 1960, all extension activities, Agricultural Extension and Continuing Education, were combined in one Extension Division under a Dean of the University Extension Division.

The establishment of new programs and activities, as well as methods and procedures to be used, frequently come up to a president as suggestions and recommendations from below. But leadership begins where it also ends—at the top. It is a subtle thing and yet indispensable. Whatever else it involves, it is clear that leadership cannot be faked or counterfeited. A man may make a limited success without a great deal of it, but he cannot be regarded as having leadership qualities when he does not. Before the essentials of leadership are considered in a closing section, let us look here at some of the manifestations of it.

There is nothing in the laws and regulations which prescribes that the president of a university must take an active part in the national and international activities that have to do with higher education. Even leadership in local affairs of this type might conceivably be abjured. But it is accepted today that responsible and able men in such positions will spend a great deal of time in such activities. This is the educational leadership which colleges and universities furnish, without charge, to the world, the nation, and the community.

Few men, when they step into the position of president of an educational institution, are well prepared for such leadership, especially on the national and international level. But in addition to his long study of history and international affairs, President Ellis had spent a year in Europe on a Fulbright Grant before he became President. So far during his tenure as president, he has represented the Association of American Universities in England during one summer, and, in late 1959 and early 1960, visited India, where he saw the work done by the University of Missouri in cooperation with four large Indian states. His service on the Board of Foreign Scholarships for the United States Department of State has broadened this view of education in other countries.

On the national scene, he has served on important committees of the American Council on Education and has been active in the Association of American Universities, and in the Association of Land-Grant Colleges and State Universities. His activities in the Historical Section of the Army during the war prepared him for service on the Advisory Committee on the History of the Army established by the Secretary of the Army. His work on an important committee of the North Central Association may be regarded as regional rather than national in character.

His leadership on the Truman Library Board is at once national and local since it is one of the state's cherished institutions. He is an ex-officio member of the William Rockhill Nelson Trust and has close ties with the Nelson Gallery of Art. His relations have been cordial and close with the Midwest Research Institute in Kansas City and also with Community Surveys there. In addition to his appointment by the Governor as Chairman of the State Bond Issue Committee, he is also co-chairman, with Reverend Paul Reinert, President of St. Louis University, of the Missouri State Commission for Education Beyond the High School. His additional activities in Missouri are almost innumerable, since the President of the State University is regarded, and rightly so, as the state's most important educational leader.

In considering the technique of educational leadership it is necessary to analyze the president's job and find its essential ingredients. Some of the factors are personal qualities, while others are methods and techniques. The latter can be learned and used by anyone who has intelligence and a reasonable amount of patience. One can strive to acquire the former, but some have these talents to a much greater degree than others. The difference between the outstanding leader and the competent man lies here. Good men sometimes lack these talents; sometimes (alas!) men of few scruples have them abundantly. But there are other personal qualities, too, those of an ethical nature, and without them, great talents will rarely carry a man through. The methods and techniques reported by successful college presidents are undoubtedly those required for the job. But no man who has held the position can analyze his own character with the objectivity needed to discover the other qualities needed. There will be disagreements with the present analysis but none of consequence with the final judgment that President Ellis has the qualities that are demanded for the position.

As to methods and techniques, the first requisite is that the president must have ways of getting accurate information and, on occasion, he must get it on short notice. In a business organization, this might be accomplished by a regular series of production charts, balance sheets, time studies, and output graphs, all flowing regularly into the hand of the official responsible. Little interpretation is needed or even wanted since the figures tell the essential story. Either profits are being made or they are not and the reason is either that there is inefficiency here or production failure there, or both. The people stand or fall with these reports. A college or university is not like this in any significant respect. A company has produced so many thousand cars or refrigerators in a year and a certain profit or loss has been sustained. But what has a teacher done in a year? What has the president of a university done? When books have been published or buildings built, these can be counted. The number of students who were there can be enumerated, but what happened to them while they were enrolled?

The president himself must know a great deal, first hand, about his university. The outlines of the picture can be secured from recommendation and annual reports, but above all, the very meaningful details which he needs can be obtained only by talking to the right people and by asking the right questions. Hence the most dangerous staff member in such an institution is the one who consistently, either consciously or unconsciously, misleads by withholding information or by falsifying it. A president can detect this by his knowledge of the institution, but especially by his knowledge of people and of this person in particular. As any parent knows, a child when asked a question about his conduct in one tone of voice is likely to tell a lie, but when asked in another tone will probably tell the truth. This is true of adults as well. The president needs a gift, a talent, for dealing with people. His greatest asset will be the picture of himself that he has helped to build in the minds of his staff members. This is the area in which Presi-

dent Ellis is most conspicuously successful. Staff members have
no incentive to tell him anything but the truth because their
attitudes toward him are favorable, and they have no fear of
punishment. This favorable attitude toward him is a result of
their conviction that he is trying to do what is best for the institution, that he is not vindictive or personal in his judgments and
that, even when they deserve censure, they will have his sympathy
and understanding. Such a man is not an "easy mark" as an administrator. As some have discovered, he can be as tough as a top
sergeant when the occasion demands it.

The bond of sympathy and understanding rests upon the conviction that the President will see that fairness—due process is the
legal term—will always determine his decisions. There are some
men with brilliant records who can never quite convince subordi-
nates that they would go the last mile to be fair and just. Yet in
the present instance, there is probably not a single member of the
staff, high or low, who would expect the President to show any
qualities other than these. The impression his acts and personality
have made upon them leaves no room for doubt. This is, in part,
a gift or talent. It defies complete analysis, yet is one of the most
decisive factors in the whole art of leadership.

A part of the method of any leader must be decisiveness, the
ability and readiness to make a decision when it is required. A
university president may be figuratively crucified every week by
the necessity of making the type of decision that he knows could
possibly make or break him as a university president. He learns
to recognize, with a sixth sense, the types of decisions whose results may be far-reaching and utterly incalculable. He will always have at hand experienced colleagues and friends and supporters of the institution who will gladly give him the benefit of
their best discussion and advice. But the decision is his and it is
his career as an administrator that is at stake. This great weight
hanging in the balance has often caused administrators to hedge,
postpone, and temporize long after it became clear to others that

the very indecisiveness was a decision in itself, and not a good decision either. The staff members of the university know that they are not expected to make any particular mistakes, but they are aware that they will make some. They know, too, that the President is human enough to realize that mistakes will be made and that he will not only make some himself but will see them and readily admit that he, like them, shares in this common frailty of mortals. This makes good team spirit. Some types of mistakes are not readily excusable, since persons in those jobs should know better. There are other types that anyone might make since one must weigh the matter as carefully as possible and then decide and act.

There are some personal qualities that cannot be classified as methods or procedures. One of these is integrity. People see it and identify it and do not follow willingly the person who does not have it. Many men of integrity, of course, are not natural leaders, but still it is an essential quality of leadership. There is no disagreement that President Ellis has this essential quality. Few remark upon it but all act with the complete assurance that he has it abundantly. His acts and decisions prove that this confidence has not been mistaken or misplaced.

There is another quality that is essential for a college administrator, although it is not needed outside this profession. This is the ability to get the teacher's point of view and understand it. There may be no way to get it except by being a teacher and an academic person himself. The teacher can tell, unmistakably, whether it is present or not in the words and acts of an administrative officer. This accounts, at times, for the lack of understanding between teachers and business officers of a university. It is sometimes puzzling to business officers that faculty members seem to find in them a lack of sympathy and understanding of what the teacher is trying to do. This is a barrier which should not exist between a president and his faculty. No matter how well Ellis may be able to deal with board members, business and political leaders, and the public at large, no staff member ever doubts that the President of the University is a thorough teacher and an academic man. Throughout the manifold activities connected with his job, he seems to think in academic terms and keeps his attention fixed on the teacher's task.

Some university presidents have, like United States President James Buchanan, been unmarried while holding a position that requires much social intercourse and a considerable amount of entertainment. There is general agreement that it is a great asset to a man in such a position to have a wife who is gracious, charming, understanding, and truly interested in and fond of people. From this point of view, the President has in Mrs. Ellis one of his most outstanding qualifications for the job.

By its nature, the presidency of a state university carries with it responsibility for non-political and non-partisan leadership in state affairs that often goes far beyond matters of purely educational concern. Having been selected by two successive governors of the state to lead the State Bond Issue Campaign and the Commission on Education Beyond the High School, President Ellis has been thrust into a position of leadership in Missouri that carries his voice to the people on matters of general concern. When he set forth the needs of higher education (and education on all levels as well), he analyzed rather carefully the general policy of the state as compared with that of neighboring areas. He pointed out that the tax structure in Missouri was causing the state to fall further and further behind, comparatively, in the support of education and urged the people to bring Missouri's achievement in this field up to levels somewhat comparable to the economic ability of the state to pay for such services. As was inevitable, certain citizens, firmly opposed to a further tax increase, expressed the opinion that education was costing too much and that more of the burden should be assumed by the parents of students rather than the taxpayer.

President Ellis replied with great emphasis, setting forth in positive and constructive arguments, the reasons why this was not a good solution of the educational problem. Known as a friend and cordial spokesman for the support of non-public as well as for publicly-supported education, his position became the rallying point for the support of citizens in the state, the vast majority of the press, and the wholehearted following of those engaged in educational activity.

The story of Ellis' presidency remains, of course, unfinished. But the achievements and promise of the first five years indicate that his will be known as one of the great administrations in the history of a great educational institution.

SELECTIONS
FROM
PUBLISHED
WRITINGS

Editorial Note

Elmer Ellis always has been interested in the West and the part it has played in national affairs. It was natural then that for his doctoral dissertation he chose to write a biography of Henry Moore Teller of Colorado. Ellis believed that Teller "was the ablest representative of the West" during the late nineteenth century.

Born in Allegany County, New York in 1830, Henry Moore Teller attended an academy, taught school, read law, and was admitted to the bar at Binghamton, New York, in 1858. His first move west was to Morrison, Illinois, where he practiced law for three years before moving on to Colorado. Teller settled at Central City and by 1864 had become a leading pro-war Republican in Gilpin County. He developed a successful law practice and profitable business interests, and at the same time strengthened his political position. When Colorado achieved statehood in 1876, Teller was elected to the United States Senate. However, in 1882, before his first full term had been completed, he was appointed Secretary of Interior. He held the post for three years and then returned to the Senate, where he remained until 1909.

During his years in Washington, at least down until the turn of the century, Teller was the West's most prominent and influential spokesman. The following selections describe his concern for his section of the United States and show especially the part he played in the campaign for free and unlimited coinage of silver. Ellis' account of the free silver fight is one of the best and most meaningful in print. The footnotes have been omitted in the following selection.

82

4

Selections from Henry Moore Teller

THE DEFENDER OF THE WEST
1876-81

. . . . From the time Teller entered the Senate in 1876 until 1889, all the Western country now included in the states of the Dakotas, Montana, Wyoming, Idaho, Washington, Utah, New Mexico, and Arizona was under the territorial form of government. This gave each territory a delegate without voting privileges in the House of Representatives. But on the floor of the Senate they had no voice whatever, and the most pernicious legislation could be enacted without an opportunity for effective protests. In the center of this vast region was Colorado, surrounded on all sides but one by territories. Colorado was to be the youngest state for thirteen years. Her experience with carpetbaggers and the Federal bureaucracy had not been happy; and it was easy for one who

Elmer Ellis, *Henry Moore Teller: Defender of the West* (Caldwell, Idaho: The Caxton Printers, Ltd., 1941).

had lived through her territorial period to see the problems of
people in a similar position. Consequently, it was but natural
that Teller, whose law practice had frequently taken him into
these territories, should feel a special responsibility for the entire
region, and to act, at times, as though he were the senatorial
representative of the entire West. When he retired from the
Senate, thirty-three years after he entered it, Senator Thomas H.
Carter, of Montana, was to point to this phase of Teller's career
as the most significant:

> In a very broad sense Mr. Teller has represented the whole
> country, but in a special manner his voice has spoken not alone for
> Colorado but for all the great West. . . . Henry M. Teller helped to
> rock the cradle of these infant States and has ever been a watchful
> guardian of their interests.

Teller's first participation in general debate is typical of this
phase of his activity. He had planned to make his first speech a
technical constitutional argument favorable to the land-grant
railroads, but another matter came up that forced him to make
his maiden speech a defense of Western people living under a
territorial form of government. A judge had been appointed for
Wyoming Territory who was from the first exceedingly unpopular. In order to rid itself of him, the territorial legislature had
followed Colorado's example and gerrymandered its judicial districts in such a way as to give this judge a jurisdiction containing
few white inhabitants, and, consequently, one in which there
would be little legal business. The Judiciary Committee of the
Senate, intent on maintaining the supremacy of the Federal
Government and the independence of the judiciary, brought a
bill into the Senate to annul the Wyoming gerrymander. The
members of the Judiciary Committee, particularly David Davis
and Roscoe Conkling, supported their bill vigorously, calling the
legislature's action nullification and open defiance of the Federal
Government. Teller rose passionately to the defense of Wyoming.

He appealed for a reasonable consideration of the problems of a territorial government, pointing out that this was the only way in which a territory could limit the evil of an incompetent or corrupt judge. He related Colorado's experience with its judiciary as an illustration.

I have seen not only in Colorado, but in other Territories, justice dealt out by the dollar. I have seen men sitting on the bench, with the whole people of the Territory protesting, selling their judgments as notoriously as indulgences were sold in the early days [sic] of the Roman Church.

The only remedy was some action such as the Wyoming legislature had taken. In spite of his arguments and those of the two Nebraska senators, who, it might be presumed, were also acquainted with these conditions, the committee's bill passed.

This was typical of much of Teller's activity in the early part of his career. The West was misunderstood and abused by Eastern—particularly New England—statesmen, and he set himself to put them right. Frequently Senators Hoar or Dawes would chide him for his sectional orientation on legislation, and his answer was invariably to point out the underlying localism of their own attitudes.

It happened at this time that certain far-sighted individuals were becoming alarmed at the rapid exploitation of American forests, and began to demand that they be conserved for future use. Chief among these was Carl Schurz, Secretary of the Interior, who cultivated the field where Roosevelt and Pinchot were later to reap the harvest. One of his first steps in this direction was to prosecute Westerners who removed timber from the public lands. This caused vast unrest in the West, as there was hardly a miner, railroad, municipality, fraternal lodge, church, or indeed any private citizen who was not technically a violator of the law. One of the cases started was a suit for one hundred thousand dollars against N. P. Hill's smelter at Blackhawk, and he immediately appealed to Teller to have the suit stopped.

Against such a policy were lined up practically all people in the West. There was no legal method of securing timber from the public lands, and no method of acquiring timber lands in Colorado and other mining states. Had the law been obeyed, neither mining nor farming would have been possible in all the Rocky Mountain region, as fuel and shelter could be secured only from the timber on government land. To Teller the attempt to enforce the law rigidly was evidence of the East's lack of understanding of conditions in the West, if not another instance of its jealous desire to prevent the growth of the West. Eastern senators and newspapers had not hesitated to call the taking of this timber robbery, which fanned Teller's anger to a white heat:

> Since I have been a member of the Senate I have noticed on every occasion when any subject has been presented that directly bore upon the interest of the West that the Senators who live farthest from the interest to be served have always had the most to say, and that too about plunderers, thieves, robbers, and frequently stigmatized people of the extreme West in that way.

He pointed out that there was no way for a settler or miner to secure wood except to go upon the public lands and cut it; that no legal provision had been made for acquiring timber lands by settlers; and that free timber from the public lands had always been the frontier American method. "Like begets like," he warned, "and Senators should remember that when they bring up sectional issues and charges against a whole class of people it may return to them again."

For immediate protection the Senator wrote to his friend Moses Hallett, judge of the Federal District Court in Colorado, before whom such suits would probably come, and presented him with a legal argument that such "depredations," or a large part of them, were within the law. To put the question beyond doubt, he and Chaffee worked out a bill to make lawful the removal of such timber as was necessary for "domestic" purposes. They were not satisfied with the Timber and Stone Act which the Pacific Coast senators were sponsoring in order to open the Government timberlands to sale. This act, they thought, would result in individual monopolies of timber in each mining region. Hence they opposed the inclusion of Colorado and the territories within its provisions. For the region not included within the Timber and Stone Act they succeeded in securing the passage of the Timber Cutting Act, which allowed anyone except a railroad corporation to go upon the "mineral" lands and take out timber for any purpose except export from the state or territory. Nevada was included within both acts, and the territory of Washington was under the Timber and Stone Act. The Timber Cutting Act corrected the old condition that had made every miner a lawbreaker, although it failed to prevent the many abuses that depleted the timber supply.

On this and similar questions Teller's attitude was the product of his experience and that of Western people generally. It was taken not only because he was the advocate of Western interests in the Senate, but because he was a Westerner whose frontier experience had taught him to think that way. However poorly this "rugged individualism," as a subsequent President was to call it, fits the industrial civilization of today, it had been the method of the frontier, and for Westerners to deny it would be to go back on their origins, and to proclaim that their own work was not good.

Particularly was this true regarding the exploitation of natural resources. In a debate on a bill to establish titles to certain valuable springs at Hot Springs, Arkansas, Teller declared his position in words that might be considered the classic expression of the pioneer:

. . . the whole trouble in this case in my judgment arises from the United States Government attempting to set apart a piece of land and control it because it has a spring on it. The entire principle is wrong; and we should have saved a good deal of money and a great deal of time, and the people of that section would have been infinitely better off, if the Government had allowed the first man that got there to take it. That ought to be the rule in reference to valuable springs or valuable lands. The man who has the enterprise to go and put his claim on the land in accordance with law ought to take it.

There had been demands at various times in the past that the public lands containing valuable minerals should be reserved for the Government rather than be exploited by individuals. This was in essence another form of conservation, about which those who wanted the West to develop rapidly were opposed to those who wanted its development postponed.

The issue came up on a proposal to reserve the mineral rights in confirming certain land grants in the Mexican cession. Teller used all his knowledge of mining law and of Western conditions in attempting to prove that it was contrary to our treaty agreements and to good policy. Owners of land, he insisted, should be allowed to develop any mines possible. Although he failed to secure an amendment to make the title to the minerals go with the general land title in these cases, he secured the adoption of other amendments to protect the right of the landowner against damage by the owner of the mineral rights. He brought in a bill in the Forty-sixth Congress to amend the law governing the securing of a mining claim, which was passed and became a law. On nearly all legislation affecting mining and public lands he offered perfecting amendments which improved the character of the bills, although he was not at this time on either the Mines and Mining or the Public Lands committee.

At the convening of the Forty-sixth Congress the Democrats were in control of both houses. Among their efforts to make political thunder for the campaign of 1880 was an attack upon Postmaster General David M. Key, by means of the Western mail routes. This attack upon the star routes was largely sectional in its nature, and the suspicion of extensive corruption in the system —later found to be correct—made it peculiarly susceptible to attack.

The star routes were those where the distances were so great, transportation facilities so poor, and population so scattered, that the revenues did not pay the cost of maintaining the service. Eastern newspapers and senators criticized the system severely, maintaining that the postal service should be self-supporting, and all unprofitable routes should be discontinued. The attack on Postmaster General Key came because of his improvement of this system by increasing weekly to semiweekly and sometimes daily service. Teller declared:

> I know what every man ought to know who has given attention to the history of the country . . . that these star route services are the great engines which open up the Western country to civilization. We first open with slow mail. . . . In a little while come heavier settlements, more people, and they demand . . . increased facilities. . . . Is there any reason why the government should not support the postal services as it supports the Army? . . . He [Key] has given us a service infinitely better than was ever given to the people west of the Mississippi River.

Teller threatened to vote against the deficiency appropriation for the postal service unless the strictures on Key in the preamble were struck out. An amendment to this effect carried, before the bill passed both the Senate and the House.

When a bill came before the Senate to renounce formally the debt the states contracted during the distribution of the surplus in the Federal treasury in the year 1837, Teller opposed it. He had no illusions that this "debt" would ever be repaid, but an occasion to read the Eastern senators a homily upon the golden rule he could not overlook.

> My experience has taught me that twenty-eight interested States are pretty sure to find votes in the Senate and in the House sufficient to pass a bill like this. . . . But when there was a bill here that was

in the special interest of a few of the Western States, and when we were asking for the mere letter of the law, as we thought, the payment of 5 per cent on the sales of public lands, pretty much every Senator who voted for it was charged by Senators representing the States that derive the greatest benefit from this bill with being moved entirely by a desire to appropriate a portion of the public Treasury that did not belong to us.

The problem which attracted Teller's attention more than any other in this period was the Indian question, and it remained permanently as one of his principal interests. On few subjects was he better qualified to legislate. All his life he had been in direct contact with Indians. In western New York his home had been close to a reservation, and at one time he had taught a school on its very edge. In Colorado he had had experience with the aborigines in a different stage of culture, and not infrequently his contacts had been like those of 1864 when he helped to prepare Denver for an anticipated attack, or when during his frequent trips across the plains he had found it necessary to go heavily armed. To these personal contacts he added a considerable knowledge gained from the study of the history of the problem in the United States, Mexico, and Canada. Here, as in the case of the public lands, there had always been a difference in attitude between the Easterner and the Westerner, even as far back as the colonial period, when the British Government represented the East.

When Teller entered the Senate in 1876, the Indian danger was being removed by the rapid disappearance of the frontier. This same elimination of wild country made the problem of fitting the Indian to civilized life more acute than ever. Custer had been killed the same year Teller went to Washington, and the policy of "peace on the plains" was still little more than a pious wish. Like the issue of conservation of timber, this problem brought Teller in opposition to the official policy of the Department of the Interior and its Secretary, Carl Schurz. It is peculiar that these two men whose policies were alike on many questions should have been at swords' points over matters which each, as Secretary of the Interior, had a large influence in solving. Teller's opposition does not need to be put down to the political antagonism which had led to the popular sport among Republican politicians of taking "a whack at Schurz." It arose from essential difference in policy, and from the pressing needs of the West at the time.

Teller had no touch of the too common frontier attitude that the only good Indian was a dead Indian. The outbreak of the Nez Perces under the leadership of Chief Joseph roused his admiration. When an appropriation bill came before the Senate to pay for their removal to Indian Territory he opposed it as unjust to the Indians. He compared their military feat with that of the ten thousand Greeks. As to the justice of their war, he declared:

> I believe no set of men ever went to war in the history of wars who had a better cause for war than the Nez Perce Indians, and if we paid out a million dollars it was our fault and not theirs.

He offered an amendment to the bill to force their return to Idaho but that was defeated. Then he supported an amendment to make their removal to Indian Territory contingent upon their consent, which also lost. It is necessary to keep this phase of Teller's activity on the Indian question well in mind for one can otherwise fall into the error of classifying him with the enemies of that race. He had his own ideas of what constituted a statesmanlike policy, and to carry it out he sometimes worked with the professional defenders of the Indians such as Dawes and Hoar, and at other times with the more typical Westerners such as Plumb.

In his first years in Washington, no other problem held Teller's interest like that of the Ute Indians in Colorado. These natives had ceded a large part of their occupied land to the National

Government three years before in return for an annuity. This the Government had neglected to pay in any manner that was satisfactory to the Utes, and in retaliation the Indians had begun to commit various depredations upon white settlers, usually no more serious than killing cattle or burning farm buildings. As these attacks easily alarmed the settlers, who naturally feared more dangerous ones, it was a problem that deserved immediate attention.

After trying to secure a better arrangement for paying the annuities, Teller made careful inquiry in Colorado regarding the situation. When he returned to Washington in the fall of 1877 he was regularly in receipt of reports from Governor Routt regarding the situation—reports that frequently included requests to exert pressure on the War Department for troops and munitions to be used for protection. The deluge of unsolicited letters that descended upon Teller regarding the problem included everything from petitions from frightened and illiterate settlers to propositions which offered to make him wealthy by cutting him in on rich mining land then on the reservation. The most spectacular of the latter was a suggestion that if he and Chaffee would arrange the purchase of the land from the Indians, they, together with Governor Routt and James A. Garfield, would be included in a company of eight for the exploitation of the mineral land. For more accurate information, Teller made inquiries among those who knew the Ute Indians through personal contact. The story he got from these persons was usually the same—corruption and inefficiency in the Indian Service and consequent failure to pay promptly the promised annuities kept the Utes hostile. "They [the Utes] are deserving of a great deal of credit for their sensible and orderly actions in the matter," wrote Uriah N. Curtis, certainly one of the best informed and intentioned of the experts. "I fully agree with you," wrote Governor Routt, "that if the Indians are properly treated & the Govt. will fulfill its part of the contract according to treaty stipulations, we will have no trouble with them."

By March 12, 1878, the Governor was writing Teller, "You are to be congratulated upon your success in getting our Indian matters in as good condition as they are. . . . Keep up the fight for the Indian Annuities, as their payment is the only thing that will prevent trouble." What Teller had done had been to insist upon the payment of annuities and the removal of the agent. For a successor he recommended Uriah N. Curtis. "I know Mr. Curtis & think he is a valuable man. He is well acquainted with the Utes & speaks their language." But Curtis was a citizen of Wyoming, and N. C. Meeker, of the Greeley *Tribune,* was appointed, perhaps with Teller's subsequent endorsement. Meeker, formerly agricultural expert on the staff of the New York *Tribune,* was an honest and able man, but his knowledge of the Utes was distinctly limited. Soon after he reached the agency he wrote Teller a long report detailing the corruption and mismanagement that had preceded his appointment. He appealed to Teller to use his influence with the Indian Bureau to secure approval of the removal of the agency to a location to which supplies could be sent without such great cost, and where agriculture was possible. Under the rules from Washington he could not issue rations to any Indian who did not work—at farming. Actually, no farming was possible near the agency.

The agency was finally moved, and that made more trouble because of the work involved, and because the Utes naturally objected to creating a situation where they would be forced to do farm work. When Meeker tried to carry out the Bureau's orders and force the Indians to do farm work, trouble began which reached a bloody climax in the fall of 1879. One group of the Indians attacked the White River Agency, killed Meeker and his helpers, took three white women captive, and outraged them. When a body of troops under Major T. T. Thornburgh moved toward the agency it was attacked, Thornburgh killed and the Utes driven off with great difficulty. This violent culmination of the long series of Ute scares in Colorado filled the local people with firm determination that such an uprising should not occur again. Secretary Schurz attempted to find a policy that would protect the Indians and also quiet public excitement in Colorado. An army on its way to attack the Indians who had opposed Thornburgh was stopped and peace negotiations instituted through Chief Ouray. The women captives were released. Then Ouray, accompanied by some other leaders of the Utes, went to Washington in order to make an agreement with the Indian Bureau.

These negotiations went so steadily in favor of the Utes it soon became obvious that the Indians guilty of the attack would escape punishment. This was very distasteful to Teller, although it must be confessed that the principal demand in Colorado was that the reservation be opened to settlement. In the meantime, Teller had acquired a new colleague in the person of Nathaniel P. Hill, of Blackhawk. The means of his election had left many political and personal antagonisms that made it difficult for the two senators to work together. As Congress was assembling in December, Hill announced himself as a supporter of the Indian Bureau agreement. Teller, however, introduced a resolution asking for the documents and prepared to contest the "treaty" when it reached the Senate. Late in February the Committee on Indian Affairs brought in a bill to ratify the agreement, and Teller countered with a series of amendments. The Governor of Colorado wrote Senator Hill that "People here universally favor Teller's proposed amendments." The obvious practicability of some of them forced the committee to substitute for the original bill one which embodied some of Teller's proposals.

As it then stood, the principal features of the bill were that the Utes gave up a large part of their reservation, for which they were to receive land in severalty and certain annuities. The White River Utes—those primarily concerned in the recent outbreak—

were to be sent to the Uintah Reservation in northern Utah. The most notable change in policy was the granting of Indian lands in severalty. It was hoped by many friends of the Indians that severalty would result in their becoming peaceful farmers. This idea had become a cure-all among Indian reformers, and they induced Schurz—unwisely, as it proved—to make it a part of the solution of the Ute problem. The bill was popular in Colorado. It would open almost the entire great Ute Reservation to white settlement. William N. Byers wrote to Teller:

> We all admire and approve your position and pluck on the Schurz-Ute bill. But a large majority of reasoning and reasonable men with whom I talk think you had better consent to the bill which will open about eleven twelfths of the reservation and remove all question as to the right of mineral and other claims thereon. Then we will inaugurate a fight for the balance. . . . I fear if the present is rejected and Ouray continues his masterly tactics we will have to submit to an enlargement of the present reservation.

But Teller had decided that the bill should be opposed. "I am not here to be dictated to by anybody on this question," he declared when it was shown that opinion in Colorado favored the revised bill. Characterizing the plan as "an easy solution of the Indian problem in one lesson," Teller delivered what the New York *Tribune* called a "furious assault upon the policy of the Secretary of Interior." The advocates of the new policy of severalty were the objects of Teller's sarcasm:

> These men knowing nothing of the magnitude of the undertaking, assumed the responsibility without a doubt as to their success. All other men are fools! Now will the Indian be civilized and Christianized in a twelvemonth! He is to become self-supporting, and the great drain on the public Treasury for his support will cease at once.

Teller pointed out that communal landholdings had always been the Indian practice and that individual holdings were against his customs and religion.

> . . . the great trouble in our dealing with the Indian is our ignorance of his laws, customs, character, and religion. We insist on treating him as if he were a civilized man, when he ought to be treated as a savage, full of superstitions and weaknesses that belong to savage life.

He ridiculed the idea that the Indians who had signed the agreement knew what holding land in severalty meant, and his criticism of the method of dealing with the Utes was extremely severe.

> I am sick of the Department management of Indian affairs. I do not refer to the present officials, but I am sick of the management of the past twenty-five years. . . . [There] is not 5 per cent of the men who have been on the border as Indian agents for twenty years, that want to civilize the Indians. . . . They know that when they have done that their occupation is gone; their opportunities for stealing and plunder are gone. . . .

Teller showed that the Indians had won every important point in controversy in their negotiations with the Indian Bureau, that no one under the bill would be punished for the murders at the White River Agency or the attack on Thornburgh, but rather that the Utes were being rewarded by increasing their annuities for no other reason that they would understand except their depredations. The guilty Indians, Teller emphasized, should be punished severely or there would be continuous trouble with the Utes and the Colorado frontier would not be safe. He preached a harsh doctrine, and his colleague, Hill, called it a "narrow and selfish view." It is worthwhile to note that some thirty years later James McLaughlin, an expert whose devotion to the Indians is unquestioned, had this to say about the same affair:

> I say it with no bitterness toward the people themselves, but I feel certain that if the Utes had been thoroughly chastised after the Meeker massacre of 1879, they would not be the irresponsible, shiftless, and defiant people they are today. . . . They escaped retributive

justice at a period of their tribal existence when the sense of their ill-doings was strong upon them, and they are the worse for it.

The only material changes Teller was able to get into the second bill were to increase the annuities to the widows of the murdered men, and to add an appropriation to provide irrigation for the lands which were to be taken in severalty. That the lands were untillable without irrigation had escaped the Secretary and the members of the committee. It then passed the Senate with only fifteen votes in addition to Teller's against it.

Teller's prediction of failure for the severalty policy among the Utes was proved correct by subsequent developments. The place assigned to them was found unsuitable, and no land had been allotted the following summer when Teller visited those on the La Plata River. It confirmed him in his opposition to severalty. When a bill was brought in to extend that policy to certain other tribes, Teller suggested it be entitled, "A bill to despoil the Indians of their land and make them vagabonds upon the face of the earth." He quoted protests against the plan from the most capable Indian farmers, the Five Civilized Tribes of Indian Territory. Agriculture was the important thing, Teller maintained, and not lands in severalty.

As the bill would make all Indians taking land in severalty subject to state law except that land could not be alienated for twenty-five years, Teller introduced an amendment providing that no Indian should be punished for polygamy who was practicing it at the time he received his allotment of land. This was adopted. Teller repeatedly insisted that all these restrictions were of no value, because as soon as the tribal status was broken the Indian was subject completely to state law.

Teller's attitude on Indian affairs forecast his policy as Secretary of the Interior. From the first he had not taken kindly to Schurz's plan of educating Indians at special Eastern schools. In the Forty-seventh Congress, Senator Dawes proposed an amendment to the Indian appropriation bill to add five hundred thousand dollars for education. Teller supported this amendment but used the opportunity to express himself upon that subject.

> When you take these children to Carlisle and send them back they
> will be skilled in some things . . . but the danger is that if you do
> not have a mass for them to associate with who have notions like
> unto theirs they will go right back to the same condition that their
> ancestors were in and they themselves were in before they were
> taken to Carlisle. Is that to be the history of Indian education? . . .
> I will admit that it is very difficult to educate them if you allow them
> to go home and stay at the lodges overnight; and yet I believe that
> the education of the children will have some little influence upon
> the adults, and I believe that if you could bring the school within a
> reasonable distance, where the parents could occasionally go and see
> that their children were taken care of, where they could see that they
> were not improperly treated, it would add very much to the system.
> The Indian is as much attached to his children as the white man is.

Part of Teller's great interest in Indian affairs was brought about by his belief in their importance to the West. He spoke on the question frequently when his chief purpose was to defend the Westerners against charges of cruelty against the Indian. When Senator Dawes presented a resolution on the Indian question signed by a large number of prominent men and women, which directly intimated that the people of the West were responsible for the difficulties of the Indian problem, Teller arose to the defense of his chosen people:

> It is not so, Mr. President. If they [treaties] have been violated the
> responsibility is with this body and not with the people of the fron-
> tier, who have greater interests at stake, who are more concerned in
> maintaining peaceable relations with the Indians than any other
> people in the world. . . . By their side we live, by their side we expect
> to live, and by their side, if they do not expire in the course of time,
> must our children live; and is it to be supposed that we want to
> despoil them or keep them degraded? . . . I have as much regard for

the people who suffered in Colorado as for the people in Massachusetts who are sympathizing with the Indians. I can safely say that some of the people who suffered by that raid . . . are the peers, intellectually and morally of the petitioners, or at least most of them. They are not ignorant barbarians. They are made poor in property and poor in spirit by the outrages perpetrated, and the Senator [Dawes] has never found time to say a kindly word for them.

The standing illustration of the pioneer's cruelty to the Indian was the Sand Creek Massacre, and when anyone wanted an example of the unworthiness of Westerners he usually fell back upon it. It was shortly before Teller entered the Cabinet that Senator Hoar quoted a part of the Senate report on the tragedy in connection with another matter. Teller immediately attacked its validity and defended the character of the troops engaged in that affair. He gave a detailed account of the incident and its surrounding conditions. He denied that it was a massacre, although he did not deny atrocities on the part of the white soldiers.

Teller never denied that injustice had been done to the Indian, but he did insist that the fault here did not lie with the Western pioneer. Easterners, whose ancestors had killed off their Indians, were blaming the present evil condition of Indian affairs upon his section, and the senator from Colorado was not the one to let that pass.

How far Teller's attitude differed from some other Westerners' with wide experience among the Indians can be seen in the following remarks from a speech of Senator Plumb's delivered on the Ute question.

There is no possible education that can ever be given to a full-blooded Indian . . . which will ever enable him to compete in any considerable degree in an industrial occupation or employment. . . .

He is simply here to get out of the way at the proper time. . . . Within fifty years there will not be probably one single full-blooded Indian on the American continent; and within a hundred years there

will not be a single person living who in his features or in his blood
will bear the impress of a single characteristic of the Indian character.
He will be entirely gone.

One could easily think of reservation-born Charles Curtis, one
of Plumb's successors as senator from Kansas, and subsequently
Vice-President of the United States, as divine retribution.

TELLER AND THE CAUSE OF FREE SILVER
1888-91

The debate on the Bland-Allison bill in 1878 had found Teller
unprepared. He had, of course, a lawyer's and a businessman's
knowledge of finance, but his education did not extend beyond
that. He became painfully aware of this during the debate and
saw immediately that it was a subject upon which he must be
informed. As early as 1874 the value of the silver produced in
Colorado had exceeded that of gold, and the year after the Bland-
Allison Act was passed it was four times as valuable. Here, certainly, was an issue upon which a Colorado senator would need
to be an expert.

No statesman ever prepared himself upon a public question
with more care and industry than Teller did in becoming familiar
with the question of money. All his legal training and experience
and his natural aptitude for study helped to make that preparation adequate. He purchased the standard works upon finance
and began his study. Not to be too much tied to theory, he sub-
scribed to the leading American financial papers and read them
regularly. Later, he added the English *Economist* and *Statist*,
and finally the French *L'Economiste*. Like a professor keeping
abreast of his specialty, Teller followed every new development
in all phases of finance, corresponding with American and
European economists, digging into histories formerly unknown to
him for the light they shed upon the immediate problem, and
burdening the representatives of foreign nations in Washington

with requests for information regarding particular phases of their national monetary systems. It need not be emphasized that he approached the problem from a prejudiced point of view because silver mining was a local interest. He was conservative by nature, and a businessman with the business point of view. He respected the opinions of bankers, men of great wealth, and the editors of the financial papers. But his study coming in connection with the growing silver interest at home made him an intense advocate of bimetallism, and left him with a poor opinion of the financial knowledge of bankers when they got away from the immediate problems of discount and exchange.

Nevertheless, the fact that he was advocating before the public what was, in part at least, a selfish local interest, irritated his conscience, and he returned repeatedly to the charge that the silver cause was more than that. He said in 1888:

> I admit that if I had not lived in a silver-producing State I might never have had my attention directed to this subject. I might have been willing to accept the statements of doctrinaires and ill-informed people as to facts; but if my attention had been directed to it and I had studied it as I have studied it, I would have the same views if I lived in Connecticut that I have living in Colorado.

The problem that Teller saw was this: Through almost all the historic period mankind had used two metals, gold and silver, as money. The supply of these had increased as man's needs increased, and they together had supplied a satisfactory medium of exchange that kept values fairly well stabilized. The use of two metals had the advantage that with the case of a difference in the established values, the one with the lower value became the temporary standard and brought it into greater demand and the values back to something like the ratio originally set.

This, itself, helped to prevent any great changes in the system of values to the detriment of either creditor or debtor. One metal checked the other in such a way as to stabilize their comparative value. This almost ideal system had been interfered with in recent times. In 1867 an international conference had suggested that the double standard be abolished and replaced with an international unit of one metal, much as it might have recommended the adoption of the metric system by all countries. This idea was seized upon by the public and private creditor class in all countries in an effort to go to the gold standard. England was already there, and Germany went soon after the conference, bidding for gold wherever she could get it and throwing her vast amount of silver coin upon the bullion market. The United States followed in 1873 with an act that passed unnoticed at the time, for few silver dollars were in use, as the coinage ratio in the United States undervalued silver in comparison with the market price and the ratios in use elsewhere. Many of the smaller European nations followed, and soon gold was in great demand. Silver, being in far less demand, was declining in value in relation to gold.

Two other factors came in to emphasize these tendencies. The world's production of gold lessened greatly, while that of silver increased, which meant that the cost of mining gold had became greater and that of silver less. But the problem did not end with the changing value of the two metals. All other kinds of property also fell in value relative to gold, and a great change in relationships followed. Debts increased in value, and the burden of the debtor became a continually increasing one. This was the main problem as Teller chose to see it. The gold standard meant, under conditions which then existed, a continual appreciation of the standard of exchange and a steady increase in the debts of all debtors. There never was a clearer case of a debtor-creditor struggle, with the creditor having the advantage of a government-made appreciation—government-made because it had changed the legal standard in 1873. Nowhere in the world was this condition so evil as in the United States, for here the gold standard appreciation came as a supplement to an appreciation of the paper (greenback) standard of the Civil War. The resumption of specie payment, however great its necessity, had the effect of making the debtor redeem his borrowings in dollars worth far more than those he had originally received. Before this contraction was over the appreciation of the gold standard began, and the same condition of enriching the lender at the expense of the debtor continued.

It was not so much the evils of the past that Teller emphasized as the promise of continued deflation. He saw no prospect of the production of gold increasing in such a degree as to check the steady fall of prices and the steady increase of debts. This great cause of human misery could be ended in only one way that seemed just to Teller, and that was to re-establish the free coinage of silver. Free coinage of silver by the United States would encourage other nations to take similar action, and a bimetallic system would be re-established in the world. It would cause immediate inflation; we might go to the silver standard alone—Teller admitted that—but this was a small evil compared to the constant grinding of the monetary system upon the farmer and debtor.

Teller was as careful as usual in his position on this question. A few times in the heat of debate he fell into oracular statements, such as that silver had been made standard money "by the fiat of the Almighty, when He created the two metals," but these were exceedingly few. Extremists among the silver men might shout about the "crime of '73," but Teller never did; they might lump their opponents together as "goldbugs," but he would not; they might flatter with repetition such arguments as W. H. Harvey popularized in *Coin's Financial School,* but Teller never would. He addressed himself to the economists and informed public opinion, and in that lay his great strength. The opponents of free silver listened to him, and his own partisans depended upon him to keep their campaign directed at attainable goals. It was said that the English and French bimetallists read his speeches with great interest.

The Bland-Allison Act remained for a long time a popular compromise over the silver issue. It was not satisfactory to Teller or any other convinced bimetallist, but political conditions were such that any change looking toward bimetallism was not possible. Nevertheless it was urged. Teller had urged free coinage in 1882, and denounced John Sherman's conduct of the Treasury Department in purchasing only the minimum required by law. The same year he introduced a resolution declaring that the purpose of the Government was to establish free coinage, but his entrance into the Cabinet had prevented further agitation in the Senate until he returned in 1885. Soon after that, he urged free coinage in a long speech, and criticized the administration for its manner of carrying out the Bland-Allison Act. His objection here was that every administration, including Arthur's, had used every means in its power to discredit silver as money. It had administered the law in such a way as to make the smallest amount of coinage possible, and warned against the danger of the use of silver money. In the subsequent Congress he again urged free coinage, and pointed out the continued rise in the value of gold standard money, comparing it unfavorably with the silver standard in Mexico, where values were remaining fairly well balanced, and with bimetallic France, where he thought they were much more stable. But these attempts were unsuccessful, and it was anticipated that they would be. A majority of the Senate was not for free silver, though these members were bimetallists in theory almost without exception, if we can accept their declarations.

The change that raised hopes for silver legislation was the admission of new Western states, which made it possible to overcome the anti-free-silver majority in the Senate, and the election of 1888, which had given the silver men a presumptive majority in both houses of Congress, with a President who, they believed, was friendly toward silver legislation.

At the Republican convention of 1888, the silver men had demanded a platform that was favorable and a candidate who would not veto a free coinage bill. Referring to the Westerners, Teller wrote his own candidate, Gresham, "I have assured them that you are not hostile to Silver money & that you will not be controlled by Wall St. if elected." The resolutions committee framed a straddle plank on silver that many of the silver advocates believed pledged the party to positive action in the direction of free coinage:

> The Republican party is in favor of the use of both gold and silver as money, and condemns the policy of the Democratic Administration in its efforts to demonetize silver.

Senator William M. Stewart, of Nevada, asked for and received what he believed were assurances that Harrison, if nominated and elected, would not veto a free-coinage bill, and most of the silver men went to him after Gresham and Allison proved improbable nominees. With a favorable-sounding plank, and the known opposition of Cleveland to silver, the Republicans had little difficulty in piling up a larger than normal majority in Colorado. Harrison's cordiality immediately after the election led Teller to believe the remonetization of silver was possible.

When Teller returned to Washington in the fall of 1889 for the opening of the memorable Fifty-first Congress, he began the greatest fight of his career—that for free coinage. The Republicans at last had control of both houses of Congress and the Presidency. The senators from the new states were apparently as strong for silver as Teller himself. Then, too, Teller had a colleague in Wolcott, who, although about to take his seat for the first time, would soon assume first rank as an orator and debater. For help in organizing the Western silver men there were two senators from Nevada. John P. Jones, older in the Senate than Teller, was a man of unusual ability and striking personality, but ordinarily inclined to be inactive. His colleague Stewart, although badly handicapped by his record of having voted for the "crime of

'73," was, for all his Santa Claus appearance, a vigorous and an able fighter. In some respects Plumb, of Kansas, was a more effective supporter, as no suspicion of personal silver-mining interests hung about him. These with the senators from the new states and the rural Democrats of the South and West represented the real strength of silver and inflation.

But first of all there was party strength to be maintained, and if the Republicans as an organization were to enact legislation they would have to maintain party lines. There were demands from several party factions for legislation, each representing definite economic interests. Silver, tariff, trust regulation, were to compete within the party with the more purely partisan issues such as the Elections bill. Pledges had been made regarding most of them during the recent campaign, and, with complete Republican control, there would be no excuse for the party if it failed. A compromise program all around was desirable, at least from the standpoint of the party.

Such seems to have been the wish of the administration and the Republican leaders in Congress—Teller alone excepted. There is little direct evidence upon the exact nature of disagreement between Teller and the other leaders, but that it was there is clearly evident. In keeping with the compromise idea the new Secretary of the Treasury, William Windom, submitted a plan for silver legislation that was aimed at raising the price of silver, and did not, in any direct way, aim at the general price level or eventual free coinage. President Harrison in his message to Congress likewise put himself on record in words that could only be interpreted as opposing free coinage, but left the way open for some such legislation as his Secretary of the Treasury proposed.

On January 20, Teller called on President Harrison to oppose the Windom plan and urge free silver in its place. Harrison held no brief for the Windom plan, but wanted a "Republican bill." He also informed Teller that he would veto any bill "going so far as to be unsound." After this Teller knew that free coinage was impossible in that Congress. It was clearly evident that the President might be able to stop such a bill in the House, and if not checked there, he would surely veto it. Not even the Senate would pass such a bill over his veto.

But the silver men were not entirely helpless; they could hold up the tariff, if necessary, to secure some favorable action on silver. It is not likely that the Republican silver senators were willing to go so far in this as to prevent a tariff bill, for there was a strong tendency, especially among the patronage-hungry senators from the new states, to stay in the good graces of the administration.

Nevertheless, Teller determined to make a fight for free coinage. He introduced a free coinage amendment to the purchase bill under consideration by the Senate Committee on Finance, and gave notice that the Senate would have to go on record regarding it. After that the consideration of the monetary legislation was transferred to several informal party caucuses, the object of which was an agreement on legislation that would keep the Republican organization intact. A subcommittee of both House and Senate Republicans, considering the question in April, came to an agreement on a silver-purchase bill of four and one-half million ounces of silver each month, to be paid for by "silver bullion treasury notes." Senator Aldrich reported to Harrison on April 23 that all agreed on the compromise except Teller, who proposed to fight for free coinage, and if that failed, to fight for making the proposed treasury notes legal tender. He would oppose any bill that gave the Treasury the power to redeem silver certificates in bullion. The other silver men were apparently unwilling to back him to the limit in opposition to the new purchase act.

On the floor of the Senate he characterized such plans as the "Trojan horse" of the gold monometallists. "It is no answer to me," he declared, "to say 'It will put the price of silver up to 129,' or that 'it is a silver bill.' If it should put up the price of silver to 150 it would never receive my support." It was, he held, merely a proposal to redeem paper money in the commodity of silver, and would not affect the problem of an appreciating standard. It might give us a better supply of currency, but that was all. "We must be squarely upon a gold basis or we must recognize silver as money. There can be no half-way about. . . ."

The House passed a close approximation to the caucus bill, plus the legal tender provision Teller had demanded, and the Senate committee reported that as a substitute for its own bill. Plumb moved a free coinage amendment which was adopted, and the bill passed. There was no expectation that free coinage would result, but Teller was determined to make the Senate and House both go on record, and, if possible, force Harrison to veto the bill. The administration and partisan Republicans generally were very anxious to prevent the latter because of the influence it might have in the campaign in 1890. The pressure they were about to exert upon the Republican members of the House was intense. This, together with certain adroit legislative maneuvers of Speaker Reed, brought out a safe majority against the bill.

Teller informed the Senate that this was a clear repudiation of the public will as expressed in the last election.

The firmness of Harrison against free coinage, in contrast to his apparent friendliness before election, embittered Teller, and he spared neither the administration nor his party in his denunciation. The other silver men followed, and Wolcott, especially, delivered an extreme attack upon the administration—evidence of the split the party leaders had tried to avoid. This split extended to patronage matters, and from this time on there was little cooperation between the White House and the Colorado senators.

After the defeat of the Senate free-coinage amendment the bill went to a conference committee. Any hope of free coinage, or of forcing Harrison to take the responsibility of a veto, had been lost through the administration victory in the House. The silver men might still have brought more pressure by holding up the tariff or attaching to it a free-coinage amendment, but they were as a whole more inclined to maintain party harmony by compromise. Teller seems clearly to have been willing to go much further in this direction than the others, but he could not secure sufficient support. The senators from the new states, upon whom he had counted, proved to be too susceptible to party discipline and administration pressure for any drawn-out fight. Nevertheless, the silver men refused to take up the tariff bill in the Senate until the compromise on silver was agreed upon. The Republican members of the conference committee worked this out, and the silver men staked out their last trench on monthly purchases of four and one-half million ounces of silver, and legal tender quality for the resulting currency. This they got in the final draft, which was to bear Sherman's name. It will be noted that the legal-tender provision had not been included in the earlier caucus measure, and it was partly, at least, as a result of Teller's persistence that the silver men insisted on it now. The report was strictly a Republican Party measure. Teller declared that he voted for it "reluctantly" because it might raise the price of silver and be a step in the direction of free coinage. If there had been any remote opportunity for free-coinage legislation in this Congress, he would not have supported the bill. It was a Republican measure designed to maintain party harmony and to make the passage of a Republican tariff possible. Later, when the bill became discredited, Sherman and other Eastern Republicans declared it did not have their approval, but at the time it passed, it received the praise and approval of the Republican leaders and the financial press. It was, as Teller afterwards said, a "sop to the West" to keep it Republican. Beyond question some of the silver advocates thought more highly of the purchase law than Teller did, and a few Western Republican newspapers praised it as the solution of the silver problem.

The feeling within the Republican ranks in the debilitating July heat in Washington became very hostile. When the silver Republicans broke away from the caucus decision and voted for free silver, the dean of the party, Senator Edmunds, read them a lecture on party loyalty, which did not improve the situation. Senator R. F. Pettigrew, of South Dakota, was also a native of Vermont, and Edmunds took occasion to reprimand the younger man personally for his failure to follow the caucus decision. Pettigrew illustrated the party morale by answering:

> I will tend to my own affairs. Further than that, if there is any more of this bossing, enough Senators from the new states will go over to the Democrats and will organize the Senate, and you'll have to pack up your whiskey jug and get out of that Judiciary Committee room.

The party lacked unity, and Harrison failed to give it much. There is no doubt that the Republican willingness to pass the Sherman Act was due primarily to a realization that they could not maintain party unity without it, and without party unity a tariff could not be enacted.

Toward the Sherman Anti-Trust law enacted during the session, Teller manifested a lack of interest. He introduced a bill of his own to prohibit combinations from controlling the rights to patented articles, but never pushed it with any vigor. He voted for Reagan's amendment to the Sherman bill to add criminal penalties for breaking the law, but protested that as then phrased the bill would not touch the Standard Oil Company and could be used against farm organizations and labor unions. He urged that this last be corrected beyond a shadow of a doubt. "My real objection to this bill is that it is delusive." It might do some good, but he doubted it very much.

With the Silver Purchase Act passed, the legislation pressing for attention in the Senate was the McKinley tariff and the Elections bill, both of which had passed the House. The silver senators had obligated themselves to support the tariff by party support of the Purchase Act. Teller seems to have played little direct part in these trades because of his dissatisfaction with the silver legislation. As Sherman said, he was an "off ox" on all these questions. . . .

CREATING A NATIONAL CAMPAIGN ISSUE
1894-95

. . . . This piling up of issues as the election of 1896 approached is somewhat confusing, but the lines appear fairly clear for the most part. It bid fair to be the most definite and undisguised class conflict in American political history.

As far as the cause of free coinage was concerned, the continued depression and the complete bankruptcy of the argument that repeal of the Sherman Act would cure it were reacting in silver's favor, especially in the South and West. Two large propaganda organizations for free coinage—the American Bimetallic League and the National Bimetallic Union—became active after repeal, and in 1894 and 1895 carried on their campaign of education by meetings and literature. Most of their expenses were met by the silver miners of Colorado, Montana, Idaho, and Nevada, who also contributed substantially to the support of certain weekly periodicals. But it was becoming increasingly difficult to raise money for the cause. The fall in the price of silver had bankrupted many silver miners and destroyed the main resources of others. Many others doubted the possibility of success, and some began to question whether free coinage would benefit extensively the silver producer. For, if the bankers were correct, and free coinage drove the United States to a silver standard at the current market rate, silver miners could profit from the resulting inflation only insofar as they were debtors.

The decline of financial support by the silver miners was partly made up for by the pamphlet war that began over free coinage after the election of 1894. Centering about Chicago, and stimulated by the vast popularity of W. H. Harvey's *Coin's Financial School,* the tracts poured from the printers in a veritable cloudburst. Economists, journalists, bankers, college presidents, and lawyers rushed into print to support Coin or to disprove him. James H. Teller, the youngest of the Senator's brothers and now a Chicago lawyer, joined the rush with *The Battle of the Standards.* The press of the Middle West took up the contest, and it was a rare newspaper that did not have arguments on the silver question for its regular editorial fare, to say nothing of the activities of voluntary correspondents.

With control of the Democratic Party in the hands of the gold-standard advocates, and the dominant Republicans in a not substantially different position, there were demands for an independent political movement for free coinage that would unite into one group all its supporters now in the traditional parties and in the People's Party. These demands were discussed and agitated freely in Washington during the early months of 1895.

Teller may still have had some hope that the Republican Party would take a position on bimetallism in substantial contrast to Cleveland's. There had been, even during the fight over repeal, attempts to unite the causes of protection and silver, partly to maintain Republican unity, but some of them were broader in scope. Back of them was the fact that there was not a complete unity of interest between the manufacturers and the bankers, rapidly as the latter were gaining the ascendancy in the business world. In a broad sense the financial group had backed Cleveland, and the manufacturers the Republicans in 1892, and this divergency was evident in the strategy of both the Republicans and the free-coinage groups. It did not promise much after repeal, although optimistic Republican silver men kept nursing the hope that it would.

There were repeated rumors during 1895 that the free-coinage Republicans were preparing to bolt their party if it declared for the gold standard, rumors that were not believed in the East, at least. *The Nation* expressed the general view when it announced: "Of the Colorado and Montana members [of the Senate] it may be said that their bark is worse than their bite. They will threaten and bluster up to a certain point and then they will surrender. Such Senators as Teller and Wolcott have no idea of disrupting their party." An attempt was made by Dubois and Carter to secure approval for a satisfactory proposal from the National League of Republican Clubs in the summer, but to no avail.

The unanimity of the controlling factions in the party from all sections east of the Missouri River should have been evidence to the Westerners that they would get no help from them. Possibly it was. At least two weeks later a Washington dispatch to the Chicago *Daily News* related the information that a "Western Republican of national prominence" had predicted that the free-coinage Republicans would bolt the next convention. A plan, he had related, was agreed upon by Western senators and other leaders claiming to be able to control the delegations from all states west of Kansas and South Dakota and possibly North Dakota and Nebraska. They would choose delegates to the Republican convention in regular form and support Senator Cameron, or some other silver Republican, for the presidential nomination. If no free-coinage candidate were nominated, the delegates from the Western states would walk out and wait on the Democratic convention, asking it to nominate a free-coinage man, preferably Senator Morgan. If the Democrats refused, the Westerners would make an independent nomination, with the hope of throwing the election into the House and then bargaining among the candidates.

There was probably little more than talk in the proposed agreement the Westerner had seemed so certain about, but it was indicative of the trend of Western ideas as it became more and more evident that the East would stand out for the gold standard. Two days after the report appeared, Senator Kyle, Populist, of South Dakota, wrote to Senator Allen, of Nebraska:

Why would it not be a good stroke for several of us to meet at a convenient point this summer—you and I, and Senators Teller,

Shoup, Morgan and Turpie. We could find out what they would like as a basis of a combination in case both old parties declare against silver.

As far as the East was concerned, it became more unanimous in its attitude toward free coinage during 1895. Writing from the atmosphere of Washington, John Hay, in the fall of 1895, indicated to Henry Adams what the trend was:

> If you don't hurry back, there won't be a silver man in America except you and Peffer, and even Peffer said in an interview the other day that the jig was up. I think Reid and McKinley and Allison and Harrison and Morton are all good gold-bugs now. A large majority of Democrats have thought they were not, but the post-masters and "deppity marshalls" have convinced them that they are— at least, such of them as go to convention.

But the grain-farming West and the agricultural South had been given to a similar unanimity by the depression. The Democratic repudiation of Cleveland was soon to show that they were nearly as united as the East. If the cause was lost in the East, it was still supreme in the Far West and South. Only the Middle West, with its great farming interests, as well as its growing industrial and commercial centers, remained questionable ground. Whether gold or silver won the next fight would be determined in that section between Pennsylvania and the Missouri River.

In preparing for the struggle, the contestants were pointing their entire case toward the election of 1896. The Eastern press began to insist that the major parties take an emphatic stand against free coinage in their platforms. Politicians, especially prospective candidates for the presidency, wanted to avoid any commitments that would kill their chances in any region. Two questions remained: What would the parties do? What would the sections do?

REVOLT
1895-96

. . . . As the time for the presidential election of 1896 approached, there developed two very distinct tendencies looking toward a realignment of parties. One was the feeling of many silver men that the day of compromise was over. Platforms such as the Republican of 1892 did not prevent Eastern members of that party from voting against all measures looking toward bimetallism, or from taking positive action against it, as in the repeal fight of 1893. The business interests in the East, on the other hand, were just as determined that the parties should end their straddle on the question and come out for the gold standard. The trend all over the East had long been definitely away from anything looking like silver coinage. Neither of the major parties had ever committed itself to free coinage, and with a Democratic President who was completely on the other side, it seemed unlikely that either would now. To one gaining his knowledge of politics from the Eastern press it must have seemed improbable that either major party would declare for free coinage in 1896, and hence possible that both might even come out for the gold standard.

There can be little doubt that as far as Teller personally was concerned, he returned to Washington for the opening of the Fifty-fourth Congress determined to make the Republican Party declare for free coinage or leave that organization for one that would. More than that, he planned to take as many Republicans as possible with him when he left. It is quite evident that he looked forward at that time to the probability that both major parties would either adopt gold standard or straddle platforms, and in that eventuality he would unite such Republicans as he could command with such silver Democrats as would bolt their party, and go in with the Populist Party on a separate ticket committed to free coinage. That was only the extreme, however, and for the present he would try to swing the Republicans and protectionists as far toward free coinage as possible. . . .

In his efforts to weld together a large group of free-coinage Republicans who would defy the party, Teller had to work against forces that were more potent than traditional loyalty to the party. The greatest was the very well-founded expectation that pending some unforeseen political accident, the next administration would be Republican, and for at least four years the patronage in the Western states would be available to those politicians who were loyal now.

Less important, perhaps, was the declining relative significance of silver mining in the Rocky Mountain states, due partly to the low price of silver, and partly to the great increase in other types of mining, especially gold mining. Certainly it would be impossible to keep the free-coinage Republicans a unit in opposition to the party that would soon be able to offer protective tariffs on wool, hides, and lead to their constitutents. How large a group could be organized and maintained was the problem. . . .

There seems to have been a fairly definite understanding looking toward action in the Republican convention among Teller and those who were following his lead: Senators Dubois, Cannon, Mantle, and Carter, and Representatives Hartman, Wilson, Shafroth, Allen, and Charles A. Towne. This included the bolting of the party if a free-coinage plank were not adopted, and joining with such other groups as the silver Democrats, Populists, and National Silverites, in a fight for a definite free-coinage platform and candidate.

The plan meant first of all the bringing to the Republican convention of delegations which were pledged to silver uncompromisingly, and to a bolt if they could not prevent a gold-standard plank. Most of them would not go as far as Teller. His own task was to keep the contests real, and, at the same time, carry as many with him as possible.

On such a program only those men who were willing to forego immediate rewards could be included. It was obviously "yellow dog" year for the Republicans, and, barring a miracle, anyone they nominated for president would win. The choice was easier for Teller than for his colleagues. He was sixty-six years old, tired of politics, and in ill health. If he cared to return to the Senate, his position in Colorado was such that he could bolt the party and still be re-elected more easily than any colleague could, except the senators from Nevada, who had already bolted. He had mentally a free hand to make his own policy. It was not so with the others, who as a group, were very young for the positions they held, and in every case would have serious opposition when they came up for re-election. Teller felt an immense amount of gratitude toward them individually, and many of his actions in the next six months can only be understood by having clearly in mind his desire to give them the protection they had earned from him.

To carry out his part of the plan, Teller instituted an extensive correspondence with the political leaders in Colorado. He wanted a delegation to the national convention that was committed to silver above all considerations of party. The majority of the politicians were opposed to this procedure, as were the supporters of all the candidates for the presidency. Early in May the Arapahoe County convention [Denver] defeated by a vote of over two to one a motion to censure Wolcott for his stand against bolting. But public opinion in Colorado was behind Teller. It was a foregone conclusion that he would be chairman of the Delegation, but the opposition endeavored to secure the choice of Wolcott and others as delegates who were sure not to bolt. To prevent this, Teller addressed a telegram to the chairman of the state central committee, saying:

I wish to say to the State Convention, through you, that I do not desire to go to the national convention, and cannot go unless the State delegation is in accordance with my ideas in declaring that in the coming campaign the silver question is the paramount issue.

The State convention should act with the full knowledge that I do not intend to support a candidate on a gold-standard platform or a platform of doubtful construction.

The fight was bitter, and it was only by a careful struggle that his friends won. Although the victory was absolute on the surface, it was marred by the many antagonisms created. When it was over, Ammons, one of the delegates, wrote to Dawson describing the undercurrents at the convention.

There was a very strong sentiment among Mr. Teller's friends in opposition to bolting the national ticket, and I know that many of them intend to support the national ticket in any event. It was this element that made it hard for us . . . and gave Mr. Teller's enemies their support in several of the closest contests. . . . It was hard to tell where anyone stood, and there was much bitterness expressed because of the difference of opinion on the proposition of bolting.

The resolution with the implied permission to bolt was carried in the resolutions committee by a vote of 24 to 18, and Ammons thought it would have been still closer had the issue been drawn directly. This part of the platform was one of the most unusual ever adopted by a convention choosing delegates to a national convention.

. . . we declare to the Republican party of the nation and to the world that our Senior Senator in Congress, the Honorable Henry M. Teller, has our unqualified approval and support in the position he has so ably maintained in Congress for the cause of the free coinage of silver in its relation to the tariff. . . . We recognize in Senator Teller the ablest living exponent of the true principles of American finance and the most fearless and intelligent advocate in public life of the financial system which will best promote the comfort and prosperity of the whole people and the whole world, and the delegates selected by this convention are instructed to act in harmony with the views of the Honorable Henry M. Teller as to the course to be pursued by the Colorado delegation in the national convention, and that Senator

Teller is hereby selected as a delegate and appointed to lead the delegation in the St. Louis convention.

A friend wrote Teller after the convention warning him that "there is strong party feeling in the state," and one of the delegates to the national convention thought it worth while to write that he expected to stand by Teller no matter what the others did. Shortly before the national convention was to meet, former Senator Stephen W. Dorsey wrote Teller from Denver:

> I write this to say that from repeated conversations with some of the delegates to St. Louis I don't believe that the majority of them have the slightest intention of leaving the convention no matter who is nominated or what the platform may be.

The Eastern press looked angrily at the challenge Teller was forcing into the contest. The Philadelphia *Inquirer* observed, "Senator Teller is in full command of Colorado. . . . He is a member of the band of highwaymen who refused to permit the tariff revenue bill to pass without a free silver proviso." Not all of them were sure that the convention's action meant a bolt, and many were inclined to believe it indicated that Teller would try to make terms. In Montana and Idaho the Republican state conventions endorsed the action of Teller and his associates on coinage and tariff, but, as in Utah, they refused to recommend that their delegates to the national convention bolt if the coinage plank were unsatisfactory.

The contest was now transferred to the Republican convention at St. Louis. In preparation for it Teller delivered a long speech in the Senate in which he discussed free coinage and its relation to the approaching election. The cause of free coinage he based directly on the question of price levels, declaring that there had been no depreciation of the silver dollar anywhere as compared with commodity prices. On the other hand, the present gold standard meant constantly falling prices. "It means 21 per cent more of farm products than it did when you repealed the Sherman Law." No international agreement for bimetallism that had to include Great Britain was possible, and the United States was strong enough "to have a financial system of our own."

> What the Republican party will do at St. Louis I do not know, but I believe I know enough of the public sentiment of the plain people, the honest people, to know that the party which inscribes on its banner, "The Gold standard" inscribes on its banner "Defeat."

The lack of specific instructions created considerable doubt among the insurgents as to the proper course to pursue at the national convention. Some did not want to bolt until instructed to do so, and up to the hour that the small group walked out of the convention hall, no one knew how many would follow Teller. Apparently many did not make their final decision until the crisis came. As late as June 15, former Senator John J. Ingalls wrote regarding Teller's announced purpose to bolt. "To me it is hardly credible, but he has much of the Cromwell spirit and may be implacable."

While the free-coinage Republicans were making preparations for a losing fight in their convention, the free-coinage Democrats were taking control of their party away from the administration forces with a speed and completeness that was as unusual as it was unexpected. All over the South and West, and in a substantial portion of the Middle West, the Democratic state conventions were selecting delegates to the national convention pledged to free coinage and repudiating the Cleveland administration in unmistakable terms. Among the candidates for their presidential nomination no one stood out as McKinley did in the Republican, but the leading one was Bland, of Missouri, and most of the others with substantial support were also committed to free coinage. Would the Democrats adopt a free-coinage platform and nominate a silver candidate in spite of President Cleveland?

The growing prospect of this during April and May raised a problem of great importance to the insurgent Republicans. It was all very well to plan to bolt from the Republican organization and to function for a time as an independent group if the Democrats were also pledged to a gold standard or a straddle platform; but it was much more serious to bolt the old party in order to take a position in line with its chief opposition. In the latter case the bolters would be between the devil of going over to the hereditary enemy, and the deep blue sea of obstructing the success of the policy that had caused their revolt. Teller was ready to accept the first alternative, as his correspondence shows, but his younger colleagues were not, and the policy which they followed was a compromise that protected the interests of their state organizations. In this unsatisfactory position, they enjoyed what comfort company could give them, for the Populists were in a similar position. If the Democrats declared for free coinage, they too would have the delectable choice of committing suicide as a political organization or impeding the success of their most important policy. Nor did the silver Democrats, even with their remarkable successes in state conventions, have an inviting prospect. Repudiating their own party's record as they would do, and splitting their organization, they could at best have but little chance of success in the election. The only hope they could have of winning lay in a complete union of all the disaffected Republicans and the Populists behind the Democratic ticket. This made them open to suggestions of compromise.

Conferences of the factional leaders in Washington resulted in a tentative understanding among certain Southern Democratic leaders, the insurgent Republicans, the leaders of the National Silver Party, and a group of Populists. The insurgent Republicans would bolt the St. Louis convention and organize a political party. At the Democratic convention at Chicago an attempt would be made to secure the presidential nomination for Senator Teller. If the attempt were successful, the Silver Republicans,

Populists, and National Silver Party would also nominate him, and a union of free-coinage forces would be effected without destroying any of the political organizations involved. If a Democrat were named at Chicago or an unsatisfactory platform adopted, the Silver Republican, Populist, and National Silver parties would unite upon a common candidate, or, at least, so the Silver Republicans and Populists assured themselves.

The Republican convention opened on June 16, and to it came Silver Republicans who were delegates, and others like Congressman Towne, of Minnesota, who had not been so honored. Teller announced for the silver men that there would be no bolt unless the convention adopted an unsatisfactory monetary plank. In that event, however, they would quietly withdraw.

Before the convention assembled, the evidence seems clear that J. P. Morgan and other interested bankers had convinced Hanna and McKinley of the advisability of a gold-standard platform. To ensure its adoption and to prevent a disastrous bolt that might prove weakening to the party, representatives of the banking group swarmed about St. Louis as the convention opened. Indeed, they were so active that Hanna finally warned them, "You damned bankers will upset this whole thing, if you keep on." But, assured of the platform, they expended their efforts on keeping the Western delegates from bolting. McKinley would do what he could for silver, Hanna assured the Westerners, and would send another commission to Europe to try to secure an international agreement for bimetallism. Far more potent than this promise was the expectation that the Republicans would have the presidency after March 4. "Whatever we do, let's avoid a split," was the theme of their argument.

Gold sentiment was well entrenched among the delegates. Someone had revived an old song made popular by Tony Pastor, and before long it was being sung, hummed, and whistled about the headquarters hotel.

Gold, gold, gold—
I love to hear it jingle.
Gold, gold, gold—
Its power is untold,
For the women they adore it,
While the men try hard to store it.
There is not a better thing in life than
Gold, gold, gold.

The only important question was how many of the delegates would walk out, and how many of the voters could be influenced by that action. It took Teller three days to reach St. Louis from Washington, as he was having such a severe attack of asthma that he could not stand continuous traveling. When he arrived he went into conferences with various groups of silver delegates and outlined the strategy for the convention. He told the Colorado delegates that the action of their state convention did not bind them to act as he did. He was Colorado's member of the committee on resolutions, and the only free-coinage representative on the subcommittee to frame the financial plank.

The real fight over the plank occurred in committee. Of the states and territories represented on the committee, ten only were for free coinage—California, Colorado, Idaho, Montana, Nevada, North Carolina, Utah, Wyoming, and the territories of Arizona and New Mexico. As in the vote on the question in the whole convention, North Carolina, the one Southern state where the delegates represented a real political party, was the only silver state outside the Rocky Mountain region. It is not likely that the effectiveness with which the delegations from the states of Kansas, Nebraska, and the Dakotas had been made to deny their former free-coinage commitments, or the unanimity with which the delegates from the South were going against public opinion in that section, made Teller feel any more friendly toward the national party organization.

In the committee the fight was protracted. When free coinage was defeated, compromise proposals were suggested and voted down. The gold-standard plank that eventually went into the platform contained a conciliatory pledge to attempt an international agreement to secure bimetallism, a position that Senator Hoar and the majority of the Eastern Republicans had taken in the Senate during the recent session of Congress. The control of the committee, as of the convention, was secure in the hands of the gold-standard men, although they were making it as easy as possible for free-coinage Republicans to stay with the party that upheld the gold standard.

When the issue was thus definitely decided, Teller addressed the committee:

> Mr. President, I am going out. I am going to fight for the principle, and I have the belief in my heart that some day this great party that has done so much for the human race, and of whose future so much was hoped and expected, will come to a right view upon this question, and that we shall not take our declaration from Wall street or from Lombard street, but from the honest sentiment of the great heart of the American people; and if you will consult that heart and let Wall street alone, you will abandon that platform that declares for the gold standard.

Senator Lodge replied for the majority:

> I wish to say for myself, what I believe I say for everybody else, that we accept and understand his position; that we honor him as a man of courage and conviction, that he takes with him not only the profound regret of all Republicans that he should feel it his duty to act as he does, but also their sincere and entire respect.

The next day the fight was made on the floor of the convention. The real battle was already lost, but the withdrawal had to be based upon the action of the convention to make it effective. The regulars were inclined to give the bolters ample time and opportunity for their demonstration, as they had the bulk of the Western delegates well in hand, and wanted to avoid anything that looked like dictation. Then, too, Teller had announced that there would be no dramatics. After the committee chairman, Foraker, had presented the majority report on the platform, including the plank that meant the gold standard, Teller was recognized to move an amendment. The Associated Press report reads:

> The name of Teller set the Westerners wild. In little scattering squads the handfuls of delegations who had been sitting under the banners of Colorado, of Idaho, of Utah, of Nevada, California, and Montana, and some of those from Tennessee and other Western and Southern States, were on their feet waving hats, flags, umbrellas, fans, and handkerchiefs and shrieking like mad. The fire spread to the galleries and swept across them until they seemed to be almost unanimously carrying on the cheer.

It was noticed that the newspapermen were particularly vociferous in their cheering. The clerk read the substitute plank for free coinage at the ratio of 16 to 1. Teller began to speak in support of the substitute. It was, in spite of his intentions, the most dramatic moment of his life; and although he realized that it was, he had little histrionic sense, and the impression he made came largely from the situation itself and from his own personality. Wrote a reporter for the St. Louis *Republic*:

> The magnificent old man bore a look of sorrow, but not of regret, at the step he was about to take. His voice was weak, and it was with difficulty that he could make himself heard when he first began his address. He steadied himself by resting his right hand on the table, and then when the cheering began again he . . . advanced to the edge of the platform. There was no attempt at oratorical effect by the Colorado Senator. He was too weak physically for the effort which it was necessary to make. His deep earnestness was apparent to all. The respect he commanded was unbounded. . . . The political significance of the situation was lost sight of in the profound sympathy for the venerable Senator from the Mountain State.

Teller reviewed briefly and temperately the monetary question, and called attention to the past platforms of the party. The
plank declaring for bimetallism by international agreement was
impossible for achievement as long as Great Britain was the great
creditor nation. The only possible avenue toward bimetallism was
for the United States to adopt free coinage:

> I contend for it because I believe there can be no proper financial
> system in any country in the world that does not recognize this
> principle of bimetallism. . . .
>
> I contend for it because I believe the civilization of the world is to
> be determined by its rightful or wrongful solution.
>
> I am tolerant of those who differ with me. I act from my judg-
> ment, enlightened as best I have been able to enlighten it by years
> of thought and study. . . . It is a solemn declaration that the Republi-
> can party intends to maintain low prices and stagnated business for
> all time to come.

These statements were spoken in a monotone so low that it was
difficult to hear him. Continues the *Republic* reporter:

> Not a gesture was made for the first five minutes. When the
> Senator had concluded his plea for bimetallism he raised himself
> on tiptoe, and his right hand gave the same old gesture which he
> always employs to emphasize his earnestness. His strength was tempo-
> rarily restored to him by a mighty effort, and, sweeping the space in
> front of him with a long reach of his arm, he shouted at the con-
> vention: "This is the first great gathering of Republicans since the
> party was organized that has declared the inability of the American
> people to control their own affairs. . . . As a bimetallist, I must," and
> his hands were raised in defiance, "renounce my allegiance to my
> party."

There were tears in Teller's eyes as he sat down, and tears in
the eyes of many who heard him. There were also cheers from
the gallery and hisses from the floor.

Foraker's motion to lay the substitute on the table prevailed by 818½ votes to 105½. Only the states that had supported it in the committee gave majorities against the gold standard, and only Colorado, Idaho, Montana, Nevada, Wyoming, and Arizona were unanimous. When the vote was announced the gold men had their opportunity, and they staged an enormous demonstration. The gold-standard plank was then adopted by about the same majority. The expected eventuality had arrived. The gold standard was in the platform.

Teller asked that Senator Cannon be allowed to read a statement. The young Utah senator, a small man physically and rather foppish in his dress, proceeded to read. It was a truculent statement of the causes that were forcing the silver men to bolt the convention. He had to read against constant interruptions which became an uproar at his last words. Teller and Cannon started down the aisle toward the entrance. Dubois and the Idaho delegation fell in behind, as did those from Nevada and Colorado. A few other delegates joined, making twenty-three in all, but looking much larger because of the inclusion of the alternates and newspapermen. The convention was on its feet yelling and cat-calling at the departing delegates: "Go to Chicago!" "Take the Democratic train!" Henry Cabot Lodge and Mark Hanna yelled with the rest. . . .

What the bolters lacked in numbers they made up in those spiritual compensations that go with defiance of the powers that be. As they walked out, Towne reminded a reporter that it was the anniversary of Waterloo, an ominous date for the Napoleon who was about to be nominated by the Republican convention. While the feeling of exultation was upon them they met and organized the Silver Republican Party. They issued an address to the public in which they restated the argument for silver coinage, and their reasons for bolting. It invoked the union of all parties still to hold conventions in order to re-establish bimetallism. To these conventions they offered the name of Henry M. Teller as a candidate for President, upon whom all of them, Silver Republicans, Democrats, Populists, and the members of the National Silver Party, could unite.

> It is not merely as the exponent of monetary reform that we present this man to the people. It is true that he had waged a mighty war for the restoration of the money of the Constitution, and his name has been identified as that of no other living man with this great cause. But had his services been less demanded and less noticed in this direction, the people would still have recognized in him for other labors a statesman of the purest type.

It was signed by the bolters, with the exception of Teller. Spurred on by Dubois, Cannon, and Pettigrew, they were offering the Democrats a candidate that the Silver Republicans could support. Then a group of Populists, led by H. E. Taubeneck, chairman of that party's national committee, who had been in St. Louis by prearrangement, issued an address calling upon the Populists and Democrats to make Teller their candidate for the presidency. With the bolting Republicans, and the Populist Party, which carried four states in the last election, behind him, Teller was a political factor to be reckoned with. . . .

JOHN THE BAPTIST FOR W. J. BRYAN
1896

. . . . It is clear that the Silver Republicans and Populists were agreed to try to induce the Democratic Party to nominate Teller—and, failing that, to nominate him anyway through the Silver Republican and Populist parties. If the Cleveland administration controlled the Democratic convention, the new party could, it was reasonably sure, carry the bulk of the states west of the Missouri, and might even displace the Democrats as a major party. At least a clear-cut fight on the silver question would follow. It is not likely that there was any impetus given to this movement simply by the hope of making Teller president. It was done to unite the silver forces in such a way as to save the faces of the bolting

Republicans and the Populists. Senators such as Dubois, Cannon, and Pettigrew had been fighting Democratic political machines at home too long to think that they could expect any mercy from them if they bolted the Republican organization and supported the Democratic nominee for president. The Populists were in a similar predicament. If they united with the Democrats in support of a Democratic candidate, their party was forever dead. This was especially true of the Southern members of the party. The nomination of a bolting Republican was a different matter, and they were anxious to avoid the necessity of choosing between supporting a regular Democratic candidate pledged to free coinage, and opposition to such a candidate. Teller, although a Republican, was the best-known advocate of free coinage on July 1, 1896, and had endeared himself to the Populist senators by his friendly treatment of them and by many lapses from regularity and support of such causes as the income tax. Patterson, in the *Rocky Mountain News*, emphasized these, and stressed Teller's record on railroad legislation as reason for Populist support.

How far Democratic leaders were involved does not appear, but it is clear that many of the senators of that political group were favorably disposed. Most of them were either personal friends of Teller, or primarily interested in finding a candidate who had a bare chance to defeat McKinley. There was a newspaper story early in June that a group of Democratic senators had canvassed five hundred party leaders in the South and West by letter, asking if they were willing to support Teller if he were nominated. Out of 423 replies all but eight expressed a willingness to help make him president. It was repeatedly charged both before and at the Chicago convention that a senatorial clique was trying to bring about Teller's nomination, and this manipulation claim was used by other candidates as an argument against Teller. When Senator Vest, of Missouri, was accused of being ostensibly for Bland and actually for Teller, he replied that he would not vote for anyone for the nomination "in the convention" who favored woman suffrage, and that included Teller. Josephus Daniels, probably W. J. Bryan's principal supporter for the nomination, made this explanation of the convention situation:

> The coterie of Democratic silver Senators who are on the ground, recognize Teller's great individual strength and his towering figure as a great champion of silver and privately most of them would like to see him nominated, but there is a general fear that the rank and file of the Democratic party would rebel against the selection of a man who so recently walked out of the Republican Convention.

This was the one great obstacle in the way of Teller's nomination by the Democrats. The obvious fact that a free-coinage plank would mean a bolt of the Easterners from the party, larger even than the bolt from the Republican, meant also that should a Republican such as Teller be the nominee, these bolters would have a weapon that would be effective in splitting the party. Senator Morgan wrote Teller on July 4, stating his own view of such a nomination:

> If you are nominated at Chicago, I will give you the most earnest and cordial support of which I am capable. Yet I have some doubt if I, or anyone, could avoid a serious difficulty in answering the objection which the gold democrats would urge in this form, viz.: "You are invited to leave your party and its honest money creed, and vote for a republican in order to get an opportunity of paying your debts with inflated, unsound, and dishonest dollars, worth in fact, only 50 cents." That tirade is answered, if we hold to the organization of which we have control, and put the gold men in the category of bolters.

A different reason was given to Arthur Dunn by Senator Cockrell.

> Young man, when we win a Democratic victory we want a Democrat. I have served long in the Senate with Mr. Teller and I respect

him, but the next Democratic President will be a Democrat and fill the offices with Democrats.

The fact that the administration now expected a free-coinage platform and candidate on the Democratic ticket, and was preparing to assist the Republican ticket, both directly and through a separate gold Democratic Party, is an indication that Teller's nomination would have placed this group in a strong position to harm the free-coinage campaign.

To Dubois, Pettigrew, Cannon, Hartman, and Mantle it was a choice between nominating Teller at Chicago, or bringing him out as the candidate of the Populists and Silver Republicans. In no other way, they insisted, could the silver forces keep such states as California, Oregon, and the Dakotas from going Republican. A free-coinage Democrat as a nominee would mean a serious problem for the Republican bolters. Teller's nomination by the Democrats would strengthen the bolters immensely at home. It would unite the Republican organizations in the Western states behind the bolters from the St. Louis convention. Even at the time of the bolt it had been freely stated by those Westerners who refused to leave the party, that if Teller were nominated by one of the other parties, there would be no opposition to him in their states. To carry out their plans, Dubois had gone from St. Louis to Springfield, Illinois, to interview Governor Altgeld, who would dominate the Illinois delegates to the convention. He was optimistic after the interview. Pettigrew went to Arkansas to see Senator James K. Jones, a leader among the silver Democrats, and returned to Chicago with him. From here he wrote Teller that Jones was working to secure his nomination.

It all depends upon Illinois and Ohio. If they will say that you can carry those states you will be nominated. . . . If the Democrats do not nominate you then the silver and populist conventions must do it. And we will defeat McKinley any way and unite the electors on you after election.

At Chicago, the Silver Republicans established headquarters from which to make their fight for Teller. As the convention was assembling here were gathered the important Silver Republicans, a number of prominent Populists including Taubeneck, Patterson, and Weaver, the leaders of the National Silver Party, as well as several free-coinage Democrats who had declared openly for Teller. They tried to accomplish their purpose by two arguments. Without Teller as the presidential nominee, they urged, neither the Silver Republicans nor Populists could be induced to support the Democratic ticket. Furthermore, Teller was the candidate most likely to carry certain necessary states, such as California, Michigan, Illinois, and Ohio.

The attitude of the Democratic leaders toward Teller's nomination was frankly utilitarian. The Southerners were generally for him, as his candidacy, even though it did not strengthen the national ticket enough to secure a victory, would at least make sure that their present dangerous rival in local politics, the People's Party, would be placed in a very weak position. Many of them also had grateful memories of the death of the Force bill. On the other hand, the Western delegates did not want Teller, even though they admitted that it would strengthen the ticket in their region. They could see no profit in naming a candidate who might help turn their state organizations over to the bolting Republicans and Populists.

A substantial number of Silver Democrats issued statements for Teller. Congressman Joseph Sibley, Pennsylvania Democrat, not only replied to Bryan's appeal for help by writing that he was for Teller, but issued a public letter in which he urged that the only hope of Democratic victory lay in nominating Teller; for with him as a candidate the party could carry Illinois, Indiana, Michigan, and possibly Ohio. He was positive, he wrote Bryan, that Teller would win.

As the delegates began to assemble, only Bland and Governor Boise, the two candidates with the largest number of pledged delegates, were as prominently mentioned as Teller. The press reported that his supporters were receiving unexpected aid through letters and telegrams to delegates from local leaders who had become convinced that it would be a strong nomination.

Teller did not make the task of the managers at his headquarters easy. He seems never to have taken his own candidacy very seriously, or, if he did, his lack of ability to "dissemble" hurt enormously his chances for the nomination. He made statements repeatedly which ruined the strategy of his managers. When asked by a reporter if he thought the Silver Republicans would support either Bland or Boise, he replied, "Yes, I think our people would support either of those gentlemen or any other man of good character and ability, who is recognized by those favoring the free coinage of silver." Immediately after his Denver reception, while starting for Central City, Teller told a reporter that he expected that Bland would be nominated. Repeatedly he was quoted as saying that he thought his nomination by the Democrats would be "injudicious." To prevent further such statements, Dubois addressed Teller a long note shortly before the convention opened:

> In my judgment you will be the nominee of this convention, and will be endorsed by the conventions at St. Louis. Judge McConnell of Illinois is openly outspoken for you, and it is a reasonable probability that Gov. Altgeld will declare himself in your favor soon. Senators Blackburn, Daniel, and Jones are for you, and also ex-Senator Walsh, and Mr. Howell of Georgia.
>
> The contest is between you and Bland. . . . McLean of Ohio is also for you.
>
> The serious obstacle which confronts me is the statement, repeatedly made, that you will not accept a nomination at the hands of this convention, and that you will support the nominee of this convention.
>
> In case they should nominate a Democratic candidate here it will be necessary for us in the interests of silver to join forces with the Populists, and nominate you at Saint Louis. In this way we can hold our western states away from McKinley on the gold standard, and in this way only.

The Populists have been a tower of strength to us, and we have
assured them that we will not desert them, but that in the event of a
Democratic nomination here that we would unite with them in your
support.

He added that he wanted Teller to telegraph and write to him
that he would co-operate with the group at Chicago and work
with them. Other members wrote in a similar vein.

On July 5, a letter from Teller was made public, which could
hardly have been to his managers' liking, although it did admit
the right to use his name as a candidate:

> I have not changed my attitude from what it was at St. Louis in
> the least. There at the earnest solicitation of many gentlemen . . .
> I consented that my name might be used in connection with the
> Presidency at Chicago. I told them frankly that I had no claims upon
> the Democratic party; beyond that I did not consider my nomination
> by the convention as possible; nevertheless, if, as my more partial
> friends thought, the Democratic delegates might believe that my can-
> didacy would more likely bring to the ticket the necessary electoral
> votes than would that of one of the life members of the party, I
> would leave the matter in their hands and trust wholly to their
> discretion and patriotism.

Teller's prospects of the nomination ebbed and flowed during
the opening days of the convention. The coolness of many Democratic delegates from silver-mining states was in evidence, and a
Colorado delegate was accused of "acting badly in a quiet way."
When H. E. Taubeneck declared that the Populist Party was
opposed to Bland and would entertain no proposition for a
compromise which did not "include Senator Teller as the head
of the ticket," Teller's prospects brightened. Later, to supplement
individual statements, the Populists united on an ultimatum:

> To nominate a straight Democrat in a divided party, when millions
> of honest citizens stand ready to support a nonpartisan candidate is
> mere reckless experiment. . . . We feel confident that the People's

party is willing to open the path of union upon Henry M. Teller. . . . We cannot be induced to indorse any candidate for President who has not severed his affiliations with the old political parties.

There was talk of various compromises such as a Teller-Bland ticket and later of a Teller-McLean ticket, to strengthen the Ohio campaign. A Washington delegate declared Teller would make the strongest campaign of any candidate in his state. Others made similar claims for Ohio, where Teller had strong support among the delegates, and where the favorite-son candidate, John R. McLean, was openly urging the nomination of the Coloradan. On July 7, it was reported that most of the Southern delegations would cast their votes for him—after complimentary votes for Democrats on the first ballot.

On the other hand, it played against Teller that the managers of his canvass began their campaign early, and created opposition from most of the other candidates. The campaign managers for both Bland and Boise turned their weapons on the outsider. The senatorial cabal story was used as a background for an appeal to let none but tried Democrats be considered. This plea was reinforced by appeals to party history, and the ghost of Horace Greeley was brought into the convention strategy to frighten the delegates away from the temptation Dubois was holding out to them. Misfortune hampered the Silver Republicans in cases like the Illinois delegation, where antagonism between Altgeld and some other delegates forced them to declare for Bland before they were ready to make a record. The impression persisted until long after the convention was over that Altgeld intended to start a stampede to Teller, but his statement of July 7, that he did not think Teller could carry Illinois, was a severe blow to the hopes of the Silver Republicans. It seems, too, that Altgeld thought it more important to secure for the Democratic Party the unity that a regular party nominee would give it, than to conciliate other parties.

Another important factor was the dark-horse candidate, William Jennings Bryan—a dark horse only to the press and public, it happens, as his papers reveal an astonishing number of pledges of support from individual delegates, the result of two years of active campaigning. He was on excellent terms with the Populists, the Silver Republicans, and the National Silverites.

Patterson's *Rocky Mountain News* favored Bryan next to Teller as the silver candidate. Shortly after the convention opened, Josephus Daniels succeeded in swinging the North Carolina delegation, which had been suspected of Teller sympathies, over to Bryan. This gave the Nebraskan's candidacy possibilities, and the delegates and observers became interested.

Now the question of supporting Bryan as the Democratic nominee was put to the Populists and Silver Republicans. The Republican bolters announced their refusal, but they did not sound as threatening as they had the day before. The Populist leaders at Chicago were in a serious quandary. They realized that they were gambling wildly on Teller, and if Bland were nominated they would be in a difficult position. Bryan as a candidate was much better. He had advocated bolting the Democratic ticket if the convention failed to declare for free coinage, and in that way had classified himself with those who put the issue above partisan advantage. Furthermore, they had not publicly declared they would not support him. Reluctantly, some of the Populists had to admit, on July 8, that they could not oppose Bryan.

Here, then was the logical candidate—the one lifelong Democrat who could unite the silver forces behind him. The strategy and labor the Silver Republicans had put into the Teller boom were now deflected to Bryan. The definite declarations of the Populists that they would not support Bland or Boise had gone a long way toward preventing the nomination of either, and to the Democratic leaders, Bryan—provided that he could develop substantial strength among the delegates—was an escape from the apparent logic of nominating Teller. As Teller's chances declined, Bryan's increased. Some of the Southern delegations prepared to support Teller shifted to Bryan. The morning of July 9 found Bryan with Bland and Boise among the probable nominees.

Teller's only chance now lay in a deadlock which might, by good strategy, be turned to his advantage. But before the day of July 9 was over, Byran had upheld the cause of silver before the convention with his masterly "Cross of Gold and Crown of Thorns" oration. The silver delegates were wildly enthusiastic, and confident that here was the Moses who could lead them out of the wilderness of defeat. Everywhere among them it reinforced Bryan's persistent solicitation of support for the nomination. This, added to the evident fact that he would in all probability unite the other silver parties behind him, prevented any deadlock by making Bryan's nomination a practical certainty.

As far as the Silver Republicans were concerned, the contest was over after Bryan's oratorical triumph. Teller's supporters did not even place him in nomination, although Colorado cast its votes for him on the first two ballots. The other votes that had once seemed so certain for Teller went to Bryan and made the bulk of his total on the first ballot. The Silver Republicans had made Teller a John the Baptist for another savior of the people. . . .

Editorial Note

On rare occasions in American history an individual writer has captured the interest of millions of readers and exercised an unusual influence upon his times. Such a man was Finley Peter Dunne. During the 1930's Elmer Ellis became interested in the creator of Mr. Dooley and edited some of Dunne's best writings in *Mr. Dooley at His Best* (Charles Scribner's Sons [New York, 1938]). This task logically led to the preparation of a full-scale biography of Dunne, a book which brought Elmer Ellis widespread acclaim.

Finley Peter Dunne was born in Chicago in 1867. Upon completing high school, he went to work at the Chicago *Telegram*. His natural talent for writing soon brought him an offer from the managing editor of the *News*, and before long Dunne was writing short, pithy comments on current affairs. He later accepted positions with the Chicago *Times*, the *Tribune*, and the *Herald*. In 1892 he transferred to the *Evening Post* and soon began experimenting with humorous editorials written in Irish dialect. Late in 1893 his famous character Mr. Dooley began to evolve, and by the following year Dunne's clever and witty comment on men and affairs became a popular institution around Chicago. Two years later Hennessy entered the Dooley sketches as a characteristic day-laborer of Archey Road. Here was created the team of Dooley and Hennessy. Dooley's comments were not only attracting national attention but were later known to be read at presidential cabinet meetings. By 1899 the Dooley essays were widely syndicated and they also appeared in national periodicals. By the turn of the century Finley Peter Dunne had made Mr. Dooley a national figure and his comment the source of amusement for millions. As Ellis has written, Dunne had become "The National Wit and Censor." The following selection shows the quality of Ellis' biography of Dunne and at the same time explains why the Dooley essays were so popular. The footnotes have been omitted.

5

Selections from **Mr. Dooley's America**

THE NATIONAL WIT AND CENSOR

D UNNE'S trip abroad cured him of his fit of depression, and
restored him to good health after the ravages of typhoid. He
had written nothing since the appearance of *Mr. Dooley's Philosophy*. Back in New York in the late spring, he revived the weekly
syndicated essays for *Harper's Weekly* and the newspapers, and
wrote some special articles for other periodicals. He and Robert
Russell had taken a small cottage in rural Long Island, and
there, with "a horse and a parrot and mosquitoes almost as big
as either," he lived out the summer, writing, swimming, playing
tennis, and seldom going into the city. With satisfactory articles
going out in regular sequence, the pessimism of the preceding
winter seemed very remote.

Elmer Ellis, *Mr. Dooley's America: A Life of Finley Peter Dunne* (New York:
Alfred A. Knopf, Inc., 1941).

"I feel there is prosperity and happiness ahead for all our little clan," he wrote Amelia. "Don't think . . . because I have cut loose from some of my old moorings and have made a venture of new fortunes that I have any other home port than the old friendly one of your respect and affection. . . . I am by no means rich but I have to some extent recovered what my illness cost me."

As usual, after a vacation from writing, Dunne's first essays of the new series were exceptionally fine, as if he had in the interval stored up a reservoir of wit and wisdom that he could now tap at will. The striking news events of the summer of 1901, the Northern Pacific panic, Carnegie's gift to the Scottish universities, the yacht races, and the Sampson-Schley controversy, were all celebrated in proper style. Revenge for the inconveniences which Dunne had suffered in re-entering the United States was taken in an article on the Custom House. His experience in his rural retreat gave him ideas for a satire on life in the country, which he wrote under the title: "The City as a Summer Resort." His illness of the past winter was exploited in an essay on "The Practice of Medicine," which ended with the oft-quoted opinion: "I think that if th' Christyan Scientists had some science an' th' doctors had more Christyanity, it wudden't make anny diff'rence which ye call in—if ye had a good nurse."

The great financial mergers, such as Morgan's erection of the United States Steel Corporation, and the boom and panic surrounding the Morgan-Harriman fight for control of the Northern Pacific, gave Dunne excellent opportunities to comment on Wall Street. "Glory be," Mr. Dooley greeted the Northern Pacific fight, "whin business gets above sellin' ten pinny nails in a brown paper cornucopy, 'tis hard to tell it fr'm murther." The struggle itself he compared to a fight between two local bruisers in his own saloon.

"Well, th' big lads is sthrong an' knows how to guard, an' whin they're spread out, small harm has come to thim. But th' little dhrunk financeers that're not used to th' flowin' dividend an' th' quick profit that biteth like a wasp an' stingeth like an adder, th' little lads that are carryin' more thin they can hold an' walk, are picked up in pieces. An' as f'r me, th' innocint man that let th' two burlies into me place to riot, I've got to make a call on th' furniture dealers in th' mornin'. That's what Hogan calls, Oh, Finance. Oh, Finance, as Shakespeare says, how many crimes are committed in thy name!"

For the rapid disappearance of the apparent profits of the preceding boom Mr. Dooley had an apt description:

"Th' effect iv th' boom on th' necessities iv life, like champagne an' race horses an' chorus girls, common an' preferred, was threemenjous. It looked f'r a while as though most iv th' meenyal wurruk iv th' counthry would have to be done be oldline millyionaires who'd made their money sellin' four cints worth if stove polish f'r a nickel. But it's all past now. Th' waiter has returned to his mutton an' th' barber to his plowshare. Th' chorus girl has raysumed th' position f'r which nature intinded her, an' th' usual yachtin' will be done on th' cable cars at eight a.m. an six p.m. as befure. Th' jag is over. Manny a man that looked like a powdher pigeon a month ago looks like a hunchback to-day."

In a manner much like his defense of Dewey, Dunne now defended Admiral Schley against the attacks of his enemies. He also had a warm reply ready for those who declared that Theodore Roosevelt, skyrocketed into the presidency by the assassination of McKinley, was too young for the responsibilities of that office:

"So whin I come to think it over, I agree with th' papers. Prisidint Tiddy is too young f'r th' office. What is needed is a man iv—well, a man iv my age. . . ."

"Go on with ye," said Mr. Hennessy. "Whin do ye think a man is old enough?"

"Well," said Mr. Dooley, "a man is old enough to vote whin he can vote, he's old enough to wurruk whin he can wurruk. An' he's old enough to be prisidint whin he becomes prisidint. If he ain't, it'll age him."

The principal event during the year which enlisted Dunne's strong sympathies was the controversy stirred up when Booker T. Washington was Roosevelt's luncheon guest at the White House:

> "Well, annyhow," said Mr. Dooley, "it's goin' to be th' roonation iv Prisidint Tiddy's chances in th' South. Thousans iv men who wudden't have voted f'r him undher any circumstances has declared that undher no circumstances wud they now vote f'r him."

There was some delicious satire on both Roosevelt and Washington:

> "They'd been talkin' over th' race problem an' th' Cubian war, an' th' prospects iv th' race an' th' Cubian war, an' th' future iv th'naygro an' th' Cubian war, an' finding Booker T. was inthrested in important public subjects like th' Cubian war, th' prisidint ast him to come up to th' White House an' ate dinner an' have a good long talk about th' Cubian war. . . . An' Booker wint. So wud I. So wud annywan. I'd go if I had to black up."

Then followed the realistic and meaningful discussion of the Negro in America, ending with the statement that there was only one right the Negro needed. "What's that?" "Th' right to live," said Mr. Dooley. "If he cud start with that he might make something iv himsilf."

Roosevelt well remembered this piece, and when he invited Dunne to the White House, he added that they would not talk of the Cuban War and "you need not black your face." Dunne replied:

> Your stipulations are gracious but unnecessary. A Chicago man is always "blacked up" even after a year in the East. As for the Cubian War it would be rank ingratitude on my part to forget the obligations I am under to that episode. I ought to divide my royalties with the survivors, but I hope I won't.

The best known Dooley essay of this series was that on the decision of the Supreme Court on the Insular Cases. The total effect of the Court's action was to approve expansion by making it legally feasible; in the popular phrase it decided that the Constitution did not follow the flag. Dunne had made Mr. Dooley satirize courts and legal proceedings before. In commenting on the speed with which the Puerto Ricans had become pro-American after the arrival of the army in 1898, Dooley had observed that "a proud people that can switch as quick as thim lads have nawthin' to larn in th' way iv what Hogan calls th' signs iv gover'mint, even fr'm th' Supreme Court." The essay was important for its picture of the workings of the Court, for Dunne did not use the opportunity to consider the problem of expansion itself. The doctrine of the Court's infallibility was accepted everywhere in conservative circles as the respectable doctrine. The Supreme Court was the one sacred institution of property interests in the United States, and to speak against this concept was the worst of all political crimes. It was this atmosphere to which the essay addressed itself, attempting to bring the sunlight of common sense to bear upon the Court as upon other institutions. Mr. Dooley described the action of the Court on the case in this manner:

"F'r awhile ivrybody watched to see what th' Supreme Court wud do. I knew mesilf I felt I cudden't make another move in th' game till I heerd fr'm thim. Buildin' op'rations was suspinded an' we sthud wringin' our hands outside th' dure waitin' f'r information fr'm th' bedside. 'What're they doin' now?' 'They just put th' argymints iv larned counsel in th' ice box an' th' chief justice is in a corner writin' a pome. Brown J. an' Harlan J. is discussin' th' condition iv th' Roman Empire befure th' fire. Th' rest iv th' Court is considherin' th' question iv whether they ought or ought not to wear ruchin' on their skirts an' hopin' crinoline won't come in again. No decision to-day.' . . . Expansionists contracted an' anti-expansionists blew up an' little childher was born into th' wurruld an' grew to manhood an' niver heerd iv Porther Ricky except whin some wan

got a job there. . . . I woke up wan mornin' an' see be th' paper that
th' Supreme Court had warned th' constitution to lave th' flag alone
an' tind to its own business.

"That's what th' paper says, but I've read over th' decision an' I
don't see annything iv th' kind there. They'se not a wurrud about th'
flag an' not enough to tire ye about th' constitution."

The lack of agreement with the Court's opinion was presented
in this manner:

"Says Brown J.: 'Th' question here is wan iv such great importance that we've been sthrugglin' over it iver since ye see us las' an'
on'y come to a decision (Fuller C. J., Gray J., Harlan J., Shiras J.,
McKenna J., White J., Brewer J., an' Peckham J. dissentin' fr'm
me an' each other).' . . .

"An' there ye have th' decision, Hinnissy, that's shaken th' intel-
licts iv th' nation to their very foundations, or will if they thry to
read it. 'Tis all right. Look it over some time. 'Tis fine spoort if ye
don't care f'r checkers. Some say it laves th' flag up in th' air an'
some say that's where it laves th' constitution. Annyhow, something's
in th' air. But there's wan thing I'm sure about."

"What's that?" asked Mr. Hennessy.

"That is," said Mr. Dooley, "no matther whether th' constitution
follows th' flag or not, th' Supreme Court follows th' iliction returns."

This last phrase was a capital hit, and translated into non-
dialect it became the most quoted and most influential line in all
of Dunne's writing. The plain implication was that the Supreme
Court was not some institution of supernatural infallibility. Supporting this view was not only a very confusing decision and a
badly divided Court, but also the great authority of the popular
oracle, Mr. Dooley, who was even less fallible than the Court.
The expression became part of the American language of political discussion the truth of which was not to be denied. It was
quoted years later by persons who had never heard of Mr. Dooley,
and even the upholders of a sacred character for the courts would
not go so far as to deny its essential truth. The probability of

making the Court a symbol too sacred to be the subject of discussion or of change went out with the acceptance of that concept. No idea contributed more toward rationalizing the discussion of the place of courts in American politics than this almost accidental phrase of Dunne's.

Although Dunne had written less during the past year than any year since he had created Mr. Dooley, he put the essays together into a new book, *Mr. Dooley's Opinions*. After seeing it through the press, he and John Grier accompanied Henry White Cannon, president of the Chase National Bank, on a long railroad journey to the Pacific Coast and Mexico. They spent nearly six weeks on the trip, Dunne visiting for a short time in Chicago on the way. By the first of the year Dunne and Grier were back in New York. Cannon was going to Florence, where he had remodeled an old monastery into a luxurious dwelling. Before he left he invited Dunne and Grier to visit him there. Dillingham and Charles Frohman were going to London, and Frohman was still talking with Dunne about a Dooley play. Dunne needed little urging; he and Grier went to London with the producers. From there Dunne went to Paris, and then with the Abbotts to Florence to visit Cannon. The week after Easter he was in Rome, and he was invited to an audience with Pope Leo XIII, whom Dunne had seen the year before.

Dunne was impressed deeply by these two visits to Rome. Although not a pious person, he found the reality of the Catholic Church's power impressive, and the sincere piety of the aged Pope near overwhelming. After the public audience on his first visit, he and Laurence Hamill, who was with him, were invited to a private audience with a small group of men. Afterwards Dunne comforted his sister Charlotte with the opinion: "I don't understand how anyone can be a Protestant after a visit to Rome." His impression of the second visit was recorded in some detail to this same sister:

It was at a public audience given to the Piedmontese pilgrims and the huge Sala Rejia was crowded with persons of high and low degree from cardinals to peasants. You never heard such a roar of "Viva Il Papa Re!" as went up when the Holy Father was carried in, high on the shoulders of the Swiss Guard. . . . He rose as the crowd cheered and smiled and bowed repeatedly and blessed us but he looked, oh, so old—a thousand years older than when I saw him last year. He delivered an allocation from the throne, which I could hear but not in the least understand. Dear soul, he can hardly last much longer. Yet when one of the foreign cardinals said to him: "May your Holiness live to be a hundred," he said, with a smile, "Why put a limit on the goodness of Almighty God?" Isn't it beautiful. I send you some beads blessed by him.

A favorite story of Peter Dunne's to illustrate the transition from the sublime to the ordinary came from the first of these audiences with the Pope. As he liked to tell it, he was in an antechamber awaiting the appointed moment and vastly moved by the solemnity and dignity of the occasion. When the feeling of religious emotion was heaviest upon him, a most unprepossessing minor cleric sidled up to him and said: "You're Dunne from Chicago aren't you? How's young Carter Harrison making out as mayor, anyhow?"

Back in Florence again at Cannon's beautiful and comfortable palace, Dunne relaxed in the warm Italian sun. The tourist colony, which included many literary people, made a pleasurable setting. To Amelia he related these things:

Gabriele D'Annunzio the great Italian poet lives a few miles from where I was. I met Villari the Italian historian, whom a good many people consider the greatest of living Italians. I don't. My money goes on Duse, the actress. But tastes differ. At all events he was clever and agreeable. Also came one Alfred Austin, Pote Laureate, a really nice little man, about as tall as Stubby's boy. He also was disposed to be friendly but his wife spoke of the immortal hero of modern humor as Mr. "Tim" Dooley. Ignorance. Some day they will speak of Shakespere as "Clarence" Shakespere or William Hookway as "Gus."

After a restful and pleasant time Dunne returned to New York by way of London. Before he left Paris, he had proposed to Margaret Abbott, and a marriage date was set for the following winter. Dunne would be thirty-five years of age in July. Margaret Abbott had been a mere school girl when he had first known her in the nineties, and was much younger than Peter Dunne. But friends recalled that he had greatly admired her beauty back in the Chicago days before 1898, and that admiration had not lessened with her growing maturity, as he had seen her on his three trips abroad. She was an athletic girl, with a substantial education in art and music, abilities and interests which were the converse of Peter Dunne's.

Dunne did not plan to tell his friends of his engagement until shortly before the wedding. He returned to New York, and plunged back into the task of writing, now having an office in the city, where he boasted that he worked from "early morn till Dooley eve." He took on the added work of supplying *Collier's Weekly* with editorials. Most of the summer and autumn he spent in the company of Charles Dana Gibson, the illustrator. Dunne had become an intimate of the Gibsons the year before, and when Mrs. Gibson, the former Irene Langhorne, decided to spend the summer at her parental home in Greenwood, Virginia, Dunne and Gibson joined forces for meals and recreation for Gibson's period of temporary bachelorhood. Although Dunne did more and better work during this summer than he had done during either of the two previous years, his routine must have presented a contrast to that of the hard-working Dana Gibson. One of his duties, perhaps his sole one as the illustrator's companion, was to keep Mrs. Gibson informed of her husband's health, work, and recreation, and of the news of New York City. This he did in a series of mock-romantic letters that were as entertaining as the letters of a humorist should be. A fairly typical report on the news from the city in this collection of nonsense, the blanks being, of course, Dunne's own:

Very little news in your set. I see John D. Rockefeller in the
Journal every day. Morgan has gone abroad. George M. Pullman is
dead. So is poor, dear Mr. Armour. John W. Gates is disconsolate
without you and Russell Sage says he would give thirty cents to see
you & he would kill a man for twenty-five. The stock market is
dull but there is a movement in corn on foot and lard is firm in spite
of the weather. That is all I know that would interest you now.
There was a time when you cared for other things but it has passed.
I might tell you that Mrs. Dodge ——— ——— and that Tommy
Hastings ——— ——— and that Ethel ——— ——— and that Tom
McIlvaine—but what's the good? It would only bore you. I saw———
at Sherry's last night. She said that little ——— ——— denies it and has
threatened to sue any one who repeats the story but ——— swears he
saw them—*in a cab!* He says it was the funniest thing he ever saw,
——— had just ———. But why go on. Did you get the cards for ———
———? But I forgot They are no longer friends of yours. It was very
pretty or would rave been but for the scandalous behaviour of———.
I never could bear that woman! The idea that she should come to the
altar in tights! Bourke Cockran was furious. He told Smalley and
Smalley wrote a little song about it. He and Bourke are singing it
this week at Hammerstein's. It goes like this ——— ———. But never
mind. . . .

Dunne accompanied Gibson to Greenwood in September,
where he spent a very pleasurable week with the Langhorne
family—the father, "the Chauncey Depew of the South" as
Dunne called him; the mother, their daughter Nancy, who was
soon to become Lady Astor; Dana and Mrs. Gibson—and several
other friends. Shortly after he returned to New York, Dunne
received a letter from Mrs. Gibson, written in verse, and he replied in what was an imitation or forerunner of Walt Mason's
rippling rhymes. "Our Bob" was the publisher Russell, whose
laugh was one of the toasts of New York publishing circles. The
"Lennoxes" were the Lord and Lady Algernon Gordon-Lennox.

I never knew, Irene my dear, that you could versify. Although it
really should be clear to me, at least, you needn't fear to fail at anything you try. The Sapphic fragment from your pen is worthy of a

loftier theme. To ask Apollo's helping when you write inflammable men, does not a generous heart beseem. I'm really crushed enough, God knows, at thinking I must stay in town. I hardly could resist your prose and now you try to rhyme me down. The Lennoxes avant-hier, were at the Albemarle hotel. I felt that Dana should be near to valet Algy but I fear he acted, in a word, like Hell. He never once went near the pair till half past ten o'clock or more; meanwhile "our Bob" had set a snare and lured them to his lodgings where he loosed his fearsome sea-lion roar. It must be fine for those who come across the sea to pleasure quaff to land at Bobby's princely home and hear the steady roar and rumble of that ingrowing laugh. But so they did & now they're off to where my lady Irene reigns. How grand it is to be a toff, do nothing else but laugh and chaff and go to any place one fains (obsolete). I wish I were of noble birth; I wish I wore a coronet. I'd travel all around the earth, I'd fill the world with endless mirth, I'd surely whoop it up, you bet. But now I think of it, I'd not. I never would to Shivaz go or Timbuctoo or Tommyrot. For me there's but one garden spot. It's Greenwood on the C&O. And there I'd thrive, mild and serene, consume the Colonel's mountain grog, play squash and drive with dear Irene, hold hands with Nanny, fair if lean; and kick the moist and faithful dog. But here I sit to toil condemned, beside the many voic-ed sea; in sheets of Irish dialect hemmed, my temper sadly sawed and phlegmed (new word), my brow with perspiration gemmed, my chin unshaven my hair un-kemmed, my hatred of the world unstemmed; by doubt distraught, by fear o'erwhe'med. Oh, this demnition grind be demn'd! Come back, Irene, come back to me. From Algy Gordon-Lennox flee; from Fleming and from Fitzhugh Lee. Come back, Irene, to

F.P.D.

Through the year of 1902, Dunne was producing a steady stream of Dooley essays, most of which went to his syndicate, but a few to periodicals. Many of the important events of the year were discussed in his happiest style. Perhaps none of his single essays was as good as that on the Supreme Court's decision of the year before, but the general level was higher and his productivity was much greater. His readers laughed at the pretentiousness of Newport society, the Sherlock Holmes stories, the visit of Prince

Henry of Germany to the United States, the controversy over imported and native art, the reading of books, the movement to restrict immigration (or at least the arguments used to support it), King Edward's coronation, Arctic exploration, and the home life of literary geniuses. By far the greatest number of essays were upon American politics, and these included most of the better ones.

Although Dunne was becoming a regular visitor at the White House, there was no indication of any tendency on his part to change the tenor of his writing because of it. During 1902 he vigorously satirized many things connected with the Administration. He was especially prone to ridicule the President's habit of speech when he was dealing with an economic issue. This was Dooley's play upon Roosevelt's statements on the trust problem:

> " 'Th' thrusts are heejous monsthers built up be th' inlightened intherprise iv th' men that have done so much to advance progress in our beloved counthry,' he says. 'On wan hand I wud stamp thim undher fut; on th' other hand not so fast. What I want more thin th' bustin' iv th' thrusts is to see me fellow counthrymen happy an' continted. I wudden't have them hate th' thrusts. Th' haggard face, th' droopin' eye, th' pallid complexion that marks th' inimy iv thrusts is not to me taste. Lave us be merry about it an jovial an' affection-ate. Lave us laugh an' sing th' octopus out iv existence. Betther blue but smilin' lips anny time thin a full coal scuttle an' a sour heart.' "

Toward the end of 1901, General Nelson A. Miles received a rebuke from the President for publicly criticizing the decision of the Naval Court of Inquiry in the Schley-Sampson contro-versy. Of course, Roosevelt had been known to criticize his mili-tary superiors in the "round-robin" of 1898. With two such fig-ures as Roosevelt and Miles, it was a natural for a Dooley essay.

> "Man an boy Hinnissy, I've taken manny a chanst on me life, but I'd as lave think iv declarin' th' sentimints iv me heart in an Orange meetin' as dhroppin' in f'r a socyal call at what Hogan calls th'

ixicutive mansion. . . . There was me frind Gin'ral Miles. No more gallant sojer iver dhrew his soord to cut out a patthern f'r a coat thin Gin'ral Miles. He's hunted th' Apachy, th' Sioux, th' Arapahoo, th' Comanchee, th' Congressman an' other savages iv th' plain; he's faced death an' promotion in ivry form, an' no harm come to him till he wint up th' White House stairs or maybe 'twas till he come down. . . . 'I've come,' says Gin'ral Miles, 'to pay me rayspicts to th' nation.' 'Thank ye,' says th' prisidint, 'I'll do th' same f'r th' head iv th' army, he says, bouncin' a coal scuttle on th' vethran's helmet. 'Gin'ral, I don't like ye'er recent conduct, 'he says, sindin' th' right to th' pint iv th' jaw. 'Ye've been in th' army forty years,' he says pushin' his head into th' grate, 'an' ye shud know that an officer who criti- cizes his fellow officers, save in th' reg'lar way, that is to say in a round robin, is guilty iv I dinnaw what,' he says, feedin' him his soord. . . ."

Sardonic Henry Adams chortled when he read this. "The round-robin was neat. . . . I am curious to know how Theodore took it. Poor Miles never had the faculty of taking a joke. . . ."

There was, moreover, one subject on which Dunne laid into the President and his administration with vigor and frequency. That was his militaristic-imperialistic habits of thinking. A friend of Dunne's once asked him how such an inveterate enemy of poseurs was able to enjoy the President's company, and Dunne replied that he enjoyed every minute of it, with the exception of those times when Roosevelt began to glorify war as a good in itself. Then he had to leave. This theme of criticism runs through the Dooley essays of these years, whether Dunne was sniping at Roosevelt in an entirely humorous way about appointing gunmen to offices in the territories, or less jocularly about his attacks on anti-imperialists at home. When General Funston took it upon himself to damn and threaten all anti-imperialists, Mr. Dooley satirized Roosevelt's gentle rebuke:

" 'Dear Fred: Me attention has been called to ye'er pathriotic utthrances in favor iv fryin' Edward Atkinson on his own cuk stove. . . . So I am compilled be th' reg'lations iv war to give ye a good slap.

How are ye, ol' commerade-in-arms? Ye ought to've seen me on th'
top iv San Joon hill. Oh, that was th' day! Iver, me dear Fred,
reprovingly but lovingly, T. Roosevelt.' "

Then followed this representation of the career of a general,
presumably Funston himself:

"Now suppose Gilligan's father whin he was young had looked him
over an' said: 'Agathy, Michael's head is perfectly round. It's like a
baseball. 'Tis so pecoolyar. An' he has a fightin' face. 'Tis no good
thryin to tache him a thrade. Let's make a sojer iv him.' An' he wint
into th' army. . . . 'Tis Gin'ral Gilligan he'd be be this time—Gin'ral
Mike Gilligan suspinding' th' haveas corpus in th' Ph'lippeens an' th'
anti-imperialists at home; . . . Gin'ral Mike Gilligan abolishin' th'
third reader; Gen'ral Mike Gilligan discoorsin' to the public on 'Books
I have niver read: Series wan, Th' Histhry iv th' United States.' "

As for William Howard Taft's report on the Philippines, of
which he was now governor, Dunne did not spare the administration, for the reports of atrocities by American forces attempting
to subdue the insurgents had sickened Dunne more than ever
of imperialism. Mr. Dooley paraphrased Taft's report:

" 'All th' riches iv Cathay, all th' wealth iv Ind, as Hogan says,
wud look like a second morgedge on an Apache wickeyup compared
with th' untold an' almost unmentionable products iv that gloryous
domain. Me business kept me in Manila or I wud tell ye what they
are. Besides some iv our lile subjects is gettin' to be good shots an' I
didn't go down there f'r that purpose. . . . Ivry wanst in a while whin
I think iv it, an iliction is held. Unforchnitly it usually happens that
those ilicted have not yet surrindhered. . . . It is not always necessary
to kill a Filipino American right away. . . . We are givin' hundherds
iv these pore benighted haythen th' well-known, ol'-fashioned American wather cure. Iv coorse ye know how 'tis done. . . . He is thin
placed upon th' grass an' given a dhrink, a bynit bein' fixed in his
mouth so he cannot reject th' hospitality. Undher th' infloonce iv th'
hose that cheers but does not inebriate, he soon warrums or perhaps I
might say swells up to a ralization iv th' granjoor iv his adoptive

counthry. One gallon makes him give three groans f'r th' constitchoo-
chion. At four gallons, he will ask to be wrapped in th' flag. At th'
dew point he sings Yankee Doodle. . . . I have not considhered it
advisable to inthrajooce anny fads like thrile be jury iv ye'er peers
into me administration. . . . Ivrywhere happiness, contint, love iv
th' shtep-mother counthry, excipt in places where there are people.' "

No issue since 1900, not even the cruelties practised on weaker
peoples by the imperialistic Powers, had roused Dunne's indignation as did the blind and selfish attitude of the owners of the
anthracite coal mines in the fall of 1902. Subject to a strike by
the United Mine Workers, the management refused all proposals
for compromise or arbitration, and insisted that if people suffered
from a coal shortage with winter near, it was the fault of the
Union, and the management had no responsibility in the matter.
In fact, George F. Baer, President of the Philadelphia & Reading
Railroad, who was the leader of the operators, issued public statements in which he upheld the sacred right of ownership to do as
it pleased regardless of public interest. These revolution-stimulat-
ing statements of ownership were capped by a letter in which
Baer declared: "The rights and interests of the laboring men will
be protected and cared for—not by the labor agitators, but by the
Christian men to whom God in His infinite wisdom has given the
control of the property interests of the country. . . ."

"It'll be a hard winther if we don't get coal," said Mr. Hennessy.
"What d'ye want with coal?" said Mr. Dooley. "Ye'er a most
unraisonable man. D'ye think ye can have all th' comforts iv life an'
that ye mus' make no sacryfice to uphold th' rights iv property?
Ivrybody will have plinty iv fuel this winther. Th' rich can burn
with indignation, thinkin' iv th' wrongs inflicted on capital, th'
middle or middlin' class will be marchin' with th' milishy, an' th' poor
can fight among thimsilves an' burn th' babies. I niver thought iv
babies befure as combustible, but they are. At wan stroke ye can
keep th' baby warrum an' th' rest iv th' fam'ly comfortable. Befure
th' winther is over I expict to hear ye callin': 'Packy, go out to th'

woodshed an' bring in a scuttleful iv little Robert Immitt. Th' fire is burnin' low. They'll be nawthin' else to burn. . . .

"List, will ye, to what Baer, th' great Baer, Ursa Major as Hogan calls him, has to say iv th' histhry iv th' wurruld an' th' ways iv Providence as revealed to him wan day as he was readin' th' Scriptures on th' ticker:

"'Years ago,' says Baer, 'Nature decided that some day, afther she'd had a long peeryod iv practice an' got her hand in be makin' th' stars, th' moon, th' sun, th' stock exchange an' other divine wurruks, she'd compose me,' he says. 'It was no aisy task, an' she had to make a lot iv preparations f'r me arrival. . . . An' she plied mud an' rock on th' timbers an' washed thim with th' floods an' cuked thim with fire an' left thim to cool, an' through long cinchries she wint fr'm time to time an' patted thim an' said: "Afther a while a man with whiskers will come along an' claim ye. Don't laugh at him. That'll be Baer."

"'Thin she mannyfacthered a lot iv dilicate people that had to keep warrum or die, an' she taught thim how to burn hard coal, an' thin I come. I call it Nature,' he says, 'but ye know who I mean. I am th' agent iv Divine Providence in this matther. All this coal was enthrusted to me be Hiven to look afther. Some say 'twas Morgan, but I know betther. I'm th' agent iv Providence—Providence Coal Comp'ny, Limited; George Baer agent. It's thrue I haven't made anny accountin' to me principal, but that'll come later. In th' manetime I stand as th' riprisintative iv visted inthrests, th' champeen iv ordher an' th' frind iv th' rights iv property. Great inthrests are at stake, as th' Southern lyncher said at th' burnin'. I'm a wondherful man. An' funny, too,' he says.

"So what are ye goin' to do about it? If thim lads on'y got to own th' coal be th' same way that I own th' part iv this house that ain't got a morgedge on it, an' ye own ye'er hat an' shoes—because a lot iv fellows come together in th' ligislachoor an' decided 'twas a good thing that a man who had shoes an' a hat shud keep thim—'twud be diff'rent. But seein' that th' Lord fixed it, there's nawthin' f'r us to do but pray. . . .

"But I'm with th' rights iv property, d'ye mind. Th' sacred rights an' th' divine rights. A man is lucky to have five dollars; if it is ten, it is his jooty to keep it if he can; if it's a hundherd, his right to it is th' right iv silf-dayfinse; if it's a millyon, it's a divine right; if it's more thin that, it becomes ridickilous. In anny case it mus' be proticted.

Nobody mus' intherfere with it or down comes th' constichoochion, th' army, a letther fr'm Baer an' th' wrath iv Hivin.

"If I own a house I can do what I plaze with it. I can set fire to it anny time I want, can't I? Ye may have foolish sintimints about it. Ye may say: 'If ye set fire to ye'er house ye'll burn mine.' But that don't mine anny coal with me. 'Tis my house, give me in thrust be th' Lord, an' here goes f'r a bonfire. What's that fireman comin' down th' sthreet f'r? How dare he squirt wather on me property? Down with th' fire departmint! I've some gun powdher in me cellar. I'll touch a match to it. I'm uncomfortable in summer. I'll take me clothes off an' go f'r a walk. Th' sign above th' dure belongs to me. I'll loosen it so it will fall down on th' top iv ye'er head. Ye want to go to sleep at night. I'm goin' to have a brass band sur'nade me. I own a gun. I think I'll shoot me property into ye. Get out iv th' way, f'r here comes property, dhrunk an' raisin' Cain. . . ."

On another essay of about the same time, Dunne tied a better-humored tag that was perhaps as effective as his denunciation:

"What d'ye think iv th' man down in Pinnsylvanya who says th' Lord an' him is partners in a coal mine?"

"Has he divided th' profits?" asked Mr. Dooley.

But the coal strike and the attitude of the owners had not been a thing that was humorous to Dunne, and he had not found it easy to write lightly about it. To Roosevelt, he confided: "The strike situation must have been funny to one on the inside, but to those of us who saw only the ignorance and selfishness and blank stupidity of the operators, it was a tragedy. I confess that I made several attempts to deal with it as comedy but I had to give it up." There is no doubt that Dunne would have agreed with the many who felt that Roosevelt's dealing with the situation was the most masterly feat of his entire career.

For the fifth consecutive year, Dunne planned a volume of his essays, which Russell published in November of 1902 under the title, *Observations of Mr. Dooley*. As he had been more industrious during the past year than the one before, he had more essays from which to choose. The book was published on schedule, and was reviewed freely. The comment on both the *Observations* and the *Opinions* of the previous year was laudatory. None contrasted the books unfavorably with the first two, although they were not quite as good. A selection from the two would have been, but each one alone included too many of the poorer pieces to maintain that standard. Rather, the comment was more likely to be amazement that they held up so well, and that in their peculiar form Dunne succeeded in treating so many aspects of American life. Many of the reviews were merely a choice selection of quotations, always good copy for a newspaper or periodical. But the accepted literary critics of America paid unanimous tribute. W. P. Trent, in an essay on the older humor of America, remarked that the school of political humor had culminated in the *Biglow Papers*, "but has surely suffered no grievous decline in the hands of Mr. Dooley." William Dean Howells, in *The North American Review*, commented upon the entire series: "It is upon a review of the whole course of Mr. Dooley's musings on men and things that we recognize Mr. Dunne as of the line of great humorists. . . . To have one's heart in the right place is much; it is in fact, rather indispensable; but to have one's head in the right place, also, adds immeasurably to the other advantage." And H. W. Boynton wrote in *The Atlantic*: "I do not think anything like justice has been done to the literary merit of the Dooley books."

The English reviewers were equally friendly. *The Spectator*, always laudatory, was now unrestrainedly so:

> And what an example of Irish improvidence we have in Mr. Dunne,—pouring out these amazing improvisations week after week, each of them containing enough wit and sense to set up an ordinary journalist for life, carefully husbanded as they probably would be. . . . It is time to take seriously a man who can so discriminate—time to recognize that Mr. Dunne is a profound and farsighted critic. No man who cannot write good sense can ever get a reputation as a humourist, and it is not until he writes inspired sense that he is considered a great one. Mr. Dunne is a great humourist; his books

are packed with true words spoken in jest. And he has the great
humourist's instinct for what is universal, elemental. Whatever his
subject, he strikes his fingers on its essentials. . . . He misses nothing.
The whole pot of civilization, so to speak, boils in his pages all the
time. . . .

The only criticism was the comment that Dunne seemed, in
the words of a reviewer in *The Nation,* to lack "fundamental
political conviction. . . . To him Imperialist and Anti-Imperialist,
Republican and Democrat . . . are equally ridiculous. . . . He belongs to the great class of those who live to make us laugh at ourselves in all our aspects." This point was certainly not true of
"fundamental political conviction," for the Dooley essays were
mere entertainment apart from their consistent attack upon humbug, pretentiousness, and cruelty. But, of course, it was true—
although no reviewer pointed it out—that Dunne did pull his
punches a little when he put the essays into books. He did not re-
print, for instance, the essay on the coal strike, although he did
the one on Taft's report on the Philippines. But Dunne's basis
of judgment was, at least in part, that the former was not great
humor, while the latter was. That he was not partisan as between
Democrat and Republican was true. But it is also true that the
differences between the two parties in 1902 were nothing that
would appeal to Dunne as fundamental; certainly not nearly so
significant as the hollow pretensions in both organizations.

On December 9, Peter Dunne and Margaret Abbott were married quietly in an apartment which Mrs. Abbott had taken in New
York. The prominent Jesuit, Father William Pardow, performed
the ceremony, and Ethel Barrymore and John Grier were the at-
tendants. After a brief trip south, the couple returned to New
York for the winter. The press, which had discovered the plans
for the marriage a few weeks before, generally covered it by
quoting Mr. Dooley on the subject of marriage, not an entirely
happy choice for the bridegroom's peace of mind. It would seem
that Dunne had expected it, and his last essay before his marriage

was a delightful piece in which Mr. Dooley speculated on the
nature of women, and admitted his ignorance. But too often before
had Dooley made good copy by boasting of his bachelorhood. And
this had been the one and only point on which the quiet Mr.
Hennessy had always been permitted to score:

"But th' childher?" asked Mr. Hennessy slyly.
"Childher!" said Mr. Dooley. "Sure I have th' finest fam'ly in th'
city. Without scandal I'm th' father iv ivry child in Archey road fr'm
end to end."
"An' none iv ye'er own," said Mr. Hennessy.
"I wish to hell, Hinnissy," said Mr. Dooley savagely, "ye'd not
lean against that mirror. I don't want to have to tell ye again."

It would be over twenty years before Mr. Dooley would hazard
the opinion that "th' on'y good husbands stay bachelors. They're
too considerate to get marrid."

6

The Dilemma of the
Social Studies Teacher

THE SHARPENING of the economic conflict in the United States since 1929 has made the philosophy underlying social studies teaching a matter of general concern. Although the activity of the utility groups in the twenties would indicate that this recognition is not entirely new, pressure groups and vested interests have become more conscious than ever before of the influence which the social studies teacher has upon society. We have only to recall the teachers' oath drives of the past few years for testimony that certain groups have come to fear the power of the classroom.

At the same time that we have this renewed acknowledgment of our influence, we teachers ourselves are being forced into a re-evaluation of our work. This results partly from the increased importance of the social studies, but chiefly it is from the serious

Social Education, II (February, 1938), pp. 79-85. Presented by Elmer Ellis as his presidential address before The National Council for the Social Studies in 1937.

conflict in the counsels with which we have been assailed. Contradictory advice has been leveled at us and has destroyed our once calm assurance that we knew exactly what our purposes were and the precise ways of accomplishing them. There have been many to urge that we should indoctrinate for a new but indefinite social order; there have been more to insist that we should indoctrinate to retard the processes tending toward change; and finally there is the force of our own tradition which echoes that we should not indoctrinate at all. This confusion is the result of the changing concepts of our vocabulary. The history which we were taught to revere paid lip service, at least, to Von Ranke's standards. Economics, as most of us were taught, was a completed system of theory. Sociology and government were deemed only slightly less coldly objective in character. The impact of intellectual and economic change has destroyed this structure; objective history seems an already ancient cult without a single follower. With it the foundations of most of our classroom practices seem to be slipping from under us, if, indeed, the roof is not already about our heads.

This same force has also attacked the popular meanings of our terminology. The meaning of "propaganda" has broadened to include not only the efforts of selfish interests to impose their views upon society but all attempts to influence the action of people, including education itself. "Indoctrination" is no longer limited to the preaching of a set doctrine but has come to include the selection of curricular materials. With the broadening of these formerly reprehensible terms to include the very things we have been accustomed to do, thoughtful teachers have found their assurance lessened; their professional stability has been weakened; and many are hopelessly at sea over the fundamentals of their work.

If there is no objective social studies teaching, but only indoctrination and propaganda, our entire point of view needs rethinking. Is it our job to turn out pupils with a group of established attitudes which correspond to the ideas of the makers of an official list? Is it desirable, or even justifiable, for us to teach our social studies classes so that pupils will have reproductions of our own conclusions upon public questions? Are we no longer professionally bound to develop controversial questions so as to avoid determining pupils' reactions? For the intelligent social studies teacher these are not academic propositions, but questions upon the answers to which hang the very essentials of what goes on in the classroom every day. Until they are answered by each teacher, social studies can not have significant meaning to us or to our pupils.

The necessary logic of our own situation forces us to the conclusion that, at least in the Von Ranke sense, purely objective history is impossible—not alone impossible to write but still more impossible to teach. These conditions apply to the other social studies and to present society as well as to history and past society. The broadened definitions of "propaganda" and "indoctrination" must also be accepted as rational, although at the same time we need to avoid reading into them the unfavorable reaction that accompanies their accepted meanings. In the popular and narrow sense, propaganda has meant the attempt, by hidden and unfair means, to indoctrinate with a particular belief considered profitable to the person carrying on the propaganda. When we broaden this to include even the general framework of ideas and values upon which our society is organized, the terms can not carry the same connotation, and we naturally and sensibly begin to make other distinctions—"unfair propaganda" and "narrow indoctrination"—to describe the older concepts. But it is inescapable that some general philosophy—legitimately called indoctrination—is behind our selection of facts, generalizations, and attitudes to be acquired in school. When, for instance, we decide to include a study of the French Revolution in tenth-grade history, a definite pattern of indoctrination, which assumes the desirability of action by citizens in the light of this knowledge, lies behind that selection, even though we consciously try to avoid determining which of several interpretations of the revolution each pupil accepts. If we are trying to achieve the permanent inculcation of an attitude of tolerance toward races other than our own, we are engaged in propaganda toward that end. These concepts of indoctrination and propaganda imply a planned education that consciously attempts to shape pupils according to a preconceived model. This conclusion is true even if the model runs along extremely individualistic lines, for even an education designed to fit people into an anarchistic society would have to have a scheme of indoctrination. Moreover, contrary to the accepted theory of a few years ago, the kind of social studies teaching that has been general in American schools has not only been broadly indoctrinating but has embodied an immense amount of very narrow, although unacknowledged, indoctrination. Questions that split local communities have usually been kept out of the classroom, but the general framework of values of our dominant upper middle class has generally been indoctrinated, even to such fundamentally reprehensible ideas as the belief that money income measures the social value of individual effort. That our citizens have been able to make modest adjustments in spite of that indoctrination is probably more of a credit to their native common sense than it is to their education.

The illusion that our social studies teaching has been non-indoctrinating seems to have passed with that of purely objective social science. With its passing has come a strong draft of realism into the discussion of social studies teaching that promises much for the future.

This was the fundamental change made by the report of the Commission on the Social Studies in the Schools. It is not unlikely that in a historical perspective its influence will be seen as bringing about this Copernican revolution in the thinking of social studies teachers. In place of the older type of social studies philosophy, the Commission recommended a frame of reference, which was far less specific than the one in use in most schools.

It took no great insight to see that the most emphatic objections to the report came from those accustomed to think in terms of this still more specific, but unacknowledged, frame of reference, which was believed to result in a different distribution of privileged positions within society. But of course the attack was upon the idea of having a frame of reference, or perhaps one should say more upon the fatal admission of having one.

It is no discredit to the better social studies teachers that they held to the theory of objectivity in their work. That was the reflection of the efforts of scholars in the social science fields to develop principles of objective validity, attempts which are significant milestones along the highway toward sound scholarship. The error lay in the assumption that it was possible to rule out questions of value entirely, that we had done so successfully on the research level at least, and that only greater care and effort were necessary to do likewise on the teaching level.

With the destruction of these assumptions, now evident to everyone, the question of which philosophy to substitute is the great dilemma of the social studies teacher.

Our rejection of the pure objectivity of Von Ranke's history, of John Stuart Mill's economics, or of Herbert Spencer's sociology, need not carry with it the still more fallacious assumption that there is no difference in the degree of validity among histories and social theories. The most regrettable effect of the disruption of the teacher's concept of objectivity has been the more than occasional complete swing to the idea that scholarship is only a defense mechanism and has no relation to ultimate social understanding or value. The conclusion from this is that it is the immediate attitude that is wanted and not an understanding of society, and that this attitude may be based upon a statement of so-called fact from a demagogue seeking to exploit, as well as upon the considered opinion of a trained and respected scholar seeking to explain. That we refuse to credit the latter with superhuman objectivity is no reason for crediting the former with a suspicion of ordinary veracity. All God's "chilluns" may have wings, but not all of them are equally trustworthy witnesses as to the difference between a horse chestnut and a chestnut horse.

There is grave danger that in our reaction against an imaginary objectivity, we may deny the desirability of objectivity itself; that we may assume that an action designated as correct may be as desirable from a person indoctrinated directly for it as from one whose trained intelligence and high ideals lead him to that decision. Such an assumption denies the very essence of democracy itself and paves the way for demagogues and dictators. It merely brings recruits for that foundation of fools which William Bennett Munro has said is the basis of every successful political party —a great mass of unthinking voters who follow tradition even to the extent of voting for a properly sponsored yellow dog.

While it may not be much of an exaggeration to state, as our anti-intellectuals do, that human intelligence is a mere speck afloat upon a sea of emotion, democracy as a way of life depends upon that speck. And that important speck is the special charge of the social studies teacher. There are many institutions besides the school which concern themselves with the emotional side of the individual's education, and within the school all teachers are charged with it. The development of social intelligence is the sole responsibility of the social studies, and it would be a sad day for democracy if these teachers went over to any type of emotionalism that would lead in directions other than those of tested scholarship.

This becomes a basic assumption in our entire scheme of social studies education—that the picture of society presented to the pupil shall be the most realistic that specialists can give. It must be recognized that this is no simple matter, because in many respects scholars do not agree either about present society or its past, and where they do not agree the teacher is not justified in keeping a pupil in ignorance of either opinion. A description of society such as the *Recent Social Trends* is not subject to successful attack in its general outlines, but when translated into a school curriculum there is room for many interpretations. Only when there is a substantial scholarly agreement is our teaching problem solved.

In the light of our own democratic frame of reference, we have selected this picture of society as the one to be taught, but our dilemma returns in the question: What can we teach, as conclusions, beyond the areas where scholars agree?

The nature of the learning process answers this, in part at least. In teaching any unit within these fields of knowledge, one assumes for the learner other ideas and conclusions about related units that are essential to an understanding of the first. These conclusions are taught as conclusions—indoctrination. Further study will bring the learner back to many of them in order to examine the assumptions on which they are based, and to condition and limit them. For the time being, however, some one thing is to be learned, and most of the concepts that surround it must of necessity be accepted without much critical analysis. The amount that is assumed is in inverse ratio to the maturity of the pupil.

In such indoctrination it seems unobjectionable to lay down one general rule, namely, that only those conclusions which are well grounded in scholarship shall be assumed as true, and that the reader shall recognize a professional responsibility to protect pupils against generalizations that have no substantial foundation. The desirability of encouraging pupils to examine all generalizations critically does not make the teaching of a vast number of them as simple conclusions less necessary.

When we come to consider indoctrination in matters that do not so readily lend themselves to objective proof or to scholarly verification, such as ideals and loyalties, the difficulties of the problem increase. Yet, even in this instance, large fields can be marked off where certain standards are assumed to be beneficial for society. In the fields of morals, as narrowly conceived, teachers have always assumed conclusions in line with popular opinion. Such indoctrinations belong so completely to our society's "frame of reference" that they are not usually regarded as such. They are imposed less by plan than by the very climate of opinion in which we live. Nevertheless it is desirable even here that high school pupils gain experience in evaluating ethical concepts in terms of their social significance. The citizen who is moral only because of a climate of opinion, which in the modern world is subject to substantial change, may prove to be a weak support to a democratic state.

Having agreed that the ideas and ideals which seem to meet little challenge are legitimate material for standards of value, we soon return to controversy concerning which ideals are not subject to challenge. In this matter objective proof is not nearly so available as in the generalizations in the more definite social science fields. Yet substantial agreement is possible. For example, we all favor improving the ability of the pupil to think realistically about society, for it seems improbable that the quality of citizens in a democracy can be increased substantially without enlarging the influence of critical intelligence. For that reason, among others, it is generally assumed that indoctrination with attitudes of racial, religious, and political tolerance, the teaching of the historical method, and the development of the habit of suspending judgment until a reasonable amount of evidence is available all result in a more desirable citizen. Were these qualities not a part of the democratic ideal they would still be justified, because they increase the citizen's ability to think realistically about society.

Where objective proof is not possible, and where no generally accepted moral standards are available, what other specific attitudes can be designated as suitable for general indoctrination? Here we might begin with the "choices deemed possible and desirable" by the Commission. Personal preference, however, favors the following somewhat different expression:

Favorable attitudes toward all qualities of mind that improve the individual's ability to think realistically about society.

President and Mrs. Ellis in the President's House, 1955.

Towner (North Dakota) High School Basketball Team, 1920.

Favorable attitudes toward policies that do not involve the loss of human life or the increase of human suffering over all policies that do, no matter how remote the people to die or suffer are from the pupil in space, time, or social environment.

Attitudes that make the habitual test of policy the good of the entire group, rather than the interest of part of the group, status, vested interests, or tradition.

Favorable attitudes toward rational consideration, and unfavorable attitudes toward attempts to obtain action by stimulating emotional group reactions.

Favorable attitudes toward the preservation and enlargement of civil liberties in their most complete forms.

Beyond these there is a substantial group of narrower indoctrinations that seem to be clearly justifiable. They are for the most part specifically desirable conditions, such as a better merit system of civil service or resistance to the boss and machine type of irresponsible political control. No one would oppose such suggestions publicly, much as they are delayed in practice. The justification for these indoctrinations lies in the fact that they are acknowledged as desirable improvements by all experts, and so clearly in line with democratic theory that a public defense of them is never, or almost never, made.

Beyond these, what other types of specific attitudes can be designated as suitable for general indoctrination? The most superficial answer, as well as the most common, is the proposal to indoctrinate with the American ideals and traditions of government. This seemingly helpful suggestion proves disappointing upon closer analysis. Outside of a very narrow area of agreement, are Jeffersonian or Hamiltonian traditions to be accepted? Or, if we accept the Jefferson tradition, as most social studies teachers do, is our problem solved? Anyone familiar with current political controversy knows that the most divergent policies are justified on Jeffersonian grounds, and, admitting that much of this is highly questionable, still the mere acceptance of a general statement helps us very little when it comes to specifying desirable attitudes. Beyond a strong tendency to favor democratic aims and methods over undemocratic, what can one do that will not be disguised indoctrination regarding contemporary partisan politics?

The relatively modest group of indoctrinations listed is democratic in character. Any teacher or group of teachers could defend it before a representative group of citizens anywhere in the United States. But it does not satisfy everyone. As a frame of reference it is not detailed or extensive enough for many. Generally these dissatisfied ones are persons attracted by the successful efforts of the totalitarian states to indoctrinate pupils with a closed system of detailed dogma; perhaps they themselves are unconsciously affected by the glitter of uniforms, the tempo of band music, and the agreement that is indicated by thousands of "Ja!" votes to one "Nein!" As such states are able to define objectives with great clarity—they are not bothered by the realization that a few years of technological change may force a revision of goals—their success in achieving their immediate objectives is very evident. The less clearly defined democratic purposes, in terms of skills, knowledges, and emotionalized attitudes, are not only more difficult to teach but less susceptible to measurement. This gives to non-authoritarian education an appearance of confusion and indirection, an appearance, incidentally, which may indicate a closer relationship to the reality of modern life than does the clocklike precision of a military parade. But to the lover of system and order there is a fatal attraction in united action and uniform thinking that may easily overshadow all other values.

Then there are others who are horrified by the fear that large numbers of our poorly trained citizens may become victims of totalitarian ideals of government. These see the problem as one of fighting fire with fire. The answer to fascist propaganda is a great program of detailed propaganda for democracy. Both groups unite in a demand for an adoption of these authoritarian methods of teaching, albeit for different objectives. That is, this last group would indoctrinate for democracy, in the same manner and in similar detail as do the totalitarian states for their systems of ideas. All too often the immediate proposals to indoctrinate for democracy center about developing hatred for the symbols of authoritarianism. It is the labels "Fascist," "Jap," "Red," "Nazi," and "Communist" against which unthinking hatred and anger are to be developed; it is the names of Hitler, Stalin, and Mussolini that are to be elevated to satanism in the mentality of the citizen. It should be evident that such a procedure makes an ideal background for exploitation by demagogues and expert propagandists for selfish interest; the only real influence of such teaching is to make citizens the willing sheep of the experts who know how to shear them by clever manipulation of symbols. How can a citizen reach an intelligent conclusion about foreign policy when he is conditioned to react with blind emotion toward the symbols he must use in his thinking? It would be far better for democracy if the hatreds were directed against the fact of injustice, the fact of exploitation, and the fact of inhuman cruelty. But these are not immediately effective enough to satisfy Mr. Educator-in-a-Hurry.

A more fundamental objection to these detailed programs of indoctrination is that they cannot help but be undemocratic. The nature of democracy is the peaceful compromise of interests that make up the state; when we go beyond a very general program of indoctrination we immediately begin to determine the relative place of each class in society. First, the emotionalist insists, the American tradition must be "clarified" or "integrated"; then direct and complete indoctrination can follow. What is overlooked is that the process of clarification or integration is a process of deciding the controversial issues of modern life, and to integrate these traditions in any real sense would be to create a totalitarianism that would differ in educational kind very little from that prevailing in the authoritarian states. How can we integrate Jeffersonian and Hamiltonian traditions except by deciding fundamental current controversies? A necessity of any extensive program of official indoctrination is the control, open or disguised, of a single unified group within the state. It makes little difference whether the group is an economic class, social group, or a political party; the method of indoctrination is the same. Moreover, it is a relative matter. The less specific the program of indoctrination, the more freedom of choice among the elements in the society; the more specific, the more real the domination by one interest or group of interests.

As long as democracy remains a peaceful method of compromising the struggle of various elements seeking to gain prestige, the program of indoctrination must remain small, and the area of pupil choice large. So long as democracy is to remain a society adjustable to the winds of technological and social change, just that long must its intellectual framework remain flexible.

There is one other aspect of the problem that needs clarification. It seems to be a common assumption that the one institution for training citizens should maintain an exact balance in its teaching on any controversial issue, even when the forces outside of the school may all be on one side or the other. Such an assumption is surely one of the most short-sighted imaginable as a guiding principle. The social studies classroom is the single agency of democracy in which trained experts attempt to prepare citizens to deal with such issues in a rational manner. The experiences within the classroom must be set within the general framework of the social mores of the larger community. If there is a balance to be obtained the classroom teacher must make that balance, taking into account these traditions and all the contemporary forces in the community that influence the minds of young citizens. The teacher must visualize goals in terms of this total experience, and adjust classroom techniques accordingly. To do less is to follow a program completely lacking in realism, but it is not easy. The different backgrounds of pupils frequently make the problem one of individual instruction. To make each pupil conscious of the sources of his ideas about society, and to force him to re-evaluate his entire set of prejudices in the light of what knowledge scholarship is able to give him, is no easy task, but it is the most important and most difficult feat of teaching. It calls for the finest statesmanship, the highest ideals of democratic life, and the best minds that society can produce, for it is here in the social studies classroom, day after day as pupils are trained in democratic ways of living, that the future of American society is being determined. To engage in it is the greatest adventure this turbulent world affords.

With this opportunity for high adventure go the responsibilities of a noble profession. These lift the social studies teacher's purposes above the details of special programs, and the dominating philosophy becomes a faith in the ability of American schools to train pupils who understand modern society, who have the ability to think with reasonable objectivity about it, who are motivated by enlightened ideals and sympathies, and who are possessed of such faith in democratic processes that active participation in civic affairs becomes the normal condition. To this teacher a citizenry so trained is the fundamental reform that is needed to make America a better place in which to live. Such an ideal takes precedence over whatever specific programs may be favored or opposed. And it is on this broad ideal that social studies teaching must be based if the historic American democratic ideals are to be maintained and fulfilled.

7

Public Opinion and the Income Tax, 1860-1900

T HE HISTORY of taxation from the earliest ages has been
the history of the attempts of one class to make other
classes pay the expenses, or an undue share of the expenses, of
the Government. Aristocrats have always been trying to shift the
taxes on to the people, and the people on to the aristocrats; the
landed interests on to the commercial and the commercial on to
the landed."

In these words the famous editor, E. L. Godkin, philosophized
about income tax history after the Supreme Court had declared
the law of 1894 unconstitutional. This viewpoint contrasts
sharply with the lack of realism that characterized press comment
on the subject during the preceding fifteen years, comment which
includes that written by Godkin himself. Certainly no other

Reprinted from *The Mississippi Valley Historical Review*, **XXVII** (September,
1940), pp. 225-42. The footnotes have been omitted.

issue in this period, except the nature of the monetary standard, roused such denunciation as did the income tax.

The income tax problem was in many ways a strange development. In some states income taxes had been in operation for several years before the Civil War. Indeed, the closely related faculty tax was common in the colonial period. So general was experience with income taxes that both the Union and Confederate governments used it freely during the war period. Statesmen, then, committed themselves to it in theory, as did political parties by group action. When the situation was changed these same individuals and groups, although they were able to rationalize an about face upon the concrete proposal, hardly could be expected to repudiate the fundamental justice of the tax under the conditions prevailing when they first approved it. The Republican party which sponsored it in the North was to become the most consistent defender of those economic interests which would gain by having no income tax, and it would be expected that the force of its attack would be lessened by its record on the question. Actually, it was lessened to some degree in the sixties and early seventies. After that, however, these moderating factors were less potent and the issue became a raw, undisguised class conflict.

In the summer of 1861, members of the federal Congress, particularly the Republican leaders, were searching for new sources of taxation to pay for the unprecedented expenditures the war was demanding, as well as to make up the loss entailed in revenue secession. The taxation plans centered about a high tariff and an increase in the internal revenue duties. This was for practical purposes close to a per capita levy, and it was to be expected that such a program would meet opposition. An income tax was introduced as an amendment to the pending tax bill, and urged as a means of "equitable apportionment of the burdens of taxation" in proportion to ability to pay. "I cannot go home," declared Schuyler Colfax, "and tell my constituents that I voted for a bill that would allow a man, a millionaire, who has put his entire property into stock, to be exempt from taxation, while a farmer who lives by his side must pay a tax." Roscoe Conkling took a similar stand, although most easterners seemed to be against and the westerners for the new tax. No very serious opposition, however, came into the open. "We do not strenuously object to direct taxes," declared the New York *Tribune,* "though we prefer to raise money by Excise rather than by an indiscriminate Income or Property Tax." Commenting upon the income and luxury features, the New York *Herald* pointed out: "Millionaires like Mr. W. B. Astor, Commodore Vanderbilt . . . and others, will henceforth contribute a fair proportion of their wealth to the support of the national government." There was no public criticism when the amendment was adopted and the bill passed.

As the time for the first payment of the income tax approached—and this was not until 1863—those affected most directly awoke to what had happened and raised an immediate cry for relief. Certain western manufacturers, very apparently under the instigation of their eastern colleagues, sponsored a call for a meeting at Chicago to consider the problem of the new tax as it affected them. This location was expected to give the meeting a better sectional appeal. The meeting took place on June 4, with representation chiefly from the East. The resolutions adopted were plain spoken, and included a demand that the secretary of the treasury suspend the operation of the law—as far as it affected income from stocks—until Congress assembled again. The reply of the treasury department, written by Edward McPherson, was a stalwart defense of the duty of the administration to carry out the intent of the law. McPherson, moreover, was not without the support of the better class of opinion among the business interests. The New York *Tribune* printed and editorially approved a letter by a prominent manufacturer who declared that the tax was "eminently just, patriotic, and statesmanlike,"—particularly in light of the existing tariff protection. These sentiments were echoed by the merchants, who, though they may have actually disliked the income tax, felt still less friendship for the new tariff protection the manufacturers enjoyed. Throughout the sixties the merchant group represents the one business interest which supported the tax consistently. Merchants were undoubtedly motivated as importers by opposition to the tariff which they saw as a competing system, and also by fear of an increasingly unbalanced budget that would mean more inflation to drive down imports. "Is it fear," the *Merchants' Magazine and Commercial Review* was to ask in January, 1865, "that leads our official men to recommend a three per cent tax when it should be thirty per cent, if there is no better way to raise money?"

Congressmen joined the press in pointing out the weakness that lay in its failure to distinguish between earned and unearned income, and the fact that it was inquisitorial in character. The most vigorous opposition in Congress came from James A. Garfield, but even he was not yet ready to discontinue it. On the whole there was little public criticism of the fundamentals of the law during the war.

The close of the war, however, changed the situation in that the danger of further inflation seemed more remote and the pressure for income lessened. Taxation could very easily be reduced, especially as there was a general feeling that the coming generation should be made to pay as much of the public debt as was possible. Immediately the question was raised as to which war taxes should be reduced or abolished first. The *Nation*, at this time, noted that there was no immediate demand for repeal of the income tax, although it expressed its opposition to an extended continuance of the tax. Merchants wanted the indirect taxes removed and the direct taxes retained. They were against any reduction of the income tax, at least in the first years following the war. "No tax," they pointed out, "is collected so economically as this, and with so little injury to the taxpayer." Bankers, on the other hand, wanted it repealed. Manufacturers, intent on maintaining the high tariff rates, had a double reason for advocating its discontinuance, and with striking regularity opposed the income tax throughout the entire period.

A new type of argument was set forth at this time which was to become popular with opponents of the tax later. In a letter fittingly published in the *Bankers' Magazine* of May, 1866, Goldwin Smith, the Oxford professor, pointed out among the evils of the income tax, "a socialistic tendency" in "a tax imposed expressly on the rich, and capable of indefinite expansion and class graduation." In England, he believed, this tendency was kept in check by the fact that the income tax paying group had all the political power, and, as yet in the United States "by the absence of any sharp class division."

The following year Congress began a series of changes which removed the slightly graduated feature of the income tax and moved the date of the termination of the law forward to 1872. During these contests the interests opposed to the tax organized in twentieth century fashion. An "Anti-Income Tax Association" was organized in New York, and a similar group started in Philadelphia. They sent representatives to appear before the committees of Congress, not only to prevent renewal of the law, but also to urge its immediate repeal. These and other enemies of the tax carried on an organized campaign of propaganda against it, which included prepared petitions and ready-made editorials for the friendly press. Their pressure upon the administration also became more effective as 1872 approached and President Grant needed their support. "I wish the income tax could yet be repealed," one wealthy New Yorker complained to the secretary of state. "Our Union League has denounced it unanimously. They contribute very largely at elections, and . . . it is unfortunate this income tax is now to be called for." At least some of the mercantile interests were still on the other side of the argument, but the fire had gone from their opposition.

Within Congress the contest developed along sectional lines with the East generally opposed to the tax and the West and South generally, but far from unanimously, in favor of it. John Sherman offered the best and strongest defense of the law in Congress when he pled for its continuance on the ground that it was the only tax which distinguished "between John Jacob Astor and the humblest citizen in the community." Among the opponents of the continuance of the tax, it is worth noting that its fundamental justice was seldom denied. One senatorial opponent, William A. Buckingham of Connecticut, admitted that "it is right to impose upon them (the rich) a larger proportion of the burdens of taxation than the value of the property which they own bears to the total value of the property of the community." His objection was that it did not work out that way because of the ease of dodging the tax. Usually the argument went that it was a war tax only, odious in times of peace, inquisitorial, and provocative of perjury. Inquisitorial was the most popular description among those opposed. Few went as far as Garfield to deny its essential justice.

There was more emphatic opposition, however, to any action which might make a graduated tax. A substantial group of western congressmen was favorable toward such a proposal, and its plans met vigorous opposition. Congressman James A. Garfield declared that it was not only unconstitutional but that there existed "just as much right to demand that the rich men of this country shall give all their income, and a bonus besides, as to demand that they shall pay twice as much per dollar as others pay." A suggestion that graduation might go up to twenty-five per cent on incomes of sixty thousand dollars brought Justin S. Morrill to his feet to declare that such a proposal could "only be defended on the same ground that the highwayman defends his acts."

The highly organized business groups, active in Washington, and backed by the eastern congressmen who declared that their states had to pay a disproportionate share of the tax, were able to prevent any further extension of the law. Should they fail they were prepared to bring a test case against it in the courts on grounds of unconstitutionality.

In sharp contrast to the interests opposed to the tax during these years were the professional economists. Amasa and Francis A. Walker, certainly as distinguished scholars as there were in the country, were its vigorous defenders. Francis A. Walker had defended the existing law, and insisted that a highly graduated tax was in the direction of justice. Likewise, the most widely used college textbooks in economics, Professor Arthur L. Perry's *Elements of Political Economy*, upheld the law, declaring that an income tax "is the fairest of all possible taxes" and suggesting that perhaps it might eventually supersede all others. Perry also favored publicity for income tax returns. The opinions of the Walkers and of Perry had been used by the friends of the tax, such as John Sherman, to bolster their arguments, but this was not enough to prevent its abolition. A situation developed here, as it often does when scholars, with their unusual freedom from the force of traditional symbols and from the definite economic interests of most observers, make a logically powerful case for a policy in their professional journals and before their classes, but which is defeated by organized interests. The economists continued to teach the soundness of the tax to their students, and history may be said to have been on their side, but the fact remains that it did not bring about the success of the proposal during the lifetime of that generation of scholars.

After the efforts to continue the tax had failed there was a breathing spell of six years before agitation for the law was revived. Up to this time the controversy had been conducted in a reasonable manner with but few blood-letting adjectives of the types that were to become common in the nineties. The only groups who kept the income tax cause alive during these years were the economists and such political organizations as the Greenback party, which favored a graduated tax. Nevertheless, the latent strength behind it, mustered chiefly by western and southern congressmen, was to concentrate on an attempt to revive it in 1878 and 1879. Several bills to that end were introduced.

Immediately the pressure of its opponents upon Congress was increased, and petitions began to be presented chiefly from the large cities and bearing the names of well-known leaders of business. One signed by Cyrus Field, Peter Cooper, and others was spread broadcast over the country and presented to Congress on several occasions. The support for the tax was slower to become organized, but eventually a large number of petitions appeared from Grange members and others in the South and West praying for its adoption. As all of the bills were opposed by the official leadership in the House, the only votes taken were on motions to suspend the rules which required a two-thirds majority. This proportion was not attained in any case, but as substantial majorities were, it is quite clear that the tax had strong support in the popular branch of Congress. The votes were sectional rather than partisan, and its supporters seem to have had little faith that even with a House majority of two-thirds any law could be carried through the Senate. This was to remain true until the increase in the number of the western members in that body that came in 1889 and 1890.

This activity in Congress, although it was not accompanied by extensive debate, stimulated discussion in the press and among the public. For the first time the opposition to the tax began to resort to rabble-rousing denunciation. This was partly a result of the bitterness against the western and southern congressmen for their insistence on silver coinage, just recently expressed in undiplomatic language in the debate on the Bland-Allison bill. The *Nation*, which had been opposed to the tax in 1865 and rather favorable to it in 1869, now came forth bitterly and uncompromisingly against it. It was merely part of the Grangers' "communistic" attacks upon wealth. The cause of the bill was laid to the silver agitators. "The present silver agitation has produced among the farmers and laborers of a large portion of the country hostile feelings towards bankers, merchants, and all that class of persons who do the business of exchange, and this has more than anything else caused the attempt to revive the income tax." According to Godkin, it was the result "of European Communism."

The *Nation*, however, was just one of many opponents of the tax who were beginning to use the term communism as an epithet to damn any economic proposal with which it disagreed. Not all the opposition was so extreme. One temperate writer in the *Bankers' Magazine* called attention to favorable features of the income tax in Great Britain. "Use," he wrote, "has caused it to be borne with more equanimity, especially as it exempts the turbulent and dangerous classes, and presses most on the intelligent and superior orders of society who have something to lose." This same writer pointed out as one of the principal arguments for the tax that New England had paid only $4,000,000 in internal revenue duties in 1875, when proportionate to population the region would have paid $9,350,000, and proportionate to wealth it would have paid $14,000,000. In contrast to this the case of the northwestern states was cited. This region had paid $43,-500,000, while proportionate to population it would have paid $30,333,333, and proportionate to wealth only $27,500,000. It is small wonder that there were protests against the intemperate denunciation of the tax. "We fail to discover in the proposed legislation any evidence of the communism which is so great a bugbear to the Eastern press," declared the editor of the conservative St. Louis *Globe-Democrat*. "An income tax, when fairly adjusted and properly scaled, is one of the least objectionable methods of raising internal revenue. . . . The capitalists and wealthy creditors of the country are able to bear their share of the public expense."

In spite of such examples of temperate discussion, it can safely be stated that this contest of 1878 and 1879 definitely started the practice of substituting denunciation for argument against the proposal. The motive behind these desperate tactics was not perhaps opposition to any law then possible of enactment, but rather

a growing realization of the possibilities of increasing the graduated feature of the tax, once it was accepted as part of the system.
Opponents had an example placed before them by Felix Adler in
1880, who, in an address before the Society of Ethical Culture,
advocated an income tax that would be graduated up to 100 per
cent on all income above enough to supply all of the comforts
and "true refinements of life." Perhaps few took this seriously,
certainly the advocates of the recently attempted legislation did
not. Nevertheless, it was part of a climate of opinion, out of
which David A. Wells brought together the recent denunciations
of the tax and gave them logical exposition. Taking the tack that
Goldwin Smith had suggested, more recently and less temperately
exploited by Godkin, he thundered effectively against the tax;
his article, "The Communism of a Discriminating Income Tax,"
in the *North American Review* became the source of innumerable
editorials and orations against the tax. Any exemption of income,
he held, made a graduated tax—the theory of which no one would
dispute—and an exemption of $2,000 would exempt "more than
nine tenths of the entire property" and "more than ninety-nine
hundredths of the property owners." "Unmasked confiscation" and
"flagrant spoilation" were the only terms he could use to describe
such a tax. "Any government, whatever name it may assume, is
a despotism, and commits acts of flagrant spoilation, if it grants
exemptions or exacts a greater or less rate of tax from one man
than another man on account of his owning . . . more or less of
the same class of property which is subject to the tax." Taxes, he
held, should be paid out of consumption, that is, added to the
price if collected before the retail sale, a theory that meant that
all should pay alike regardless of wealth or income. Where the
shoe pinched was that income taxes could not be passed on to the
consumer. This to Wells was all wrong—"any form of tax which
compels a person to advance taxes in gross to the Government
without some appropriate legislation to protect and enable such
tax-advancers to collect the tax from those who use and consume—

should be regarded not as taxation, but as spoilation and an invasion of the rights of property."

No other serious fight for the income tax was made in Congress until after the admission of the states of the Northwest increased the western interest in the Senate. Bills, however, were regularly introduced and petitions for and against such legislation were received. The major parties dodged the issue regularly, and only the minor political parties were unqualifiedly committed to it. There can be little doubt, moreover, considering the support the tax had in 1878-1879, that it was still more acceptable to the public as an alternative to tariffs or excises. When Joseph Pulitzer took over the New York *World* in 1883 his ten plank editorial platform aggressively demanded both income and inheritance taxes. Nearly all of the academic economists continued to support it, and agreed that the technical objections raised to it were superficial. Young economists, as, for example, Richard T. Ely and Edwin R. A. Seligman, followed the lead of the Walkers and Perry as advocates of the tax. One notable exception appeared among the younger economists. J. Lawrence Laughlin followed Wells in holding that the objections to the tax were overwhelming, and that in practice it was an "unjust" tax. The tax reformer, Henry George, was not favorable toward the income tax, although he approved of its purpose in so far as it was aimed at "the reduction or prevention of immense concentrations of wealth." In general, the growing single tax movement considered it only slightly better than the usual indirect taxes.

Beginning with 1890, the agitation for an income tax increased, stimulated by hard times, the organizations of farmers and laborers, and the growing antagonism in the West against the eastern section of the country. It was discussed more freely in magazines and commented on more frequently in the press. In the summer of 1891, the Ohio State Democratic convention adopted a plank in favor of a graded income tax. The chorus of the eastern press, always excepting the New York *World* and the

Springfield *Republican,* was loud in denunciation of the idea. "Class legislation on a tremendous scale," was what the *Republican* and New York *Tribune* called it; while the Democratic New York *Sun* declared that it was "a final outrage in the way of class legislation." To most of the eastern press it was bait to catch the Farmers' Alliance support, and continued to be called such until it was finally adopted.

The pledged Democratic revision of the tariff in 1893 and 1894 caused the income tax to be brought forward as a means of meeting the deficit in revenue, with partial and tentative support from President Cleveland. Its prospective adoption loosed a flood of press argument and propaganda that was more extreme than any heretofore used. There was no unity to the argument against the tax—many, including Wells himself, stating that the theory was all right, but it would not work in practice, and then turning about and shouting "class legislation" and "socialism." Others, more consistent, took the ground that there was no justification in a tax that discriminated against large incomes. "The principle that one small class of the people shall be made to bear a distinct and extraordinary burden of taxation, solely because they are rich . . . is the very essence of that Socialism against which civilization protests, and which good judgment and high conscience condemn," declared the Philadelphia *Public Ledger.* "It would be placing a premium on idleness and shiftlessness, and a tax on thrift and industry," added the Des Monies *Iowa State Register.* The arguments used in favor of the tax "are communistic, and only communistic," insisted the Cleveland *Plain Dealer,* which claimed not to object to what it called a "fair" income tax. "The record of history is that it is the tax of tyrants," recalled the Milwaukee *Journal,* adding also that it was "a bid for dishonesty and a bounty for perjury and fraud." Its popularity seemed appalling. "As it is," sorrowfully concluded Wells when its adoption seemed assured, "a system of class legislation, full of the spirit of communism, seems to find favor with the American people."

On the other hand a large number of newspapers in the South and West defended the tax. Four out of five Democrats in those sections favored the tax, declared the *Ohio State Journal,* after quoting favorable comments from the New York *World,* St. Louis *Republic,* and the Atlanta *Constitution.* "They like it," announced this partisan Republican organ, "because they think it will chiefly strike the so-called 'capitalistic' class, which they imagine to be composed of Republicans almost exclusively, and which they are convinced is a menace to the country anyhow and ought to be taxed out of existence." "Taxation," argued the Kansas City, Missouri *Times,* "has been levied upon articles of common consumption, and as the proportion of a poor man's income spent for such articles is several times greater than the proportion the wealthy man spends, the inequality is obviously worse than any inequality in the collection of income taxes would be. . . . Under the present system the South and West pay an excessive share of National taxation and get a deficient share of the benefits. The Northeastern States have reaped nearly all of the benefits, and have escaped much of the taxation." "A tax upon incomes bears justly upon those who can best afford to pay it," added the Chicago *Times,* giving voice to the most common argument of those in favor of the tax.

The debate in Congress was no less extreme than in the press. Sherman, who had fought for the tax in 1871, declared he still favored it if it were necessary for revenue purposes, but as a protectionist he did not think it was at the present. Much more extreme were those who had shorter memories or no hampering record to make their opposition inconsistent. "This proposition is a war upon honest industry, honest wages, frugal living, and moderate gains," declared Senator George F. Hoar. "It is a combination of aristocrat and Populist, of the millionaire and the tramp, which is forcing this policy upon us against which the honest, the simple, frugal American spirit expresses its dissent and its loathing." Senator David B. Hill, Democrat of New York, who had not only the financial center as his constituency, but also a desire to embarrass Cleveland, became the most violent opponent of the bill. In terms of a modern Hearst editorial he declaimed: "European professors announce to American professors, who publish and believe it, the birth of a brand new political economy for universal application. From the midst of their armed camps between the Danube and the Rhine, the professors with their books, the socialists with their schemes, the anarchists with their bombs, are all instructing the people of the United States in the organization of society, the doctrines of democracy, and the principles of taxation. Little squads of anarchists, communists, and socialists cross the ocean and would have us learn of them." Most of the speeches against the tax were deservedly classified as "argument by epithet" by one advocate.

The only ground upon which the more conservative advocates insisted upon the justice of the tax was that "it was an equitable distribution of taxes, and that the men who had the wealth of the country should pay in proportion as they call upon the Government for their protection and preservation." The Populists were more abrupt in their statements. "The time has come," declared Senator William A. Peffer, "when we propose to stop that kind of work. We are going to make you men of the East bear your burden of taxation." To accomplish this he offered a substitute which would have lowered the exemption from four thousand to one thousand dollars and graduated the tax from one per cent to five, remarking that "while Senators smile at the idea it is based upon exact justice." It received five votes—three Populists and two silver Republicans. Commenting upon the debate in Congress, the outstanding exemplar of moderation of editorial tone, the Springfield *Republican* observed: "The advocates of no cause in Congress were ever able to summon such an array of classical economic authority to their support as were the so-called Populists and Communists in defense of the income tax. . . . their arguments were simply overwhelming. They are in the main sound and reasonable arguments, and it is but fair that the case, as thus presented by the South and West, should be heard in the East."

The tax was adopted as part of the Democratic tariff bill, and became a law amid Democratic praise: "The passage of the bill will mark the dawn of a brighter day," predicted De Armond of Missouri, when it passed the House, "with more of sunshine, more of the songs of birds, more of that sweetest music, the laughter of children well fed, well clothed, well housed."

In spite of such roseate promises of a new day, certain large income receivers rushed a case to the Supreme Court based upon a claim of unconstitutionality. Public attention was immediately fixed upon the Court. In addition to the definitely constitutional argument, distinguished counsel for the large income receivers, Joseph H. Choate, warned the Court that if it upheld the law "this communistic march" might go on and the rate become twenty per cent; and one of the opposition counsel, James C. Carter, reminded the Court that the great majority of the American people who favored the law would not willingly accept an adverse decision. The opinions of the Court were in not dissimilar temper, as it divided five to four to declare the tax unconstitutional. "The present assault upon capital," declared Justice Field, "is but the beginning. It will be but the steppingstone to others, larger and more sweeping, till our political contests will become a war of the poor against the rich; a war constantly growing in intensity and bitterness." The majority opinion was described by Justice Harlan as that of a conscious economic class acting in its own interest and contrary to the Court's own precedents.

The opinions of the judges made new opportunities for the press to express itself on the tax. "The overthrow of the income tax is the triumph of selfishness over patriotism," declared the New York *World*. "Great and rich corporations, by hiring the ablest lawyers in the land and fighting against a petty tax upon superfluity as other men have fought for their liberties and their lives, have secured the exemption of wealth from paying its just share toward the support of the Government that protects it." The Augusta (Georgia) *Chronicle* returned to the charge that the decision left the system of taxation one which "robs the masses . . . for the few who own the wealth of the country." The Detroit *Free Press* insisted that the law "was regarded very generally as a commendable effort to compel the rich to bear some share of the burdens of the Federal Government." "A wonderful thing is our judicial system," sarcastically exclaimed the Louisville *Courier-Journal*, while the *Post-Dispatch* of St. Louis proclaimed, "Today's decision shows that the corporations and plutocrats are as securely intrenched in the Supreme Court as in the lower courts which they take such pains to control." On the other hand, the *Nation* announced that Judge Harlan's dissenting opinion "expounded the Marx gospel," the *Journal of Commerce and Commercial Bulletin* headlined it "Socialistic attack on the Constitution," and the Cincinnati *Enquirer* declared it "would have come more naturally from a Debs or a Coxey." Of the decision itself the Cleveland *Plain Dealer* declared, "The overthrow of the Socialistic income tax by the supreme court was the greatest endorsement for the principles of historic Democracy ever made in the United States." The decision was "gratifying to a large majority of the people" agreed the St. Louis *Globe-Democrat,* because the tax was "peculiarly obnoxious to the American sense of justice and propriety." It was a "Democratic blunder" agreed the moderate *Daily Inter-Ocean* of Chicago. The tempo of victory was considerably higher in certain other editorial offices. "The great compromises which made the Union possible still stand unshaken to prevent its overthrow by communistic revolution," exulted the New York *Tribune.* "The fury of ignorant class hatred, which has sufficed to overturn absolute power in many other lands . . . has dashed itself in vain against the Constitution of the United States, fortified by the institutions which a free people have established for the defense of their rights. . . . It is probable that the decision just rendered will not only stand, but will prove strong enough in public appreciation to crush all who may dash themselves against it." "The wave of socialistic revolution has gone far, but it breaks at the foot of the ultimate bulwark set up for the protection of our liberties," agreed the New York *Sun*. The decision, echoed the Philadelphia *Inquirer*, "deals a fatal blow to an insidious form of communism." "Congress . . . will not again mock justice by a general income tax law," predicted the Cincinnati *Enquirer*. The Brooklyn *Daily Eagle* was not so confident. "Western repudiators and Southern ex-rebels struck hands to punish, through the income tax law, those who had brought them to naught. The supreme court has brought these hostiles to naught. That they should have any apologists, defenders or allies in the court is a national danger and disgrace. Whether that decision be the end or but the beginning of the war between civilization and loot in this country, welcome is the decision and ready are the friends of civilization to meet whatever is yet to come!" Probably the Springfield *Republican* commented most intelligently upon the editorial and judicial opinions: "Nothing remains to be said save that quite as interesting as the decision itself, or the tremendous remonstrance of the minority judges, is this display of blood-red wounds by the victorious enemies of the deceased law."

The decision, however, marked a very substantial check to the movement. The Democrats in 1896 denounced the decision and proclaimed their intention to enact such a tax as soon as they assumed power. The Republicans said nothing about it. It was to take twenty years after the enactment of the tax in 1894, unquestionably desired by a majority of the voters at that time and very likely in 1878, before the slow process of amendment, followed by legislation, would again establish an income tax. In the meantime the national government was supported by what was close to a per capita tax falling equally upon Sherman's "humblest citizen" and John Jacob Astor. When it came, it rapidly grew into such a discriminating tax as many of the opponents of the nineties feared. Communism, however, did not come, nor were all comforts and riches quite lost; but an emotion-stirring epithet that could be used against any and all attacks upon the special privileges of capital was discovered, and for many years it continued to be as successful a defense of the economic status quo as it was in the nineties.

8

The Profession of Historian

AMERICAN history as a field of teaching and research is
largely a development of the period since the founding of
graduate schools and seminar training. The notable historical
scholars before that time were distinguished literary craftsmen,
some of whom, such as Henry Adams, were college teachers. But
the profession as we know it is a product of the graduate seminar,
with the Ph.D. training the standard for the teaching and writing
of American history. It is only sixty-four years ago that the first
detailed survey of the study of history teaching in American colleges included a plea that all colleges offer "an undergraduate
course in American History and Economics."

This paper was presented as the presidential address at the forty-fourth annual
meeting of the Mississippi Valley Historical Association in Cincinnati, Ohio, on
April 19, 1951. *The Mississippi Valley Historical Review,* **XXXVIII** (June, 1951), pp.
1-20. The footnotes have been omitted.

Since then the growth of higher education and the popularity of history as a college study have increased at a rate that has absorbed into teaching positions the growing number of young historians coming from our graduate schools. At least this was true until the depression of the thirties, when declining college budgets and enrollments left many a promising young scholar without a professional opportunity, until various federal programs such as the Federal Archives and the National Park Service were able to provide positions that saved the technical training and ability of many.

Our best estimate indicates that there are about 6,700 history teaching positions in American colleges. At the rate we conferred doctorates upon history scholars last year, it would take twenty-four years to replace these teachers by holders of doctoral degrees. The latest list of doctoral dissertations in progress includes approximately five for each degree that was conferred last year, indicating a much larger potential supply. At least this is true if we assume, as it seems we must, that candidates for doctoral degrees enter the teaching profession, whether or not the degree is conferred. Moreover, at the rate we conferred masters' degrees last year, it would take only five years to replace every one of these teachers, should we replace them with teachers having this level of training. At last year's level of production, it would take less than five years to replace all our present college teachers with doctors or masters providing that all of these sought positions in colleges. The number of Ph.D. graduates from the larger universities is greater than in the twenties or thirties, and the number of graduate schools offering advanced work in history is increasing. The very large number of college teachers needed for American history in the small university makes that field, from the administration's standpoint, the most promising for advanced graduate work, at least in the social science field; and hence, it is one of the first to be developed when real need, normal expansion, or local prestige require that advanced graduate training be undertaken. If adequate libraries are lacking, historical records of some type are available locally. Costs are a factor, too. The social sciences cost less to teach than other areas of knowledge, and of the social sciences, history costs the least—if judged by present practices as embodied in university budgets. As long as the standards for graduate work in American universities are a matter of individual interpretation this condition will continue. And, too, as long as our larger graduate schools in the American Association of Universities oppose any kind of accrediting of graduate work, the only standard that exists will continue to be the not very effective opinion of scholars.

There is no doubt that we can count on a steadily increasing demand for college teachers of history. While the recent Commission on Higher Education overestimated the effective demand for higher education, the growth curve itself is there and its continuance is about as certain as any similar predictions based upon American experience and prospects. There are, too, substantial prospects of finding positions for teachers trained on the doctoral level which are now held by teachers trained on the master's level, specifically the junior college and to a less extent the large high school. We can, I think, reasonably expect an increasing demand for teachers of history in the future.

In addition to the outlets in teaching, there are growing opportunities in full-time research, archival, library, museum, and editorial work that the graduate school historians have largely ignored in the past. The historical society is a case in point. From an institution staffed originally by self-trained scholars, it is in the process of becoming one that at its best rivals the university in the scholarship of its staff. These institutions are probably as important to the historical profession as the university department. The graduate schools can serve a professional need here by providing better graduate training for these positions, but the problem really goes deeper than that; for nowhere, I believe, has there been worked out the degree of desirable cooperation and coordination between the work of the historical society and the university. The coordination between undergraduate teaching and graduate instruction is relatively easy because both are administered by a single department, but it is no less desirable between graduate training and the historical society. So much of the future of American history is involved in the library resources of these societies; such a large proportion of the publication of scholarship is in their hands; such great possibilities in adult education are open to them, that they deserve more attention from all professional organizations than has been common. The purposes of the department of history and the historical society are essentially the same, and neither should be neglected by the profession. We have only touched the numerous possibilities of cooperation between the two in achieving these purposes. This cooperation was one of the purposes for which this Association was founded, principally, it happens, by the historical societies.

The greatest prospective growth in the professional services of historians is not in teaching but in governmental agencies and large business corporations. Each decade sees a much deeper appreciation of the uses of history as a practical guide to the administration of government departments and private corporations. The usefulness of history in the military branches of the federal government seems to be one of the more spectacular examples of a growing interest on the part of federal agencies in competent historical branches. Much slower are state and local governments, whose archives in many cases remain relatively uncared for, and private corporations, where with a few very notable exceptions little use has been made of the services of the historian. As large corporations grow in age, appreciation of the value of their history grows upon them, and they begin grudgingly first to take better care of their archives, then to provide facilities for the research of others, then to begin haltingly a teaching program for their own employees and their public through museum techniques and publications, and finally in a few cases to subsidize basic research.

It is an ironical phenomenon that no type of large institution is more backward in its uses of history as a technique of self-study and evaluation than are those institutions most directly under the influence of professional historians—the colleges and universities. In their relations to history the universities should exhibit more of the characteristics one might expect from a management with superior professional advice at hand. Instead, they respond almost exactly like a private corporation or government agency with no historical counsel available. Archives are neglected until the problems of storage force a consideration of the basic problems of selection and arrangement. No plans for research and writing are developed, except as some superannuated teacher for whom employment must be found is designated historian, sometimes, it seems, on the sole ground that, if his memory is good, it might save the labor of much research. As in the less intellectual institutions, it takes an important anniversary, such as a centennial, to force serious attention to the general problem, and most of our better university histories grow out of such occasions. What university or college history department is able to give a new instructor a useful history of the department, the undergraduate or graduate school in which it is located, to help him orient himself to his work? And where do academic historians have enough prestige in their own institutions so that their discipline is used intelligently as one of the tools of wise planning? Perhaps the appreciation of the uses and values of history may some day creep back to the universities by the successful examples in the business corporation and the government agency.

Every worthy profession is concerned with the recruitment of new members. Historians need to be so concerned. Circumstances now bring into the ranks of our craft a reasonable proportion of the more able students, and along with them a larger share of the mediocre. What happens is largely a result of pure chance, since the profession has no plan or program. This policy of drift accounts in part for the situation that the historian receives his doctorate nearly eight years after his baccalaureate, an educational program that theoretically could be completed in three years. Several factors combine to cause this delay, late professional choice—frequently the senior year in college or even later—and scarcity of graduate fellowships being two of the more important.

Not all the delay is lost to the historian, provided the time is spent in study of related fields, in teaching, or in other vocational activity which widens one's experience with society. But it is also true that a high proportion of the more productive scholars receive their doctorates earlier than the average. Whether those who take more than average time become better or poorer teachers, no one knows. Scholars in the natural science fields make their choices earlier in life than historians, and they take their doctorates at a younger age. Some of this advantage grows out of the essentially romantic appeal science makes to intelligent boys and girls today, but there are also organized movements that encourage it, including the science talent searches. Historians possess the means to achieve similar results for their profession in the junior history movement, best exemplified by its Texas organization. This type of organization could, with the cooperation of historical societies, social studies teachers' councils, and historians generally, maintain on a high level similar movements in each state. Through these organizations we could discover interests and talents at an early age and begin to plan the student's education for the historical profession much earlier. Historians need a greater breadth of training than most other scholarly specializations, and it is reasonable to believe that we could plan that education more adequately if we started earlier than at present.

At a recent meeting where graduate training in history was discussed, one of the most distinguished scholars in our Association pronounced the sweeping generalization that there was nothing wrong with our graduate training that better teachers and better students would not cure. I think we can all agree with this. But we may feel that just as the statement that there was nothing wrong with West Texas that more water and a better class of people would not cure led to the reply that this was also true of hell, so it might be replied that there is nothing wrong with education or indeed life itself that better teachers and students could not cure. What we need are the means of getting better teachers and better students, and, unless I am badly mistaken, as we get better teachers of history in the schools and colleges as well as the graduate schools, we will get better students. At least there is one aspect of this problem that we of the profession can do something about; we can improve the experiences of students of history, directly and without outside encouragement. There are several possibilities of such improvement available to all of us:

Our graduate training would be improved if we had better education in history for the undergraduate major. This training could be made to lead more directly toward scholarly maturity. History in the undergraduate college is such an excellent vehicle for general education that much of our offering is designed as cultural background for undergraduates who plan no career in scholarship, and these same courses also make up the program of the prospective scholar. A course in constitutional history designed for pre-law students without much history, one in economic history in which the major objective is the needs of the large group of students planning to be businessmen—these are not the best possible training for the scholar. The prospective historian can no doubt use some of these general education courses profitably, but a higher level type of course with a progressive sequence that leads from the relatively simple to the more complex should also be included in this program. It is from this large group of courses that the usual master's program is selected, and any increase in maturity here would be still more apparent on the beginning graduate level.

It should be emphasized that the A.M. degree represents a level of training that is important to scholars and teachers of history. A large amount of instruction in junior and senior colleges is done by teachers with this level of training. A majority of our citizens and future leaders are gaining their concepts of the historical process and of historical scholarship from these teachers or those with less training. And there are fewer standards here than at the doctoral level. Any college can offer a program leading to an A.M. degree in history, regardless of its staff or library resources, and there is no agency in the educational world to say that its training is inferior to any other. Usually in these institutions the degree represents a fifth year in which the student takes those courses in the department he did not take for his major, with perhaps a thesis, directed by a teacher already overloaded with undergraduate courses. At the other extreme we have the large graduate school where work for the doctorate is heavy and the A.M. program has become obsolescent. It seems impossible for a department to become heavily involved in graduate training for the doctorate without virtually abandoning the master's program as far as standards are concerned. Here, too, the program is one of senior level courses, of better quality, perhaps, but the master's thesis is usually dropped, not because there is anything better to put in its place, but because the staff is so busy with doctoral candidates that it has no time to direct the lowly masters. A considerable body of informed opinion holds that the strong department in the small university or large college which offers no work beyond the master's provides the best work at that level. These conditions are not peculiar to history, but there is no sign of any movement in American higher education to improve them. The scholarly training of college teachers on the master's level is not going to improve until the leaders of higher education assume a larger responsibility for standards.

Our training program for the doctorate is now under severe attack for two alleged deficiencies: one, that it does not result in well-trained research scholars, and the other, that it does not turn out competent college teachers of history. While both of these criticisms are frequently exaggerated, we have no reason to be satisfied with our results. Changes in our programs have not kept pace with changes in the social sciences themselves. Some of the requirements are relics of a day when the definition of history was much narrower than anyone would propose now, and others are based upon other objectives than those we now acknowledge. History, as a field of scholarship, has changed much faster than our training program for the profession. Like most professions and all bureaucracies we have comfortably believed that the type of education we experienced ourselves was so highly successful that no more than trifling modifications were worthy of consideration.

Consequently, it is not surprising that we have to face illconsiderable demands for changes. The separation of prospective research scholars from prospective college teachers as is so frequently urged is a counsel of desperation and ignorance. To some extent it comes from vested interests albeit unconscious ones. There is the agency research director or great university specialist with ample funds to employ research assistance. Their needs for technicians who can do routine tasks of specialized research, regardless of their general competence, leads them to be severely critical of the graduate schools' insistence upon breadth as well as depth of scholarship. In a similar way shortsighted college administrators are beguiled by a concept of an ideal teacher so filled with information and understanding that he can teach anything, and do it eight hours each day without pause. This demand is also promoted by people with a panacea to sell, the panacea being a program of professional education courses, in its most extreme version to be required for the legal certification of college teachers.

It should be said again and again that a college teacher who is not a scholar is a college teacher who cannot fulfill his proper function; nor is a technician, master of some esoteric technique, a scholar. No one would deny that we should have special emphasis in our training for historians going primarily into society work, for those going into archives, and for those certain to be teachers. But it does mean that the basic training for scholarship and teaching is the same; that the major difference that sets off college teaching from secondary school teaching is scholarship; that to abandon scholarship in teaching is to give up the one claim the college teacher has to survival, which is that he has something fundamentally more sound to offer than the popularizer on the radio and in the Sunday supplement. To abandon scholarship as the basic requirement of college teaching of history or any other field is to abandon scholarship everywhere. If college students are not taught by scholars, there will be neither the understanding of scholarship necessary to its support among our citizenry, nor will there be developed advanced students able or willing to become research scholars in history. What would happen to the quality of social science concepts, I am unable to predict.

Our more thoroughgoing critics assert that the research scholar and teacher are separate entities. The teacher in this view is a sort of guerrilla who operates between the lines of the research workers and the college students, making available to the latter whatever the former knows that is useful. They use the term "scholar" for this guerrilla as someone apart from research who has never been contaminated by direct contact with that fascinating, soul-wrecking charmer whose greatest desire is to destroy the young and innocent college teacher.

The history of higher education, of scholarship, and of advances in all fields of learning, I believe, directly contradicts this. There is no scholarship without research; there is no productive teaching without understanding. More important than breadth of information, significant as that is, depth of understanding of the nature of scholarship itself is learned only through service on its firing line, which is research. It is only through participating in research that the college teacher gains some understanding of the limitations of our knowledge about society and of our tools for understanding established facts. It is the only experience that we can be certain has a reasonable prospect of making a teacher a sound enough scholar that he will not mislead his students into naive beliefs that encourage the shallow optimisms and pessimisms that curse a democratic society. There are too many nostrums in the social sciences to risk teachers who cannot stand the test of scholarship.

Scholarship has just this to do with the research training for the doctorate. No teacher can teach a college level course, which goes beyond the narrow confines of a textbook, without resorting to research. He cannot prepare a worthwhile lecture without research. The validity of the generalization to which he leads students will be just as sound as his research, and nothing else will make it better.

The thesis and other research training we require for the doctorate guarantees a minimum of ability to conduct research in a way adequate by modern standards. It also promises a minimum of interest in research and a desire to do it. College teaching certainly demands the minimum, even though it does not demand continued published research. Research there must be for all sound teaching, but published research is not required. Publication is highly desirable. It is a real, perhaps the only, guarantee of continued and growing scholarship. In publication, research must meet the professional standards of editors of journals, or be subjected to the reviews of other scholars. Those are usually good tests, but a teacher can mature his scholarship without them, and many become so burdened with teaching tasks that they must. Overemphasis upon research can harm teaching by monopolizing the attention of the scholar and narrowing his interests. Several bad, but widely known, illustrations of this unfortunate development are the major basis upon which the case for the antithesis "scholar v. teacher" rests. The good teacher must be aware of these dangers and divide his attention between the two phases of his single task.

The soundness of our traditional position that the college teacher needs to be a scholar, familiar with real research, should not blind us to the weaknesses of many of our practices in training historical scholars. Our graduate training programs were framed in their fundamental aspects when history was past politics, a relatively definite and exact content, limited in concept, and not too difficult to master. Since then history has expanded not alone in the geographical areas involved, but still more in its interests. Great areas of economic, social, and intellectual history have been annexed, and they are less precise bodies of information than the older history was. In fact, political history has changed greatly, and we now are more interested in depth, with what lies under the surface which we used to study, and this is by its very nature less definite and less susceptible of easy mastery.

The graduate training program in history in most of our universities would be improved if the spread of content mastery, as represented by the lecture courses that must be taken to prepare for the preliminary examination, were reduced. It was not such an enormous problem in our earlier graduate schools. There were fewer kinds of history, and fewer professors each inclined to insist on a high level of information in his field. In many graduate schools these fields cover nearly all of the chronological span of European and American history, with most of the currently popular specialties, such as economic and intellectual history, included with each period. Such is the lack of uniformity in courses from one graduate school to another, that training in a field on one campus is not usually thought sufficient by the candidate, and he must needs have his work, even repeat work, with the person who is to set and read his examination. The lecture courses which prepare for these examinations remain, for the most part, the senior college level surveys. These accumulations of facts demand too large a share of the student's attention and retard the development of mature scholarship. Depth of scholarship in selected areas, with considerably less attention to the mastery of facts in many of the intervening areas, surely leads to a more mature scholarship.

Our training programs would be improved by greater insistence upon work in related fields, primarily other social science areas. In addition to work in at least American and European history, work in other fields is desirable in some instances because certain students will eventually teach in some field in addition to history. But its major value is in what it adds to the student's ability to interpret history, and the stimulation it gives to historical research and teaching. The outside field requirement that now exists is too exclusively a factual mastery to meet the requirements of the preliminary examinations, and while at least some of this is desirable, seminar work in the field should also be required. Historical research and teaching usually lack ideas for interpreting the development of society. It is by using concepts from the systems of general analytical theory developed in other social science disciplines that new light and stimulus come to historical thinking. Frederick Jackson Turner used concepts of a "new" geography and economics and applied them to historical development to give us a series of concepts that stimulated research and teaching as has no other single scholar in American history. Thorstein Veblen used anthropological concepts to make unique contributions to economics. One does not underrate the historical method itself when he asserts that the most fruitful new concepts and explorations are to come from the application of social science hypotheses to historical situations under the rigid control of historical methodology. There is a great deal for the historian to learn about the past by observing it in the framework of concepts and with the tools which scholars who specialize on the present have developed. Public opinion survey techniques cannot be applied directly to historical controversies, but a clear understanding of them can aid the historian in evaluating the evidences of public opinion that appear in the contemporary records. Urban history which fails to use the tools developed by the urban sociologist and geographer is singularly barren of useful fruit. History scholars can profit in their doctoral training from experience in using the research techniques especially of cultural anthropology, economic theory, and social psychology.

A major improvement in the research training, and especially in writing and teaching resulting from research, lies in the type of guidance that develops a thesis subject about which the student will be enthusiastic. We are not apt to develop significant scholarship unless we can inspire students with considerable emotional drive toward the solution of some of the problems that lie on the frontiers of historical research. This means not only the exemplification of these qualities on the part of the graduate professor, but also a willingness on his part either to accept subjects which are difficult and laborious to direct or a willingness to send the candidate to another university where there is a scholar who can and will direct that thesis properly. Research enthusiasm is too precious a quality to risk its loss by forcing subjects within the narrow groove of the graduate professor's immediate interests.

A larger amount of shifting from university to university by students would improve the education of graduating historians by widening their experience with teaching procedures, with older scholars personally, and with research collections. At present this shifting is inhibited not alone by inertia but by practices relating to our examining system, so that virtually the only students who move are those whom no department wants. Graduate student opinion that it is safer to take as many courses as possible with a professor who will be one of his examiners is too widespread to be ignored. The student who begins his acquaintance with his examiners as an undergraduate is better prepared for his doctoral examinations than one who starts that acquaintance as a student with a master's degree behind him. This pressure to confine training in one department leads to an impoverished scholarly education. The smaller the department the worse the practice, but even with the largest and most distinguished it still handicaps the scholar. A department which holds a large portion of its students for all their training is not giving them the best training available.

There are few dissertation subjects on the doctoral level in history which do not also involve another field of scholarship—political science, economics, literature, geography, sociology, or any of several others. It would improve research training if such theses were jointly directed by a historian and a scholar in the related field. In practice such joint direction requires a degree of cooperation that regrettably is not always possible. But its value to the student and to research projects is incalculable. More and more thesis direction should become joint rather than individual. Where this can be done, and the smaller graduate school has some advantages here, the resulting research training is on a higher level.

There is a persistent problem presented by the sheer size of dissertation projects frequently undertaken by students. Projects that are too large either delay completion of the work toward a degree to an undesirable extent, or lead to superficial work. On the other hand, subjects are frequently so restricted that they add little to the students' scholarship. To solve this problem one frequently meets the idea that subjects should be chosen from problems involving only synthesis. It is difficult to see what these problems could be if research training is what is needed. Certainly it is unlikely that a student is capable of much synthesis unless he is familiar with the more elementary factors of selection and analysis; one who does not have realistic conceptions of the nature of historical knowledge is not in a position to make valid syntheses involving that knowledge.

The problem here is one of balance and proportion. It seems to be met with reasonable efficiency in most departments. The procedures usually followed can be used by others. The dissertation subject can be isolated as a part of a larger unit, the remainder of the unit to be done later and then the entire study published. The dissertation may be an expansion of a master's thesis on the same subject, and hence grow into a larger study than would have been feasible on a new subject selected much later in the student's training. Smaller subjects are sought where the sources can be exhausted and a definitive study be completed without making unreasonable demands on the time available for training.

The language requirement probably brings up more strongly emotional reactions than any other common practice. For the students who work in European history there is never enough language ability. For those whose research is in several phases of American history, some languages other than English are necessary; in most areas of research in the American field no languages except English are useful tools. The question is not foreign language versus no foreign language, but rather what tools are needed to make a graduate student a scholar in American history. If we had some guidance of the prospective historian during his undergraduate years, his language training would be assured. As the problem comes to us in the graduate school, however, the student has usually had substantial training in one foreign language. The question then is, will we require him to acquire sufficient mastery of a second foreign language to pass the examination. The best argument for the traditional language requirement is that the student does not know definitely where his research interests may lead him. But the choice is not between languages or no languages, it is one between a specific language tool, and an alternative tool of research he might acquire with the same expenditure of time and effort. As against substantial training in the research methods of cultural anthropology, as the equipment of a historian whose research will be in social history, the balance will not be for a language he did not study as an undergraduate.

Certainly here is one area where we need more realism in our thinking.

The proposition that if research training for the college teacher could be abandoned, it could be profitably replaced by a large program of professional education, raises several questions besides the desirability of research training.

One fact that is usually overlooked is that a substantial proportion of college teachers of history have had a program of professional courses designed for teaching in the secondary schools. That this proportion is so high is a result of the complex manner in which the college history teacher is recruited. An examination of a large number of transcripts of graduate students indicates that it is much higher than we or our critics have realized. As one examines the training patterns of those who have had this training, one is struck by the sheer waste involved for the college teacher. Not all of it, of course, because the practice teaching, the methods, the psychology, and the history of education at their best probably have a high carry-over value to the college classroom. But the many faddist courses that are specified by certification regulations in some states, by many college curriculums in this area, and by the advisers of undergraduates, add up to a large loss for college teachers trained in this way which could have been put to much more profitable use.

That there is a threat that something of this nature may be required for college teacher preparation is just punishment, I fear, for the lack of realism with which we teachers of advanced graduate students have approached our program. Correctly convinced that the basic preparation for the college history teacher is scholarship, we have ignored other significant factors, and at times have put ourselves in the position of defending the proposition that any trained scholar can teach his subject, regardless of whether he can speak, understand students, or become part of a faculty team for the liberal education of a group of young men and women.

Here is one of the most clearly overlooked opportunities for improving the teaching of history in college. While no young Ph.D. assuming his first college teaching position is near his maximum teaching efficiency, regardless of what his training has been, we could short-cut his arrival at a high level of efficiency by more careful planning of his graduate work. As most of our students do some college teaching while they are taking their graduate training, this teaching presents our greatest opportunity. All too often it is merely experience for the student-teacher from which he gains only so much as his ingenuity can fashion from it. It can be, and in some places is, made a rewarding experience. It is then designed as a learning activity, in which the student-teacher is given some preparation for his task and then supervised in such a way as to enable him to avoid ineffective practices and to attempt more successful ones. Such preparation and supervision, if carried on systematically and intelligently, adds little formal training time to the student's program and accelerates his acquisition of a respectable classroom technique. Bad teaching habits frequently begin out of the timidity and embarrassment at assuming the leadership of classes for the first time, and a little sympathetic supervision then can prevent most of them from becoming established.

With minor exceptions for the handicapped, who will never try to teach, and perhaps a few whose research positions outside of teaching institutions are already assured, why should not a semester of supervised teaching experience become standard for all Ph.D. candidates in history? Too much of it, so much that it delays unduly the completion of graduate work, is undesirable although at times a financial necessity. But each advanced graduate student can spare the time for one course for one semester.

We should not stop there. There is a substantial body of thought and a significant body of literature dealing with the history of higher education, the place of the study of history and related fields, the purposes of teaching history, the various organizations of historical knowledge, the ways in which students learn historical concepts, and the possibilities and limitations of testing and rating student learning. These are only the fundamentals of what must be comprehended if a young teacher is going to have a professional approach to college teaching, and will grow rapidly into a highly efficient teacher. One organized course, coming preferably before the guided experience in teaching, and taught by a competent historian with enthusiasm for teaching, can make a world of difference in the quality of teaching done during at least the early years of a career. Whatever else we do in our doctoral programs, we can surely find time and place for this addition.

One of the major difficulties we face, and the basis of much unreasonable criticism, grows out of a highly utopian concept of teacher training. This is, in short, that our doctoral program should produce that paragon of all virtues, the ideal teacher: an inspiring personality, an original scholar, and a master of classroom procedures. We might as well be realistic and admit that the young Ph.D. in history still has a great deal to learn about both teaching and research, and that any college administrator who proceeds on any other assumption is extremely gullible. In no profession are practitioners near the peak of effectiveness when they complete their required training. The professional societies and the great foundations interested in scholarship provide means for improving research and writing skills, and research institutions continue the education of their own staffs. The college must realize, too, that it has an obligation to improve the teaching effectiveness of its faculty. When it employs a young Ph.D., it must learn to proceed on the understanding that the college must place him in an environment that will encourage him to become an effective teacher, and give him helpful supervision as long as he needs it.

A longer training period in the graduate school would, of course, result in a more finished product. But that is virtually impossible. Unless we have a revolution in our relative salary scales, and who sees such a prospect, the major effect of a longer period of training with its consequent postponement of an income would be to exclude a larger proportion of the more talented students from the ranks of prospective college teachers.

The solution here is to recognize that the new Ph.D. in history is neither a complete scholar nor teacher. This takes more years than he has had to give to it, and it is the gradual development from experience, study, and reflection, all of which take time. What we need is generally beyond the scope of the graduate school and in the hands of the employing college and professional organizations and foundations.

Our present practice too often is to meet the new teacher with a full program of teaching his first year out of graduate school. Not only a full program, but all too frequently a teaching program made up of the unwanted odds and ends of courses of which the older members of the department are anxious to unburden themselves. Instead, then, of our young teacher starting off with a teaching experience, in which he has time to work at the job of becoming an effective instructor and continuing his research development, he spends his nights "getting up" his new courses, having all he can do to keep ahead of the students in his various classes. It is little wonder that he develops some sad teaching habits which may stay with him for life, and that in the exclusive devotion to preparing for classes and teaching them, his research ardor cools and his skills atrophy.

Our professional organizations, specifically the one national organization of specialists in American history, the Mississippi Valley Historical Association, have responsibilities in these matters. Our protests against other groups who move into our field and determine policy are made with bad grace when we have neglected our obligations as a profession. Up to the present we have concerned ourselves almost exclusively with research and scholarly publication. True, we have paid considerable attention to the teaching of history in secondary and elementary schools, and have done so throughout our history. But it is time that we matured to the extent of accepting responsibility for other matters of great concern to our profession. We need to devote more attention to recruiting able young scholars to our ranks. We should be studying the value of history as an instrument for intelligent planning and administration, and promoting its use in this area. We should be studying the possibilities of adult education programs in history. We need continuous study of our training programs for research and for teaching. As an Association we should be so active in these fields that others with less understanding of our profession would hesitate to attempt to speak for it.

These, I submit, are some of our professional obligations that we have been neglecting. Let it not be said that our neglect extended into the second half of the century!

SELECTED
SPEECHES
1946-1960

9

The Social Studies Teacher and the World Crisis

THE SERIOUS problems which face the American people today need little elaboration. We have had breakdown after breakdown in our productive organization because of conflicts between capital and labor. While our own consumption of food is the highest in all our history, we are decreasing our aid to the starving millions in Europe and Asia. Every major organized group, the laborer, the farmer and the businessman, to say nothing of the gluttonous consumer, have shown such excesses of greed that we cannot recall its equal in all our history. In the past twelve months virtually no considerations of patriotism seem to have modified our unashamed group selfishness. Does anyone want to suggest that the international situation is better stabilized than domestic affairs? Growing shadows here certainly threaten

Delivered before the Missouri Council for Social Studies, November 8, 1946.

215

conditions that can only lead to another world war and destruction of modern civilization.

Lest, however, we lose our perspective on these problems, I want to quote an editorial found recently in a magazine. It reads:

> It is a gloomy moment in history. Not for many years—not in the lifetime of most men who read this paper—has there been so much grave and deep apprehension; never has the future seemed so incalculable as at this time.
>
> In France the political caldron seethes and bubbles with uncertainty; Russia hangs as usual, like a cloud, dark and silent upon the horizon of Europe; while all the energies, resources and influences of the British empire are sorely tried, and are yet to be tried more sorely, in coping with the vast and deadly Indian insurrection, (and with its disturbed relations in China). It is a solemn moment, and no man can feel an indifference—which, happily, no man pretends to feel—in the issue of events.
>
> Of our own troubles (in the U. S.) no man can see the end.

This is not from last month's New York *Times*. Instead it is from *Harper's Weekly* for October 10, 1857, just eighty-nine years ago last month. It is well to be aware that our fathers had problems, too—problems which seemed to them as great or nearly as great as our own seem to us. It is also well to recall that in many cases in the past our forefathers failed. The American Civil War not only cost unbelievably in lives and property, but also left us with domestic antagonisms that still handicap our progress. The failure of our leadership after the first world war made collective security impossible and was a potent factor in bringing on the second world war and our present insecurity.

All wars have been followed by periods of reconstruction that were domestically characterized by struggles of those groups who during the war had secured increased prestige and incomes to hold their gains against the attempts of other groups to restore the old relationship. Internationally, post-war periods have been characterized by the expansion of victorious powers into the vacuums left by the defeated powers. These have resulted in antagonisms and competing alliances that indicated the line-up for the next war which inevitably followed.

In spite of these truths, we must face the fact that the problems of today are more serious. The difference in the present as compared with former periods of post-war reconstruction exists in both good and evil changes. We have, in the present instance, the following unique conditions: we have taken a large step toward international government in which every great power in the world is united. We had a similar attempt after World War I and we have capitalized upon its failures to build an organization that structurally has a much higher chance of survival. Since our experience with international government, which began with the first Hague Tribunal, is less than fifty years old, there should be little wonder that we grope considerably in trying to make it effective.

Another change is the decline of old European imperialism under the drive of democratic pressure, humanitarian sentiments, and the rising nationalism of backward areas. Whether by choice or by force of circumstances, and both elements are playing a part, Great Britain is pulling her controls out of India and Egypt in such a complete manner as would have been considered astounding ten short years ago. Similarly, The Netherlands is trying to compromise on commonwealth status for the East Indies. France is experimenting with the extension of political privileges, and of representation in the French Parliament to its more advanced colonial areas; and the U. S. is breaking its political connections with the Philippines. Such a program after World War I might have made an enormous difference in the history of the twenty years before the outbreak of World War II, but one can only speculate as to what its effect will be at this time.

Another change is the revival, temporarily, we all hope, of Russian imperialism and the use of the Communist parties as a means of extending that control. There are unique elements in this extension in that these Communist parties form fifth columns to whom Russian success is the highest good and takes precedence over the good of the state of which the party members are citizens, and also over the good of any international organization. While these groups are not a serious problem in the English speaking countries, they are a powerful weapon for extending Russian control in most European countries. This element is relatively new, and like the Fascist fifth columns of the thirties it is a most disturbing element in the international picture.

While we have always had to repair and rebuild in other post-war periods, the need has never been as widespread as it is today with virtually all of Europe, China, the Pacific Islands and Japan in a condition that cries out for speed and generosity on the part of nations whose standard of living is as favorably placed as our own. The need for rehabilitation, the means and speed with which it takes place are potent factors in our post-war situation. Lastly, and most significant of all in the present post-war world are the new weapons of tragically destructive power. They need, I hope, no elaboration here.

We are not without strong defense against the perils that exist in these changes. The great race between education and catastrophe is not yet lost. Whether it will be lost or not will depend in a substantial part on the work of social studies teachers. It is well to be realistic about this. Nothing is gained by exaggerating the role of teachers in society. Neither is it desirable to rest content with the present role that these teachers play.

All social studies teachers now realize that the mere existence of an international organization approaching a type of world government is not a guarantee of world peace or security, as some optimistic individuals seemed to believe after the San Francisco Conference. The existence of machinery to solve problems does not in itself indicate that the problems will be solved. When Lord Robert Cecil, who next to Woodrow Wilson had the most to do with the structure of the League of Nations, returned home, his brother, Hugh, asked him whether the new organization would work. "You have got the wrong idea, Hugh," he is reported to have said, "a spade doesn't work." The United Nations too is a mere tool that, with sufficient desire, energy and willingness to sacrifice on the part of the citizens of the great powers of the world, can be made to work. But it will not work by itself. Then we all realize that the great problems before the United Nations Assembly today, questions like the veto and the treatment of colonial areas are not going to be solved in our classrooms, certainly not in their short run aspects.

What, in the light of this situation, is the duty and obligation of our social studies teachers?

First, it seems to me, there is a modest long-range program for the improvement of social studies teaching that should be promoted by our group. We all know that large programs are accomplished only when some group educates the general public, promotes and pressures, if you please, until it is accepted by the public. The foremost item on this list is for better teachers. I am not disturbed about the quality of the teachers who come to these meetings year after year, who read the professional journals and are alert to improvements in their teaching, but I am concerned about the great majority who are rarely touched by these forces. And there is a still much greater group yet to be induced to become social studies teachers, where the hope of real improvement on a large scale exists.

We are, I believe, all agreed that we must attract more high-ability students for social studies teaching than we have in the past. Then we must insure that these students receive a training that is superior to any now being administered. This is not the occasion to detail what these improvements might consist of, but it is proper to point out that a professional organization of social studies teachers should concern itself with this problem, and exert its influence to increase the material and social rewards of social studies teachers, otherwise the better rewarded and less strenuous occupations will continue to drain away too large a proportion of our better talent. I see no easy way to accomplish this. All teaching salaries, must, and will, increase in relation to other incomes. But the need of citizenship training for the general good is so apparent and of such national and international importance today that special efforts should be made in order to assure that teaching rewards are at least as substantial as those in any other. One possible approach would be to follow the example set in vocational agriculture, vocational home economics and trades and industries education. These teachers, as you all realize, teach on federally subsidized programs, which make salaries higher than in other areas of teaching. Surely there is as great a claim for a federally subsidized program for citizenship training that would bring to the work abler and better trained teachers! Increased federal aid to elementary and secondary education seems certain to come in some form. We should see to it that at least part of this is devoted specifically to citizenship training, by making social studies teaching positions so attractive that we can fill them with high-ability people who have been adequately trained for their tremendous jobs

To achieve these and other goals, we need to make our professional organization of social studies teachers stronger and give it a more positive program. This organization must play a larger part in professional life than any teachers' organization has in the past. It should be a means of protecting social studies teachers against unjustified attacks from special interests. It should exercise self-discipline over its members to insure that they follow recognized professional codes of ethics which they themselves help formulate and revise from time to time.

Another long-range measure is involved directly, I believe, in legal changes in the status of the citizen which influence his training. The most important of these is the voting age. A young citizen finishes high school, and unless he belongs to the minority who go to college, he has completed there his last organized

instruction related to political citizenship. It is three and sometimes five years later that he becomes a legal voter. Recognizing
that there are reasonable arguments against granting voting rights
to citizens younger than twenty-one—still, from the standpoint of
increasing the effectiveness of the political aspects of our citizenship training in high school, there are great advantages in making
the acquisition of the voting privilege coincide approximately
with the high school graduation. Social studies teachers should
make it their business to call this to public attention.

These suggestions for a long-range program seem remote from
the needs of November, 1946. Certainly they do not exhaust
the many practical things that could be done this year and next.
Permit me to suggest a few things of this type also.

One of the most helpful would be to insure that the fourth
year of high school social studies—called variously American
Problems, Economics, Civics, and Sociology—is taken by high
school students. Here we have a course that we have been using
in Missouri since 1928 as the climax of the citizenship training
in the schools. To it we reserve our pupils' most mature experience
with international relations, with government and with economic
problems. And in many of our better high schools this year not
over one senior out of four will have any experience with it! Why?

Well, the senior year curriculum is crowded! The State Department, some may say, only requires three units of social studies.
And in the meantime, young citizens are not only inadequately
trained, but they lack highly necessary training that the schools
are fully prepared and ready to give. There is no one thing that
Missouri teachers can do that would be as immediately effective
in elevating our citizenship training program as would a quiet
campaign to induce every high school in the state to make that
course the common experience of all high school seniors.

There are no social science courses which we now teach which
cannot be improved in the light of present conditions. And improvement, I insist, does not require a new course of study or

new textbooks. We should continually ask ourselves, are we getting the maximum results from this class. It is hard for instance to find a more useful social studies course than history in the hands of a competent teacher. But it can be taught with such an emphasis on traditional content and on remembering isolated information that the pupils' experience is barren indeed. It seems clear that the stress in any history course today should at least include these:

1. Problems of past international relations. What conditions were conducive to peace.
2. The influence upon society of the great technological discoveries, like those that ushered in the industrial revolution. If we are going to live in an era of atomic power, there is no better preparation than to study what lesser changes have done to society in the past.
3. The shifts in sources of world power resources in the past.
4. The history of the attempts to solve the problem of war and peace. Why should not Grotius and Vattel be presented as innovators on a par with the great scientists and statesmen?
5. The concept of a good life in past ages and how the resulting standards of value influenced the civilization of the day. In our social studies courses other than history the emphasis should include these understandings:
   a. A knowledge of world government as represented by the United Nations, its structure, functions, its probable weakness as brought out in criticisms, and its possible improvement. Since the ratification of the San Francisco charter, the United Nations is a part of our own government and merits attention equivalent to that given to other parts of our government.
   b. A better knowledge of world geography. While this can be helped in many other ways, a change in our curriculum is overdue. Such a course could well replace our present

course in high school geography and should become the standard ninth grade social studies course. This knowledge would include an understanding of the distribution of power resources, world standards of living and the means of raising them, the intellectual, religious and economic elements of world unity.

Then we need increased emphasis in our teaching upon the waste involved in the selfish competition of organized groups for a larger share of the national production. By this we might develop a higher type of patriotism, a more sensitive attitude toward what the general good demands and hold up for our future citizens the essential advantages to the entire group in lessening those competitive class contests for larger and larger shares of the national income. The American economy must increase its efficiency and the enormous losses due to labor wards, cartels and other monopolistic restrictions which bring about our "boom and bust" economic cycles must be greatly reduced or the American system is apt to fail in competition with other systems.

This all involves developing of a higher and somewhat different national and international patriotism and morality. Social studies teachers cannot do this alone. Other teachers in the school system can contribute at least as much as we can. I think we owe it to our keen sense of the need for this patriotism to re-educate some of our colleagues. We should make sure that within our own school system teachers of literature are conscious of the need of developing a sensitiveness toward right and wrong as it is involved in group conflicts and that the teaching of literature and the fine arts center, in part, about those great problems. The standards here cannot be those of aesthetics alone. Literature must be to an increasing degree vicarious experience with problems of life which involve standards of conduct. The catharsis of great art can and should be a deep emotional experience involving conflicting values.

If we can do a fair measure of these things, education can win in the race with catastrophe and only as we make our own personal sacrifices to accomplish these ends will we deserve James Hilton's famous tribute to the teacher.

If I had a child who wanted to be a teacher, I would bid him Godspeed as if he were going to war. For indeed the war against prejudice, greed, and ignorance is eternal, and those who dedicate themselves to it give their lives no less because they may live to see some fraction of the battle won. They are the commandoes of the peace, if peace is to be more than a short armistice. As in a relay race, our armed men have handed victory to those who dare not stand still to admire it, but must run with it for very life to a further and larger goal.

10

The College of Liberal Arts

Much as we have used classical models and examples for modern educational practices, the origin of our American liberal arts education is the medieval university. Through many modifications this came to the American college by way of English universities. Their example was followed to a large degree by the colonial college in America, but not as general training for all of the learned professions, as much as for professional training for members of the clergy.

Useful and valuable as this was, it so restricted the character and usefulness of the American college that in the first 80 years of our national history the percentage of our population attending college declined steadily. This decline of higher education was checked and the trend reversed by two factors—the expansion of

Delivered at William Jewell College, May 23, 1949.

professional training, and the "liberalizing" of the heavily theological training of the later colonial college by the introduction of modern languages and literature, the new natural sciences, and the social sciences.

These changes had been under way for a long time, but were painful and slow. Revising the college curriculum has always carried with it complications similar to those of moving a cemetery, and that was evident in the slowness with which the colonial college changed. The first relatively modern scientific study to break into the sacred area of Harvard Yard arrived shortly after 1800 in the form of an extra-curricular series of lectures, which were held at hours that did not interfere with classes and for which students needed the written permission of their parents in order to attend.

This dam broke in the decades of the 1880's and 1890's, and the weapon which broke it was the elective system; a system, I suspect, not founded on principle so much as upon the necessity of finding a weapon to force the newer areas of knowledge into the curriculum.

It was an effective weapon in accomplishing this purpose, however much harm it did in other ways. But the older curriculum, virtually all specifically required, had intrinsic merits that could not be ignored. The result of compromise between the two was basically our present curriculum, partly required and partly elective with its basic principles of distribution in the underclass years and concentration in the upperclass years. The result is the American arts college, a unique institution that has developed to meet the needs of our society.

Nineteen years ago [1930] next November the featured speaker at the Missouri State Teachers Association meeting in Kansas City announced that the liberal arts college was through, that its function had been taken over by the high school, and that while some few institutions would limp along for a few years, chiefly because their faculties and administrations could find no other employment, they all would soon have to become professional schools in order to survive. Today this state has three times as many students in liberal arts colleges as it did when that gentleman made his prediction. No new colleges, junior or senior, have developed in Missouri except colleges of the liberal arts. Professional schools themselves are demanding more liberal arts training than ever before in their history and are, in some cases, actually reducing the amount of professional training in order to provide for more work in the liberal arts. Several of our teachers colleges have revised their programs to become, in essence, arts colleges instead of the professional and vocational institutions they were. All in all, a realistic view seems to indicate that like the celebrated report of Mark Twain's death, that of the liberal arts college has been slightly exaggerated.

In fact, the American liberal arts college is the most completely successful institution of higher education of our day. I am speaking, of course, of the colleges as they actually operate on this and other campuses. I make no reference whatever to those mythological institutions for the feebleminded which Hollywood likes to present as the American college or even to those equally imaginary junior country clubs at which *Life* magazine likes so well to go to a party.

William Jewell College on its one hundredth anniversary is at the height of its influence. By all the objective tests one can apply, as well as subjective ones, this college is achieving its purposes more completely now than it has ever done. In general what applies here applies to other institutions with similar objectives. Academic people are highly introspective and critical. If there is one thing about which we are customarily more critical than we are about our democratic form of government, it is our system of education. Perhaps it is well that we are, for it is out of that spirit that we are forced continually to revise our procedures and renew and refine those who are relatively untouched by liberal arts ideals and standards, who rarely see the great woods because of brush and weeds which surround it. It is time that this important fact is recognized—that the general education offered by the liberal arts college has gained more common acceptance and approval than any other type of higher education. It stands today as the most discussed, the most imitated, and the most highly developed type of higher education.

The essential that differentiates American liberal education from professional and vocational training is not difficult to state in general terms. As good a statement as any is that made in 1940 by the Trustees of this College whose anniversary we are celebrating: "We believe that the Liberal Arts College should adhere strictly to its purpose of training for deeper comprehension of the civilization of the past and the civilization of the present in order to train leaders in the civilization of the future."

It is, let me interpret, education for the whole of life, not for part of it. It is Gestalt education, if we may borrow a psychological term. In the words of Montaigne, what we are training is "not the scholar but the man." Certainly, it is vocational education in a very fundamental sense, based upon the faith that breadth and depth of training in fundamentals is better for a life's vocation than narrower specialization. The liberal arts are aimed not at any narrow range of skills but at the development of "rich and many-sided personalities," as a national commission expressed it in the thirties.

It is education, too, that takes into consideration the fact that students and people differ in ability, interest, and in the backgrounds with which they come to college. It does not, therefore, assume that the best education for each person is the same, but attempts to adapt the college experience to the individual for the most effective education. It is not a program committed to one single approach. It supports no panacea, whether it be presentism, classicism, or great books. It is education that recognizes that the world is changing rapidly and that a skill useful today may be useless next year, but that real education is not something that

new discoveries or changed laws can destroy. It is also an education that helps each individual to arrive at a satisfactory and
satisfying code of ethics—one that is based upon principle and
which cannot be destroyed by the winds of material change.
Liberal arts education is fulfilling its purpose when it increases
one's disinterested self-discipline and enables a person to change
and adjust to changed conditions within a framework of an acceptable code of ethical behavior.

When liberal education is available on the college level, it
is clear that only the student who has native ability and emotional
drive considerably above the average can take reasonable advantage of it. On the college level it is education for prospective
leaders and other highly trained workers. Our facilities for liberal
arts education in college are not available in such a degree that
we can afford to squander them upon students who show little
promise of playing a significant role in society.

The liberal arts are not, to put it negatively, a specific body of
content or courses. Rather, they are a group of qualities that a
college tries to develop in students. These qualities represent
changes in our students, both of degree and kind, which teaching
tries to bring about. We try to develop these qualities in many
ways: not only through the organized curriculum, but also through
the artistic, civic and religious activities of campus life, and
through examples of intellectual integrity and moral worth on the
part of the faculty.

But we do need science. As Cardinal Newman wrote, "A
liberal education teaches us to see things as they are." There are
facts, principles, and theories that no liberally educated person
can ignore, and many of them lie in the realm of science. Dean
Gauss has pointed out that the truth often lies in making many
fine distinctions, and it is exact knowledge that enables one to
make such discriminations, or to know when they cannot be made.
The strictest regard for the claims of evidence and the suppression
of all wishful thinking are habits and traits whose development

is part of a liberal education, and the natural sciences are a useful, indeed a necessary, means to this end.

Certainly as important as our understanding of natural laws is our understanding of human society. It is basic to a liberal education, and it cannot be separated entirely from a system of values. We have often stated our purpose in the social science area as preventing ignorant change and undercutting ignorant opposition to change. Important as this is, it is essentially negative in its approach. There are two positive qualities here that a liberal education tries to develop in the behavior of its recipients.

First, it tries to develop the most scientific understanding of society that scholarship has to offer. The liberally educated man understands a large range of these concepts and they condition his thinking and acting about his own role in society. He habitually sees society with perspective in time; he has some basic knowledge of the principles of government, anthropology, economics, sociology and social psychology. He is not an expert in all of them or any one of them, perhaps, but he is familiar with their basic concepts and guides his action accordingly. As in science, we try to develop the attitude of mind that has the strictest regard for the laws of evidence, but we also recall to him Aristotle's principle, that "It is the mark of an educated man to expect no more exactness than the subject permits." Plato cannot teach us much about atomic fission, but he can help us arrive at the questions to ask about it in order to determine what we as a society should do about it. The liberally educated man has sufficient understanding of how people in groups behave to be suspicious, if not absolutely immune, to panaceas that are involved in totalitarian concepts of history and human destiny. The one master cause concept, the supreme panacea, is always a great temptation in teaching social science, for it is easy to teach, comforting to believe, and requires little intellectual energy to understand. But it is highly unscholarly, and dangerous to democratic progress. There is no magic in the area of social science, and the belief that there is constitutes the greatest danger to democratic government. One of the greatest of our popular humorists once remarked, "A man that'd expict to train lobsters to fly in a year is called a loonytic; but a man that thinks men can be turned into angels by an election is called a reformer an' remains at large." Developing mature understandings of how people and societies behave is one of the most difficult tasks of the college of liberal arts.

In addition, a liberal education tries to develop citizens who are fit leaders for our great society. This is one of the great justifications of a liberal education in a democracy. It was the chief motive behind Thomas Jefferson's efforts to bring the study of law into the university, because he saw that for several generations, at least, the lawyer was going to be the political leader. He had observed that the lawyers who were not college trained were frequently unfit leaders of a democracy, because the narrow vocational law they had studied in some practicing lawyer's office had done little to give them a perspective upon society, a sound knowledge of government, or a code of ethics that was essential to the leadership in a democracy.

In a democracy all citizens are rulers, and the few with natural ability and adequate training are leaders, or must be if democracy is to be both democratic and efficient. A liberal education must not only inform about government; it must develop democratic values and benefits, and it must produce the willingness and ability to lead in the common tasks of citizenship.

Finally, there are the value-establishing humanities, which give real and vicarious experience in arriving at standards. It is not here alone this is done, but the humanities provide us with our greatest opportunities. To be a rich and many-sided personality, a person must have a system of values, a philosophy of life. He must have a perspective upon the present, and understand the tradition in which he lives just as truly as he must understand the basic facts of nature.

It is not enough to have knowledge: to know facts, theories, and principles. A liberal education is dedicated to the cultivation of a *good* man. Here is centered the search for values in the experience we give our students. The student learns to appreciate the values in his own tradition and society, and to test these values against those of philosophy, literature, and religion. We can sum up the purposes of the humanities in a search for ethics and aesthetics, the good and the beautiful. Goethe saw their supreme place in a liberal education when he wrote: "A teacher who can arouse a feeling for one single good action, for one single good poem, accomplishes more than he who fills our memories with row on row of natural objects, classified with name and form."

No person comes to a full moral stature until he has examined and tested his inherited principles. Probably the best place to test them is against a different set held by a different advanced civilization. This need is what gives such value to the study of Athenian civilization, because of all historic societies it provides the best mirror to hold up to our own. But there are other mirrors —codes of conduct approved but never fully realized, utopias imagined by the poets and other prophets, the paradises of the world's religions.

To this must be added such experience as colleges can give their students in testing moral and aesthetic ideas against the realities of life. This is the most difficult of all perhaps, and our opportunities come from art, music, and literature. It is here that great teaching is most needed, for it is here that the real test of the liberal arts takes place. *Antigone* in a poor teacher's hands may be merely a dull exercise in translating Greek words, but in the hands of a master it can be an immense personal catharsis from which the student gains moral and intellectual stature.

The greatest weakness that prevails in arts colleges here is uninspired teaching and the identification of literary and artistic scholarship as the only aspects of art and literature that are part of a liberal education. We make the same mistake in the humanities that we do in the sciences when we assume that our courses are to prepare students for advanced scholarly study, and forget the fundamental reason why they are in the curriculum. There is an unassailable place for scholarship in a liberal education, but it does not rule out art, faith, or emotional experience.

The great basis of scholarship in the liberal arts is what gives depth to its training plan—the field of concentration, more commonly called the major and minor. No separation between this and the other objectives of the arts college is possible or desirable, and all the qualities should continue to be developed in all parts of the program. It is in this field where the student finds his greatest motivation that depth of scholarship and wisdom are most readily developed. Here also is where vocational education is most clearly evident in our plan of liberal education, for the students' choices in this field have close and definite relations to prospective vocations. There is nothing undesirable here; certainly, if the choice is well made, and the vocation later followed, it is highly desirable.

But the field of concentration is not disguised vocationalism or professionalism; rather, it is the plan by which we attempt to give depth to the educational experience of each liberal arts student. The fundamentals of student interest apply here, and the student elects to follow up that which has touched him most deeply, and to become a master of that. It is good teaching and guidance to have him follow his own interest, because it motivates his exploration in one area of scholarship and carries him far deeper into understanding or creative experience. Here the well taught arts student acquires an appreciation of scholarship, here he follows his interests as far as he can carry them into literature, or philosophy, or physics, or art, or mathematics. To him it is the mastery that will give the greatest real satisfaction in life, whether he or she later becomes a journalist, a lawyer, a minister, a public official, a housewife, or perchance a teacher of that very subject.

The weakness here of most liberal arts colleges is a tendency to lose sight of the main purposes of a liberal education and to make the specialization a variety of professionalism. Many colleges have become small universities in which each department is a professional school with little or no commitment to the purposes of a liberal education. In many cases, especially noticeable in some of the science fields, and in art and music, they frequently do become narrowly professional, and in some cases actually give less of the liberal arts to their students than some of the best of the professional schools. This is a tendency contrary to the spirit of a liberal education against which we must be constantly on our guard. It is one of the basic weaknesses in the college of liberal arts as it exists today. Through lack of faith in its own program, and through the desire to meet the competition of vocational training for students we have tended strongly to go over to professionalism, not alone in the area of the major but even in the courses taught to meet the distribution requirement.

Another weakness of considerable magnitude is the purposelessness of much of our arts college teaching. We in the liberal arts are not alone guilty of this, but with us it is, I believe a greater evil. It arises from our failure to be clear as to what our purposes are. It leads to purely factual teaching and testing, and has, I believe, grown much worse since the objective test became popular, useful as that is in its proper place. We must be more careful that we insure that our courses, and, indeed, our individual classes, are a means of changing students in the direction of the qualities we are agreed that leaders in American society need.

The other major weakness in our present practice that I wish to emphasize is our failure to adapt our programs to the individual interest and ability of our students. While it is true that we receive a highly selected group, that does not mean that they have similar interests or abilities. We are particularly inclined to ignore the differences in high school education, which varies more today than it ever did before. It is not that we do not temper the academic wind to the weaker among our students as it is that we do not challenge the very able to the maximum of their possible development. We set our standards too much to the average and fail to differentiate in a way that would make for greater progress with our more able group who have the real potentiality of leadership.

These, then, are the main features of liberal education today. The liberal arts college is at the height of its influence as an educational institution. Through its peculiar American forms it is achieving in a reasonable measure the high expectations we have of it, when we are realistic in our psychology of learning. But it has many weaknesses that should challenge us all to its improvement. It is tending strongly to abandon its birthright for a type of professionalism. Much of what we are doing in the liberal arts college is characterized by a lack of clearly defined purpose, and degenerates into relatively meaningless factual teaching, and our provisions for caring for the individual differences and interests of students are far below what they should be. The improvement of our programs in these particulars should be the immediate task of all of us to whom has been committed the future of the American college of liberal arts.

11

The Needs of Higher Education in Missouri

THE DEMAND for higher education is going up at an increasing rate. This increase is not the result of an idle demand of our young people and their parents but it arises from the fact that more and more of our occupations require increased education and training. Numerous occupations that are now professional or semi-professional did not require such training and education a few years ago. No one can foresee where this trend will end, but certainly in our lifetime it is going to mean that a larger part of our people are going to have some college education.

We must add to this trend the fact that, while today there are fewer than eight million in our population who are of college age, by 1970 there will be nearly fourteen million. And whereas there are two and a half million students in colleges and universities

Delivered before the Springfield, Missouri, Chamber of Commerce, January 10, 1955.

now, by 1970 there can hardly be less than four and a half million. In fact some careful estimates indicate that there may be six and a half million.

Anyone who studies seriously the problems of higher education from the standpoint of the needs of a state, like ours, must realize that this problem is not a small one. He must realize too that the demand for university and college training will swamp all our institutions, public and private, over the next fifteen years unless we plan carefully what we are going to do.

Missouri is fortunate in that it is well supplied with colleges and universities, both public and private, which are well distributed geographically. This is important because by far the most economical and efficient way of meeting our present and future needs is the expansion of existing institutions, not the addition of new ones. And by expansion I mean not the multiplication of programs in a college, as we have often done in the past, but the concentration on one or a few programs and the multiplication of students wanting these programs. This is particularly true of the very small college which in the past has frequently wasted its narrow resources trying to be all things to all kinds of students. Many, for instance, have spent relatively large sums trying to meet the standards of the American Chemical Society for training chemists and in the end found themselves still not able to meet these standards, and with a mere handful of students in that area.

In the past colleges have had a to compete for students, as most were under-enrolled for efficient operation. Most private colleges in this state would improve in efficiency with a 50 per cent increase in enrollment. But many of these colleges cannot expand much beyond that without very large additional funds in the form of gifts. After enrollment reaches a point of efficient operation, private colleges have to raise new funds for each new student that are about twice what the student pays in tuition. Because of this the possibility of increases here are limited for that type of college.

The availability of public funds and the ability of the public to make their needs felt will result in the public colleges and universities carrying the heaviest part of the great increase in students. One can anticipate that it will work like it did among universities after World War II. The large private university admitted as many students as it felt its plant and staff could care for—usually about 20 per cent more than before the war—and then turned down the other applicants. The public universities then felt under compulsion to care for all who came who could find housing, and on a make-shift basis did care for them. At the University of Missouri the enrollment reached twice the previous high.

There is one place where some new institutions can well be added. These will be public junior colleges, which because they permit students to live at home, can give two years of college at the lowest possible cost. Cities of 25,000 population and up which are without public or private colleges can and in several instances will, I believe, establish junior colleges in the next ten years, and that will help with our problem.

An approaching crisis in higher education in Missouri is based simply upon the fact that we do not spend the amount of money on higher education that other states spend. In 1953, for instance, Missouri spent $5.08 per capita for public higher education. Forty states spent more than that, and only Kentucky and certain New England states with many more private colleges and universities, spent less. Colorado spent three times as much; Kansas, Nebraska and Iowa two and a half times as much; Oklahoma twice as much. All of the states of the Deep South spent more per capita than Missouri. This situation and the tradition that goes with it, makes Missouri's problem especially acute because such low expenditures leave us at the beginning of a great expansion with our staffs and plants in the public institutions already stretched to the point where there is no margin left.

The principles of economy and efficiency in our planning make it desirable to go beyond state lines. The states from New Mexico to Montana have an inter-state agreement whereby the University of Colorado provides medical education for the medical students from all states, the states favored in turn paying some of the cost. A group of southern states have a reciprocal arrangement which covers medicine, dentistry, veterinary medicine, and several other fields. Other areas have regional compacts.

At the end of World War II veterinary schools were flooded with applicants and consequently many of them refused to admit any but state residents. In Missouri the General Assembly, on its own initiative, appropriated funds to expand the two-year school in the University of Missouri to a full four-year school. Minnesota also established a new school as did some other states. But now in both states we are reaching the point where our previous lack of veterinarians has been caught up, and our livestock industry is no longer suffering to the extent that it was. At the same time Arkansas and Nebraska lack training facilities. Taking a long-range view there exists in this region schools enough to educate the needed veterinarians. But our exclusion of out-of-state students may force other states to set up new schools. If new schools are set up in each state we will have tooled up more than we need to produce veterinarians and wasted valuable funds.

It would be far better for all concerned if we could make some reciprocal arrangements among states whereby uneconomic duplication can be prevented. There are many professional schools such as dentistry, pharmacy, and architecture that the University of Missouri does not have. Rather than build those, we could more economically trade with others.

It is this type of professional education, especially on the advanced level, that is so costly. Medicine, with its needs for clinical facilities and the necessity of paying high salaries for physicians to serve as teachers, is especially expensive. Veterinary medicine is not far behind. Agriculture, engineering, and all sound, advanced graduate work costs many more times than undergraduate general education.

For these reasons the greatest burden of this great increase in enrollment, in a financial sense at least, will fall on the universities. The burden for this in Missouri will fall primarily upon the University of Missouri although the private universities will bear some of it. Engineering is an example of an expensive, but far from the most expensive, professional training. On the two campuses of the University of Missouri [Columbia and Rolla] we have 2,500 students in engineering—over 65 per cent of the total in this state. Because of defense needs and because the countries behind the Iron Curtain are now training scientists and engineers at a rate higher than we are in the United States, the defense agencies of the Federal Government are appealing for vast increases in these enrollments. They have increased 50 per cent at Missouri in the last two years. They may well double by 1960. If this happens it will mean that we will have over 5,000 engineering students on the University's two campuses. The need in the way of buildings and staff will not go up that fast but it will increase greatly.

The most difficult aspect of the problem to solve is not that of plant but one of staff. The problem grows out of growth in size, but more because the inflationary economics of the day make professorial salaries lag far behind those of business, industry and government, and other types of government positions. We must be able to compensate our present staff better in order that we can hold them against offers from industry and from universities where more funds are available. Even more important, we need funds to use in the job market for young professors, in order to attract people of top quality, not only into college teaching but also college teaching at Missouri. Unfortunately our history of this in the years since the war has not been good. We have fallen behind relative to other universities until our competitive salary position is at the lowest point in our history as a large university.

We now rank behind several state universities in our salary scales, which we had always exceeded until a very few years ago. Unless the requests now before the General Assembly are met, we will fall still further behind next year and the year after.

Second only to the problem of staff is that of classroom and laboratories. Our situation at Columbia is essentially this. The Red and White campuses were originally constructed for about 4,000 students. Since the war we have added some five new buildings such as Hill Hall for Education, and new agriculture and chemistry buildings. But our main reliance to meet the needs of 1954 has been the use of army barracks and such old rooming houses as became available to us to convert into classrooms, laboratories and offices. The situation at the School of Mines is similar.

Rather than detail present needs which are stated in our appropriations requests, I might better indicate the seriousness of our immediate future, stating the adjustments we are making to care for our present enrollments within the income we are now receiving. During the last two years we have attempted to live on our operating budgets by securing funds beyond our legislative appropriations from various sources. Most important of all we raised student fees 35 per cent. We have reduced the number of our faculty in several instances and dropped the less needed programs and courses wherever possible in order to save funds from our teaching budget. We have intensified our search for outside funds for research purposes, and these are now at an all time high in the university's history.

In order to make our classroom and laboratories handle our present enrollment we were forced to reinstitute the post-war 7:30 class schedules, which gives us, I believe, the highest usage time of our facilities of any university in the country. The most disastrous step we have had to take is allowing our salary scales to decline relatively to other universities.

With our academic belt this tight we face the prospect of a greatly increased demand for university education from Missouri young people. Unless we have substantial increases in income, it is difficult to see how we can satisfy that need—difficult to see how we can avoid denying admission to many students.

At the University of Indiana where they are more accustomed to large scale building than we are, their experience shows that it takes five years from the appropriation for a new major building to its occupation for educational uses. Major buildings needed in 1960 must be authorized in the coming General Assembly in order to insure that they will be available in time. Truly it is later than we think!

12

Responsibility for the Superior Student

PUBLIC education has been under attack during the past five
years and more—an attack that is marked by an almost party-
line viciousness which condemns every change that has been made
during the past fifty years. Virtually all of the attack applies to
private and parochial education as well. No one familiar with
schools can read much of it without the conviction that most of
these writers have seen no classrooms since they finished school
and that the observations are extremely remote from the reality
of what goes on in the school and in the classroom. I think we
must admit, though, that such evidence as they do cite is from
starry-eyed writers of some faddish belief in education who have
made wild generalizations about what should be in schools with

Delivered before the Educational Policies Commission at the convention of the
American Association of School Administrators in St. Louis, February 27, 1955.

little or no contact of what goes on in actual classrooms. Like the rest of you I have read much of this literature in the past several years and have been uniformly impressed by its lack of correspondence to what I have seen in high school and college classes. The defenses of the schools against such attacks have been reasonably adequate. We are doing the best job in our history for the great majority of students and for that matter, the best job any school system in the world does for that large group. We have, however, had one weakness that has handicapped our defense. That weakness is that we in the high schools and in the colleges are not doing very well by the distinctly superior student. As an earlier publication of the Educational Policies Commission pointed out, "waste of talent has occurred in the past and is occurring at present." I think the reasons why are easily explained and I will not take time to discuss them here but an explanation is not necessarily a justification. In our concern for the education of all Americans we have lost sight of the need for a superior education for the most able. This is the one place where many European secondary schools are superior to our own. Because they restrict their attention to that top group, cut the pattern of their curriculum and teaching to it and ignore the larger group, they have less of a problem of adaptation to the superior student.

One situation that points up the seriousness of this problem relates to our teaching of science, mathematics and engineering. While our colleges of engineering are growing rapidly because the demands from industry are overwhelming, national defense interests are also heavily involved. It is clear that many of our leaders in Washington in the best position to understand, believe the Soviet school system is turning out twice as many engineers and scientists as we are and in an era of mechanized and scientific warfare that has implications that are not strictly educational. With this problem facing us our situation is indeed a difficult one because mathematics and science teaching in the high schools, and certainly the smaller colleges, is in a far from good condition.

The teacher training institutions, including the large universities, are preparing very few teachers in science for high schools chiefly because the incomes from industrial employment are so much greater than those from teaching.

I use the needs of science and engineering because they are easy to spotlight at this moment. But as educators we all know that the needs in other fields, while not so obvious in the market place, are just as great in terms of real American needs. Our problem is where are these superior students to come from if we are to take full advantage of our potentialities?

It seems to me they are to come primarily from two sources. It is a well-known situation that only about half of the top one-third of high school students go on to colleges and universities. The other half, because of a lack of motivation or funds, do not secure more formal training. Another group which does start college or university, because of a lack of motivation or financial resources or both, drop out in the first or second year. While most of these last are people of relatively low ability, there is a fair percentage of high ability students among them who simply do not have high motivation or sufficient industry. There are certain steps we could take looking toward a much tighter coordination of college and high school in the area of adapting education to the superior student and thereby increasing our supply of highly educated specialists and leaders. The European schools are solely for this student. They require of him twice as much academic work as we do of our high school students. It is relatively easy for them to do this as all students are treated alike and those who cannot measure up fall out. As the countries of Western Europe are accustomed to an oversupply of professional men, they are not so concerned with the loss of talent. But our dynamic economy puts such a premium on technical competence that we need to treasure all the talent we have.

I am not unconscious of the difficulties of trying to maintain two or more standards of work in the same school but I am sure that in both high school and college we ought to move in the direction of more challenging work for the superior student as far and as fast as we can. Programs of various kinds have been started on an experimental basis over the country including rapid promotion and early entrance to college for the very superior student and college credit for extra work in certain specified courses in high schools where the examinations are set by the university. All of these plans are based upon a belief for which there is considerable evidence that for the really brilliant student the time in going through high school and college could be reduced by as much as two years. It would be safer to say for some it could be reduced by two years and for others, one.

We all need to recognize that as the great new surge of students comes into the senior high school and college, this problem of adaptation is made more difficult. With great enrollment pressures, teacher shortages, and restricted plants, diversified programs become more difficult to administer. But our needs are great and our resources of talent limited. Neither the high school nor the college can make much progress alone. A much closer integration of high school and college work for the superior student is clearly the best answer here and I do not know that any of the plans now being used are inherently superior to any other. I have a measure of hope that we can evolve plans that will save for the professions of teaching, engineering, medicine and others, many of the top third of the high school students who now do not even arrive at college. Certainly some of their lack of motivation growing out of their school experience must be involved in the lack of challenge to superior minds of the regular program. Then I hope also that the colleges can adapt themselves to these better educated high school graduates and develop plans of their own to save those drop-outs who have high ability.

The appeal I would like to leave with you is a plea for a much higher degree of integration between high school and college in the education of the superior student, one which will see to it that our professional and scholarly needs for the future will be adequately supplied from our reserve of superior talent.

13

The Role of Higher Education in
Meeting the Teacher Shortage

THE PROBLEM of teacher supply is of deep concern to all
collegiate institutions in the State. All of the state institutions
and all of the private colleges prepare teachers for the public and
private schools. Historically the church related colleges have educated on the bachelor's level a small majority of our supply of
high school teachers, and the state institutions have educated a
large minority of the high school teachers and a great majority
of the elementary school teachers. This pattern has changed
recently only to the extent that more church related colleges have
begun to prepare elementary school teachers and help supply the
great need at that level. The responsibility for action in the
present crisis is not one for the state institutions alone, but it is a
joint responsibility for all institutions which have looked to the
public schools for the employment of their graduates in the past.

Delivered before the Sixth Annual Public Awareness Institute, Park College, October 12, 1955.

The problem of a supply of competent teachers for the elementary and the secondary schools is one of the most serious that we face in the country, and it is a problem that is especially acute in our region. For three years in succession now the enrollments in our schools nationally have increased a million and a half and they will continue to increase so long as we can be certain—which is the next six years.

In an almost comical fashion, as we look at it, our statisticians have been saying for the last several years that the crest of the wave will reach the first grade in six years—always expecting, and perhaps hoping, that the birth rate would level off next year and present some relief from this problem. That, however, is an assumption that I gravely suspect is not well founded. I have vivid memories of the Hoover report issued in the thirties on *Recent Social Trends* which based all its recommendations on a predicted declining birth rate and in substance advised potential primary teachers to consider changing their careers into some occupation concerned with caring for the elderly. These predictions that six years from now birth rates will level off or begin to decline may or may not be true, but the assumption that they will is a carry-over from the kind of thinking on population growth that characterized the Hoover Commission Report.

There are many ways of approaching the status of the teacher shortage. Perhaps as good as any other is the fact that for last year there were 80,000 teachers in the United States teaching on "emergency certificates." That is, there were 80,000 teachers with somewhat less than our rather low standard of teacher qualifications at work in the schools and this number was an increase over the year before. Similarly, the National Education Association reports that if all the 1955 college graduates who are prepared for teaching enter that work, there will be just enough for replacements of those who drop out but none at all for the increased enrollment. If Missouri could attract as many teachers from outside as it loses to other states, it would be a bit better off here than the national average. The Office of the Commissioner of Education estimates that last year we graduated a little more than enough for replacements. When we take into account however, that only two-thirds of those prepared to teach in Missouri colleges actually enter the profession, it is easy to see that these graduates are not enough for replacement of those who normally retire and would leave no margin whatever for the increased enrollment.

This will certainly be true over the next several years unless we change the trends that now exist in our college enrollment picture. The Research Division of the State Teachers Association estimates that Missouri will need about 22,000 new elementary and high school teachers in the next five years, or an average of 4,500 each year. Last year we graduated 1,500 or just one-third of the projected demand, and only two-thirds of whom actually taught for a year or more.

Moreover, we know that we lose a great many of our graduates to other states. A study of the State Teachers Association last year showed that 30 per cent of the graduates prepared to teach in state-supported colleges accepted positions in other states. At the University of Missouri we made a follow-up study of these teachers and found, as expected, that most of them report that relative salary was a major factor in their decisions to leave Missouri. They have been doing this for many years and unless we can improve our salaries and other conditions of work in the state, our teacher shortage will grow worse instead of better.

We must begin with the declaration that universities and colleges of the State cannot solve this problem alone. There must also be a concentrated effort on the part of the school districts and the State as well. If school teaching in Missouri is not an attractive career in terms of prestige, respect and income—nothing the colleges can do will develop an adequate supply of competent teachers. These are matters for the public and our function is limited as citizens to working for these conditions, and as educators in seeing that our own students and graduates are well aware of these needs.

No one can doubt, however, that one of the chief problems in Missouri is that in addition to our immediate graduates, many experienced teachers leave our state for greener pastures elsewhere, perhaps 3,000 a year or about twice the number graduated from our colleges last year. Were it not that Missouri gains substantial numbers of teachers from states to the south of us, our situation would be much worse. In a study made by the University in 1948 it was shown that of the women who had stopped teaching in the state that year, 28 per cent were teaching in other states, and of the men 45 per cent were teaching in other states. The principal reason given for leaving was higher salaries, the mean increase by the change being reported as $900. We should not overlook the fact that many who left teaching stayed in Missouri in better paying non-teaching jobs.

There are many things that the schools themselves can do to help alleviate the shortage and supply themselves with competent teachers. They can re-arrange schedules and non-teaching duties in ways to make teaching a more attractive way of life. Undoubtedly there are schools so well administered that they cannot be improved, but as in our colleges and universities, I suspect we have many fine teachers handicapped by a mass of routine duties that could better be performed by less well-trained persons. Dr. Fuson's recent article in *School and Community* gave some indication that Missouri high school teachers are more burdened than most with non-teaching duties. Our school administrators should be constantly on the alert to make maximum use of the teaching talent they have.

One of the things that handicap the complete professionalization of teaching is its temporary character for many people. By increases in salaries, providing better retirement plans, arranging sick leave and reducing non-teaching duties, they can hold their competent teachers longer than they now do. These measures will help to hold teachers against leaving to take jobs in business, the temptress that entices away more of our teachers than the salaries in other states.

Schools can do more to seek out and re-employ former teachers with good qualifications. Some of those who have dropped out for marriage could well be induced to come back, providing they have no small children. Something—not much perhaps, but something—could be done in larger centers to provide less than full-time positions for married women who cannot work quite full time outside their home.

Nevertheless, with all the schools can do it is true the universities and colleges hold the key position in solving this problem as they do in supplying the members of all other professions. Colleges that train teachers are well aware that the only permanent solution of this problem is to prepare well-qualified teachers who are committed to teaching as a career.

They realize that short-run emergency measures, while necessary to meet the crisis, may—unless they are well considered—handicap this long-range permanent solution. It takes a long time to educate a superior teacher. There are no short cuts, and substitutes for good teachers do not exist.

Let me suggest some methods which are not exhaustive and certainly are not new, but which I believe will help.

First and foremost, we must persuade more college students to enter teaching as a profession. Many factors are involved here and some of the basic ones go down into the high school. In order to provide early contact with teaching as a profession, there are organized in this state Future Teachers of America clubs in our teacher training colleges and in a number of our high schools. In the high schools these are the counterpart of the science clubs and the agriculture clubs. It seems unquestioned that these should be promoted more vigorously especially at the high school level. A recent report showed that there are fifty chapters in Missouri high schools having approximately 1,000 members. This is a disappointingly small number and certainly is a situation that should and must be improved if we are going to recruit an adequate number of teachers for our schools. Colleges which train teachers should assume the responsibility for sponsoring and encouraging these chapters in the high schools of the State—provide them with assistance and even leadership so that the clubs will give young people an adequate professional orientation and result in bringing desirable candidates into the colleges and universities that train teachers. The college campus clubs can be useful in a similar way. Colleges now receive as students about half of the top third of the high school graduates. It is among this half that do not now come that we must look more assiduously for new prospects for teachers. The half of this group contains many more girls than boys and they are our chief hope of recruiting adequate numbers of well-qualified people.

Colleges might consider, too, more adequate use of their scholarship plans in this direction. I am convinced that we are not doing a very good job of assigning our scholarships to those students who could not otherwise go to college. If we did, we might have a substantial number for the good students presently overlooked who do not actually enter college and become a prospect for the teaching profession. We could expand greatly these scholarships by appeals to philanthropic individuals, the great foundations and to large corporations. We have several large corporations giving generous scholarships for many different college specializations, but can you recall any specifically for teachers?

Another matter that is somewhat intangible but nevertheless of equal importance I believe, is the possibility of increasing the prestige and dignity of the profession of teaching on our campuses. The college that rewards superior teaching, the campus where the most effective teacher is the most admired will do more to make careers in teaching seem attractive to undergraduates than even well-organized programs. A student's attitude toward teaching is moulded by the teaching he receives and the esteem with which it is held by others. These carry a conviction of its value as a profession to society that no exhortation can equal. One problem with high school teacher training that needs immediate attention in the colleges is the training of science teachers. We are not now preparing enough to satisfy a small fraction of our needs. There is no place for them to come from in satisfactory numbers except from the science classes in the colleges. The supply of these teachers is so short in the high school that little immediate help is coming from that quarter in terms of students entering college already determined to become science teachers. But, we have large groups of students in all our science classes in college. It is no credit to us that virtually none of these are inspired to go into science teaching at least at the high school level. Of course, we can say that industry and research agencies take all the supply. Certainly it is true that private industry, which is now complaining about the lack of science and engineering graduates from colleges, has by its employment of our science graduates at salaries higher than teachers' salaries helped to kill the goose that lays its golden eggs of research and engineering manpower.

But regardless of the causes, there is no prospect in sight equal to the inspiration in the science classroom and laboratory for developing a badly needed supply of science teachers for the high school. The situation in mathematics is nearly as bad and it is growing worse in the field of foreign languages.

Every college campus should be a key factor in improving this situation. Both the denominational and the state college should oppose the materialistic drive of most students and their parents toward the larger income professions. I do not believe that in our lifetime the financial returns from teaching will equal or exceed those from business, medicine and law. They will be more stable but common sense indicates they will remain somewhat lower and in times of inflation they will lag behind many other groups. The Census Bureau recently announced that college graduates earned during their careers $100,000 more than non-college graduates. Such a statement has almost no meaning, of course, to a teacher whose extra hundred thousand dollars in his career is somewhat less than visible. If the difference in income between teaching and other learned professions is not too great it may not be too disastrous an influence. For if we recruited for our teachers large numbers who came solely because it paid better salaries than other professions, certainly we would lose a great deal of the idealism that has always marked the teaching profession. Teaching, like the ministry must, it seems to me, carry a large measure of idealism. I hesitate to say this because we all know it has been used to justify the low salaries for teachers that are dangerous to the future of our children. But the idea that the profession in society that pays the largest income is the most reputable and deserving is an idea that all educational institutions should oppose.

Colleges and universities can further assist in supplying qualified teachers for the schools by helping local schools in recruiting them from college graduates who did not plan to teach or who for one reason or another did not teach after they graduated. In the case of the former, they need professional education, and in the case of both groups they need refresher training to make them high grade teachers. Each college can seek out such individuals especially in its own community, arrange classes for them during the regular year and summer school. It is impossible to estimate how many temporary or permanent members could be added to the teaching profession by such methods but the prospects are good enough that colleges have an obligation to try. The U. S. Department of Labor estimates that there are a half million women college graduates under fifty-four years of age with no children less than five years old who are not now employed. If such procedures were used effectively, they might bring into the ranks of teachers many competent people but it will take a program and publicity to make these potential teachers aware of the possibilities. This our colleges and universities should assume.

Colleges, too, can bring summer session opportunities to at least the married teachers and prospective teachers in their communities. Married women whom we recruit to teach in the schools are usually in need of refresher or additional training and because of the responsibilities of their family find it impossible to attend a summer session a great distance from home. All colleges can do a service by providing this training in their community. In some instances universities might well establish extension centers in larger communities where colleges do not exist in order to care for a substantial group of such potential teachers.

How well we can do these simple and common sense things in our colleges and universities and how well our school districts can improve the attractiveness of teaching as a career will determine whether we can solve these problems without more heroic measures. But if these fail to recruit an adequate staff of teachers there is only one other way we can do it and that is—have a recruiting program based upon scholarships that will be given to students in return for a commitment that they will teach for a definite term in the State. This is a plan that has been tried in the field of medicine to secure doctors for rural areas with what are apparently quite satisfactory results. Mississippi pioneered this plan for rural doctors and some other states have followed. So far as I know only one state has tried this in the field of teaching. Virginia in 1948 established a plan which provided, for those who could qualify, a scholarship of about half the cost of a college education. The student committed himself to pay this back by a year of teaching for each year of scholarship. The latest report was that 96 per cent had worked off their scholarships or are working them off by teaching—this being over an eight year period. It is easy to understand how such a plan could be used in recruiting into teaching a large number of our able young women, especially, who do not now go to college. But we must be realistic and understand that state money for such a plan would come from funds that might go to schools directly, and by improving conditions there, improve the supply of teachers and the quality of the instruction in that way.

Dean Lindley J. Stiles of the School of Education of the University of Wisconsin has proposed a similar but more generous scholarship plan for teachers to be paid for by the National Government. Dean Stiles writes, "It is futile to continue to hope that sufficient numbers of young people of ability who can now afford to go to college will choose to enter teaching."

If Dean Stiles is correct that our present procedures are futile, I have no doubt that in the end we will have to go to some such plan. But its adoption would be an admission that our salary scales are going to remain too low to secure a high quality staff. With the new Foundation School Program in Missouri, I have faith that we can solve our problem without resort to such measures but to do so will require more determination and more imaginative planning on the part of the state, the school districts and the colleges, than we have had. If we can secure these, I believe that we can solve our problems without resort to a government scholarship plan. If we fail, some form of this plan is the only line to which we can retreat.

These are the principal measures that the colleges and universities should employ to help solve the teacher shortage. The education of a generation that will face more serious problems than our own is dependent upon the solution of the problem. Our professional responsibilities require that we bend every possible effort in this direction.

14

The Responsibility of the Educated

MOST commencement speakers start their thoughts on what to say, by taking a resolution that they will do something different. They will not do the same thing most commencement speakers do, namely, talk of the great problems that face a new college graduate. They make this resolution, and then even as I, they tell the graduate about the great problems he faces. What is there to say on an occasion such as this except to remind you of your duty and the major tasks you face in carrying it out?

What are these responsibilities? It is only possible to suggest some basic ones. It is important that you remember that you are an advantaged group. If our society cannot expect a superior performance from you, then indeed we are in a tragic state. What I

Commencement address delivered to the State University of Iowa, February 4, 1956.

should like you to do this morning is to dedicate yourself to repay your great debt to your country and your society, by bringing it in closer harmony with its ideals. This means facing reality clearly, and it means taking action courageously.

I will try to indicate a few of the areas where it seems to me that a better perspective is needed in order to make our nation better, more realistically based upon fact and more resolutely oriented toward our major purposes. My examples come from the fields where some of my own work and experience has been. As a university administrator I have been impressed with the irregularities in our programs for research, for certain types of education and even for medical care. Here it seems, too often, sentimentality rather than hard-headed realism determines choices of programs. This usually seems true whether we refer to legislative appropriations or to programs supported from private contributions to a worthy cause.

We see this, for instance, in the higher claims that curative programs of all kinds have over programs that relate to other phases of our life. There is now before the Congress legislation, with a good prospect of passing, that provides federal funds for expanding medical education facilities in our colleges and universities.

Back of it there is no showing that our universities need new facilities for medical education and research, more than we need them for engineering or education, or more than we need them in our libraries or science laboratories. Rather it is the same type of appeal for the relief of the immediately painful, that represents what one can hope is only a preliminary stage of a better public conception of the place of higher education in our social structure.

The problem here is not too different from that related to fundamental and applied research. Applied research in all science has almost the only effective appeal to industry, to the private giver, and to legislative bodies. In spite of all our science teaching in high schools and colleges, in spite of the steady growth of the proportion of our public which has profited from such teaching, as well as from considerable sound popular scientific writing, the appeal here is still all for applied work. This is easily understandable in terms of the American tradition of practicality. Part of this results, no doubt, from our habit of thinking that there is need to justify expenditures in terms which have financial value. Certainly there should be no disparagement of applied research. It would be the height of folly for us not to make use of the discoveries of science to improve the lot of mankind as fast and as far as possible. But behind this overwhelming preference for the applied is a nearly complete lack of appreciation of the purpose of basic research.

As Esther Everette Lape wrote recently:

> When a new drug for treating tuberculosis was found and justly acclaimed, perhaps a few stopped to think back to the research in optics that went into the microscopes that made it possible to see the germ—a visualization essential to understanding the disease. Fewer still perhaps thought of the chemical research on the glass that made possible the optics; or of the development of the stains that aided in visualization of the organism through the glass; or of the method of culture or the fundamental studies in microbial nutrition that made possible the culture media. Yet these and literally thousands of other details constituted the basic research essential to the ultimate "discovery" of the drug.

The discoveries basic to our highly productive hybrid corn, upon which the prosperity of this state depends, were made by scientists working on problems of basic plant genetics having no immediate view toward increasing our food supply. The discoveries basic to this and to atomic energy have been founded upon scientific curiosity and not the solution of a specific practical problem. It is interesting that the figure who stands supreme as our historic dedication to the practical, Benjamin Franklin, also gave us our classic defense of basic research. Watching a balloon ascension in Paris one day, a bystander inquired of him, "What value is it?" to which the great scientist replied, "Of what value is a new-born babe?"

The difference in evaluation is well illustrated by the very significant development of polio vaccine by Dr. Jonas Salk. When Dr. Salk was presented with the Presidential citation recently, like a true scientist, he modestly told a fable that illustrated his dependence upon the work of many other scientists. Dr. Salk has become with justice a national hero, but the scientists as represented by the Nobel Prize Committee, gave their prize to three other scientists who developed the tissue culture techniques for growing the virus.

One must not paint a false picture here by exaggerated emphasis. Such groups as the American Cancer Society are investing heavily in basic studies of growth and cell structure. The establishment of the National Science Foundation in 1950 was a large move in a good direction, even though the Congress supports it less than one might wish. But there is a slowly growing conception that the great need is for more basic knowledge, the scientific capital upon which all of our applied discoveries rest. It is our hope that you graduates of a great university and representing a new generation, will further the conceptions that are developing here.

The condition which under-rates basic research in the sciences, vastly under-rates research in the non-scientific fields of literature, history, religion and philosophy. The resources here are infinitesimal compared with those for science. The reasons are similar. It is difficult to show immediately valuable results. Certainly it is impossible to show financially profitable results from research and investigations in these fields. Are they less important? Only if we accept the concepts that the spiritual and the human are less important than the material, that man's beliefs and loyalties are of less significance than his power over nature, that the amount of power at man's disposal is more important than what man does with that power. None of us is willing to accept these propositions and yet, by our society's choices we endorse them. The funds available for research in humanistic fields are insignificant compared with those in scientific areas. The Federal Government makes no contributions to these ends; business and industry are equally negligent. The American Council of Learned Societies, which encourages research in these areas, has little support relative to the National Research Council which is the parallel organization in scientific fields.

We, as a society, dare not forget that man's philosophy must be equal to the demands that scientific change puts upon it. Each advance of knowledge, each new discovery that increases our power over society or nature carries with it added danger and responsibility. The more we know, the more we see that is fearful and dangerous. Alfred Noyes sees this when he writes:

> Midway between the height that crushes, and the
> Depth that flatters him,
> Man stands within a little ring of light
> He calls his knowledge. Its horizon line,
> The frontier of the dark, was narrow once
> And he could bear it. But the light is growing;
> The ring is widening; and with each increase
> The frontiers of the night are widening too.
> They grow and grow. The very blaze of truth
> That drives them back, enlarges the grim coast
> Of utter darkness.

We neglect the encouragement of investigation and discovery in the humanistic fields at our peril.

Important as it is to our life in the future these concerns are only part of the duty of today's graduate. An example from another field may serve to broaden our perspective. No problem that faces America today is more significant than its relations with the rest of the world both free and unfree, beset as we are with cold wars and the all too real dangers of atomic and nuclear warfare. No one can be conversant with these problems and believe that the answers are simple or easily found. But one can look at them from the standpoint of our policy of dealing with them, and question whether we are using our best methods of promoting our interest in world affairs and our security as a nation and a people.

One of the first weaknesses that strikes an observer is the influence of domestic politics upon foreign policy to the great detriment of our position in world affairs. This is not new. It has been traditional in America, as in most countries, to know little about other countries and to cherish our own nationalism very highly. Our ancestors of Revolutionary times, and the concentration of our attention upon the American Revolution developed, among subsequent generations, highly inflammable anti-British feeling that was re-enforced from many quarters, especially from our large number of citizens of Irish extraction who had inherited other justifiable grievances. As a result, "twisting the tail" of the British lion has been standard campaign procedure in American politics for most of the years since our Revolution. It cost us little prior to 1910 as the world and our place in it was much different then than it has become in recent decades. Let us take one form of it that now has done its damage and threatens us no longer in that same form.

I refer to what became known as McCarthyism. It was my privilege to spend the year 1951-1952 in Europe, teaching at the University of Amsterdam and visiting much of Western Europe, especially Austria and Germany, where the cold war raged. Because of my own interest as a historian, I became intensely interested in the propaganda wars between the West and the Soviet, as they were reflected in the press, radio and in intellectual circles generally. In the process I became very familiar with the United States Information Service, which was the main arm of the United States Government in the cold war. The constant attacks upon it by the local Communists testified as did many other factors, to its influence.

One year later, in the spring of 1953, Mr. Roy Cohn and other representatives of the Senate Committee then headed by Senator McCarthy arrived in Europe with the announced purpose of examining security risks among United States employees and especially to inspect the books in the Information Service libraries. Newspaper representatives were called in and statements were made by Mr. Cohn, charging that the Service was infected with Communists and that the libraries were filled with communist literature. Breathing charges and threats, his party moved rapidly from library to library. Before its arrival librarians, American all, fearfully removed from the shelves numbers of books that were there in large part to prove to Europeans that Americans were not afraid of ideas. The European employees of these libraries and our friends on the European press were astounded and dismayed. "We thought," one said, "Americans were not afraid of anybody." The Communists had a field day; it was their greatest victory of the propaganda war! "Now," they gloated, "American capitalism is shown to be no different from Hitlerism." This and subsequent actions of that senate committee were so harmful to American standing that it may well be that Senator McCarthy harmed our standing in Europe more than we had been able to improve it with the many millions we spent on our Information Service. One of the most effective organs we had developed for use against the great enemy of our way of life had been almost destroyed. The pro-Soviet forces could not have done this. Their efforts in that direction had been singularly ineffective. But sabotage—no other word is adequate—sabotage from home accomplished what the forces of Stalin could not do, and the Communists enjoyed a great victory at our and Western Europe's expense.

Why? The Senator from Wisconsin did not intend to do it! He was merely the demagogue using our foreign affairs in order to cultivate favor and secure power. It was modernized tail twisting, this time, of the Communists. That it gave them their greatest victory in Europe that year, he never understood, or if he did he knew that it would pass unnoticed at home. The real tragedy here is that for the most part he estimated American public opinion correctly. That part of our public which was both informed and influential was relatively so small that the Senator could ignore it with impunity. There is no need now of belaboring an incident that is past. It is only as an extreme example of a general weakness that I use it now.

Let us take a more recent and persistent aspect. American traditional press freedom and enterprise, American partisan politics, all have combined repeatedly in the past two administrations to create incidents, such as Secretary Dulles' recent "Brink of War" quotation, that become weapons against us.

As one of our more level-headed observers, Marquis Childs, remarked about the statement, "Among America's allies it renewed the old fear that the United States would act alone and impulsively with atomic weapons. Western Europe has lived in dread of such unilateral action in Asia. Dulles appears to confirm the deepest apprehension by saying that at least twice on the 'brink of war' the United States planned to use atomic weapons. . . . The harm is done in the further alienation of public opinion not only in Britain but in all Western Europe. Dulles' role as spokesman and champion of American foreign policy is weakened. His unpopularity both in Asia and in Europe is enhanced."

Why are we weakened in this fashion by an intelligent and patriotic public official? Largely because he feels, I think, the impelling necessity of some vigorous defense of his policy, forced on him by partisan politics and political journalism. He therefore unwisely is led into a presentation of recent diplomatic history that in effect weakens the United States' position in the world.

The incident is only one of many in recent years that result from weakness in our means of promoting our international policy. Domestic politics and vigorous news hunting combine to reveal in distorted form information about American policy that undoes much of the good the policy itself has accomplished. It is not so in other countries, and Britain, for example, or Canada, do not find that a vigorous democracy or a free press require that they present themselves before the world as blunderers in policy making, and dangers to the peace of other nations. The difference is in a different tradition of politics and policy.

The solution here is that we must rethink our public affairs in a way that we will not have to burden our policy with these terrific and useless costs. We can without weakening our democratic vigor at home, maintain a strong foreign policy conceived in our national interest and carried out so efficiently that we make full use of every natural advantage that we have! But to do so requires that you, the newer generation of citizens, become more mature in these matters than our generation has been. When we have that maturity among a large group of leaders, then and only then, will our foreign policy statements be phrased solely for the good of the nation's interest, and not for the unthinking and tail twisting mentality of part of our voters.

Times change and many of the things that were suitable for our fathers do not fit the facts and conditions of the new world of modern science and modern international relations. By accepting this education which the State of Iowa and this faculty have helped you to acquire, you have accepted many grave responsibilities. At the risk of triteness, let me add that you inherit a great tradition, wrought out by our ancestors with great difficulty and labor. It is up to each of you to promote and refine that tradition, to preserve and improve the civilization bequeathed to you against the enemies of ignorance, indifference and fear. It is a great time to be alive, yours is the most worthy enterprise in human history, and you are equipped with the best the world can give you for your task. I believe that today we can pledge for you, as that fine lady, the Queen of Great Britain, did for herself and her people at the time of her coronation—"With a new faith in the old and splendid belief given us by our forefathers and the strength to venture beyond the safeties of the past, I know we shall be worthy of our duty."

15

The State University

IN EDUCATION, as in nearly everything else, many changes have taken place the past twenty-five years, and change is going on now at a rapid pace. By way of illustration, twenty-five years ago the two big questions for many university students were (1) How will I pay for my next hamburger? (2) Can I get a job when I graduate? Now the two big questions for many students are (1) Where can I park my car? and (2) Of the several jobs offered me upon graduation, which will I take?

John W. Gardner, President of the Carnegie Corporation, pointed out in *Harper's* for January, 1957, that the hunt for educated talent, while so far having been most noticeable in technical fields, now "extends far beyond technicians and engineers. We are in the midst of a revolution in society's attitude toward talent. For the first time in history men and women of

Address delivered at the Country Club Christian Church, Kansas City, Missouri, January 22, 1957.

high ability and advanced training are not merely finding a market for their gifts; they are being pursued, flattered, and fought over."

Mr. Gardner went ahead to say, "Our present demand for talent is not a mere by-product of prosperity. It is the nature of our society that has churned up the wave of demand—the rapid rate of our technical innovation and the social complexities that have come in its wake. We are only beginning to understand that one of the marks of a modern complex society is an insatiable appetite for educated talent. It is not just technologists and scientists that we need. We desperately need gifted teachers, professional men, scholars, critics, and seers."

One further quotation from Gardner's article: "One of the most important consequences of the rise of educated talent is the wholly new position of colleges and universities in our national life. As the cradle of our national leadership, their role is increasingly weighty and powerful."

The state universities of America represent the highest expression of democratic educational philosophy. It was largely Thomas Jefferson who developed the philosophy of the state university in this country. His writings and his actual planning for the University of Virginia gave the ideological basis for each state to found one university dedicated to higher learning and outside of church control. He thought in terms of state systems of education, of which the university would be the apex. Not only the University of Virginia, but all state universities founded later, used his theories to justify their existence.

Today our universities, public and private, are our most valuable institutions. In days of rapid scientific advance and sociological change, the region or nation with the best universities is the region or nation which most improves its standard of living and its fundamental culture. Universities, continuously concerned with the problems of society, are a country's greatest asset.

Because of the nature of its support there are aims for the

American state university that are peculiar to it. It must concern itself with the total education of the entire population of the state. It must provide equal educational opportunity for all, regardless of class, creed, or financial status. It takes responsibility for the personnel needs of the learned professions, industries, and the highly trained occupations. It must gear extensive research programs to the needs of the state.

The leadership function of the state university extends to all elements of the educational system, including other publicly supported institutions and those under private auspices. The state university must fit itself into the total pattern of education in such a way as to bring about the greatest benefits to the people generally. The state university must recognize, and help make the most of, existing resources, even those resources and capacities in private institutions.

Private colleges and universities are in every sense as valuable to society as the public. Their functions and responsibilities are somewhat different, and it is the duty of the state university to so plan its work that a well-rounded program adequate to the needs of the state results from the total work of the private and public colleges and universities.

At the state university the primary responsibility is for its campus programs. The reasons for this are not only historical but also immediately practical. The state university must find funds to supply the number of properly educated professional people the state needs if they are not being supplied from other sources. Moreover, it must be prepared to offer educational opportunities to the young people of the state in all major fields of endeavor, with some variation in numbers from time to time as conditions warrant. Education should always be stressed in those areas that are in demand in the state. If, for instance, a state is not an oil producing state, there is little reason why it should invest heavily in curricula in petroleum engineering.

The state university has responsibility for the proper education of those entering its professional groups, including the responsibility for recruiting from the high schools of the state the proper types of students to enter the various professions. The state university does not meet its obligation by merely sitting proudly on its campus and waiting for proper candidates to apply for admission.

A state university should also attract a number of exceptional students from outside its borders. Rural states especially, but all states in the West and South, lose talent to the endowed universities and private colleges of the East. This large group of talented young people tend strongly to find their careers and their homes in the area where they receive their college education, and as a result the home states lose heavily in the process.

Every state university has obligations in the field of research and investigations. This responsibility distinguishes the university from the college. Extending basic and fundamental knowledge has been the obligation of all universities historically. The state university has obligations for research and investigations bearing upon problems of the state of which it is a part. Whether these are sociological, scientific, or humanistic, whether they are in the field of public health or in business or government, the state university has an obligation to take the lead in solving the state's problems through scholarly investigations.

The state university, in contrast to the private institution, has the obligation of carrying education in certain areas to the entire population, and not just to the students who happen to be on its campus. This program we usually refer to as adult education. Continued education of people in the professions—teachers, physicians, businessmen, lawyers and engineers—enabling them to do refresher work in their particular fields through conferences and short courses is a state obligation.

Universities also have obligations which involve cooperation with other state agencies—for example, cooperation between the State Department of Health and the School of Medicine, the

Legislative Research Bureau of the State and the University Department of Political Science, the State Historical Society and the Department of History, the State Auditor's Office and the Department of Accounting, and the State Highway Department and the Department of Civil Engineering. While these are developed in somewhat different ways in each state, the relationship between the state university and those other state service agencies is close, and the state gains much from such cooperation.

The state university has a role of interpreting itself to the state. President Harlan Hatcher of Michigan State University recently wrote:

> The sense of pride which is felt by the citizens in their university which they have founded and supported and which serves them in the name of their state is a source of much strength. Their belief that their state-supported educational institutions have tapped new sources of leadership and have given their sons and daughters the opportunity to become tomorrow's leaders is well founded. In order to continue successfully in the performance of its educational mission, the state university must constantly interpret that mission to the people.

In a rather commonplace way I have attempted to describe the role of the state university in America. Now a few words about the University of Missouri.

During the next several years we are going to be engaged in an extensive building program, which will be financed with funds from the state bond issue and with dormitory construction money borrowed from the Federal Housing and Home Finance Agency. The building program long has been needed and it will be of tremendous help. However, it will not supply plant facility needs for all time; in fact a good many current needs can not be supplied through funds now available.

The most serious problem we face now, and one for which the solution is not in sight, is the inadequacy of teachers' salaries at the University. We lose staff members to higher paying jobs, both in education and out of it. It is difficult, frequently impossible, to find top-flight new instructors at the salaries we can offer. Far too few young people are preparing for college teaching. This is especially serious at a time when enrollments are going to step up rapidly. The quality of the teacher determines the quality of instruction. We have asked the state for a considerable allocation to the salary budget, for we want to keep the University in a position to render effectively the services needed by our young people and by the state generally.

In conclusion I would like to leave with you the rather poetic statement of President H. B. Wells of the University of Indiana:

> I am the university of the people
> My roots reach back into the earliest days of a free
> Citizenry on the American continent. Conceived in
> Liberty and born of an unwavering faith in Democracy,
> I have been nurtured from humble beginnings to the
> Strength of a mighty institution.
> All knowledge I have taken as my province. No human
> Problem is too remote; no learned profession too recondite.
> Always I work unceasingly for the advancement of
> Human welfare.
> My discoveries have made the deserts to bloom and the
> Mines to give forth their treasure. In farm and field,
> In the marts of trade or finance, in the halls of
> Government—all have been aided by the far-flung Republic
> Of minds that ever seek to find and give light.
> My doors have been open to all those who can profit from
> My resources; no social or economic barriers have ever
> Daunted the hundreds of thousands of young citizens who
> Claim me as Alma Mater.
> I am society's best social investment. Her contributions
> Have been returned many hundredfold! in human progress,
> In wealth, and in human service. Here the strength of the
> Nation is renewed; here the noble compact of society with
> The Dead, the Living, and the Unborn can be cherished for
> A better, brighter civilization.
> As no other institution of our day, I am of the people,
> By the people and for the people.
> I am the State University.

16

Remarks at the Dedication Ceremonies
of the Harry S. Truman Library

TODAY marks an important milestone in the building of this great memorial. But it is not enough, nor are we through. The nation has a responsibility here that Independence and Missouri share. This is to complete and round out this entire project not only as planned but even on a larger scale.

There should be a continuing program looking toward expanding the museum aspects of the collection. In the next one hundred years many items will come to light that bear in important ways on President Truman's career. Some of these will be donated by owners, if properly approached; most will have to be purchased, for which funds will have to be kept available. For this development provisions must be made for exhibit space in this building.

Some day there will center in this building a project for the

July 6, 1957

publication of the letters of President Truman, such as has recently been completed or started with the papers of Washington, Jefferson, Lincoln, and Theodore Roosevelt. These are great scholarly enterprises that put copies of the most essential manuscripts in every scholar's study. These publications are expensive, and are heavily underwritten by the government or by private philanthropy. Questions of security and good taste will prevent a complete publication of letters until considerable time has passed, but in the meantime there will be small collections of selected papers edited and published.

Then there are research grants to aid and encourage research in this period of American leadership. We can probably depend upon the great scholarly foundations to promote this objective, providing we do our part in making research here convenient.

Most important of all is the great library, supplementary to the Truman papers and personal library, that must be created here if this memorial is to become the great center of research and study that this notable collection of papers deserves. That collection should include everything available that relates to the period of the Second World War and the Cold War period. It must include these:

1. Papers of as many cabinet members and other close associates of Mr. Truman as it is possible to bring together. This is not something that is brought about by merely willing it. It takes difficult labor on the part of several people to get this done, and I have no doubt that we will be adding papers in this category, although at a reduced rate, one hundred years from now.

2. Complete sets of the documents of all the governments of the world for the years 1935 to 1960, and with such others published subsequently that throw light upon the Truman period.

3. Microfilm or original files of the principal newspapers of the world for the same period.

4. Copies of histories and memoirs written in all languages, now and later, that deal in an important way with the Truman years.

5. Microfilm of unpublished research studies in university and government libraries which deal in an important manner with these same developments.

6. While these are the most important needs, we must also remember that historical study is not exclusively by periods. It is in a significant way also topical and cumulative. To study and understand the exercise of executive power from 1945 to 1953 we need to have extensive information on its exercise under previous chief executives of the United States, for in a real sense Harry S. Truman was the descendant of all the Presidents who had occupied that office before him, and what they did as history and precedent had important relationships, both positive and negative, to what he did. Thus the library of all studies relating to the Presidency of the United States is an essential for completing this library.

After that we must have a smaller continuing program of acquisitions both to the museum and the library, one that we will go beyond anything the National Archives is able to undertake. This will call for a permanent organization devoted to the growth and expansion of this institution to make it and keep it a dignified and useful memorial to Missouri's contribution to world statesmanship —a program that will insure a library that will grow in usefulness to scholars and indeed to all mankind, a benefactor of all research and scholarship.

Let us not set our sights low. Here is a cause and a project that offers the possibility of growing in importance with time. This occasion calls for dedication to the tasks remaining rather than merely congratulations on a start well made.

17

Crescendo in Higher Education

TODAY our universities and colleges, public and private, are our most valuable institutions. In days of rapid scientific advance and sociological change the region or nation with the best universities is the region or nation which most improves its standard of living and its fundamental culture. Universities, continuously concerned with the problems of society, are the country's greatest asset.

In a sense the various states are engaged in a sort of regional competition, in which each state is trying to develop its resources and its society at least well enough to keep up with the nearby states. Society has many kinds of resources, but the most important one is the supply of competent, well-trained people.

In every state a number of colleges receive public support. Why do the states and municipalities maintain these institutions?

Commencement Address at the University of Omaha, June 1, 1959.

281

The immediate answer, of course, is to supply their occupational and professional needs. The need now is most urgent. There has never been a time when there was such an overt demand for teachers, engineers, physicians, nurses, scientists, social workers, psychologists, accountants, economists, agriculturalists, etc.

The demand for college-trained personnel today is not due alone to the fact that the general economy of the country is at a high level. Our society has come to recognize that a highly educated manpower, indeed a highly educated citizenry, is absolutely necessary to twentieth century America.

There is no factor in today's economic and cultural development more important than trained manpower. The city, state and nation which has the best supply of educated people—scientists, teachers, engineers, businessmen, journalists—will be the one that makes the greatest development and maintains the highest real standard of living. College graduates tend to find their jobs in the area where they have been attending college, and consequently the better a state's total system of education is, the better future that city or state will have, both material and in cultural considerations.

One of the illusions commonly cultivated is that a low tax rate is attractive to business and industry and consequently stimulates economic and social growth. While no one would claim that high taxes encourage industry and business, it requires no very profound analysis of our recent history to show that most frequently high taxes go with healthy growth. Those states of our union which are experiencing the most rapid development are those very ones where per capita taxation is high and consequently the level of public and private services is high. Industry and development have gone in where the supply of trained people is excellent, where opportunities for education are readily available and of good quality, where research is already going on that is of value to business and industry, and indeed where all types of state and community services—medical care, highways, conservation, regulatory agencies, police, research and development—are of high quality.

Those states and municipalities which nurse their tax dollars too carefully, hoping in vain that low taxes will attract outside industry, are committing themselves to a low standard all down the line for their own people. They create a situation where the more energetic and learned leave, to go to those areas where governmental and private services in education are at a high level. This migration enriches those areas rather than the ones which are less aggressive in their support of higher education.

Competition, not only in technological development, but also in matters bearing directly upon social, economic, and political philosophies, is on a world-wide basis. I fear that as a nation we are not doing as well as we should in this competition. Apparently we have assumed that we hold a permanent superiority over all others. Now, however, we are encountering a strong challenge.

The place of science, and indeed of all learning, in today's competitive world has changed tremendously the attitude in high places for education of all kinds. As our post-war world has become divided into two camps, this competitive educational situation has assumed many disquieting aspects. The tremendous growth in education in the Soviet Union—a similar growth, I might add, is just gaining its initial momentum in Red China—has been the subject of alarmed observation by western European and American leaders. While some of these leaders may have arrived at some unrealistic generalizations and still may have a tendency to under-rate the quality of Russian education and science, Sputnik ended our tendency to under-rate it in the degree we had previously.

In their rather crude but effective way the Russians are moving toward enormous production of specialists from their universities in all fields where they think need exists. If their plans demand the production of so many thousand electrical engineers for 1962, in dictatorial fashion they provide that many—no more, no less, except for the margin of error in their calculations. Similarly they produce physicians, physicists, geologists, and language experts.

While Russia is devoting a tremendous percentage of its income to higher education, it is less than it would be if they permitted their people to have some choice in these matters, as any democracy devoted to the welfare of the individual must. The United States, as the leader of the anti-Communistic powers intellectually, politically, and militarily cannot afford to fall behind in the quality of its higher education, and certainly it cannot afford to fail to supply the needed personnel for advanced scholarly and scientific positions.

While Congress has recently been recognizing the need for federal help in this area, higher education is so much a matter of state, local, and private responsibility that we must by all means take a new look at what we are doing and make new tests of its adequacy. Are we wasting our resources on many young people who cannot make the contribution that will be demanded of them? Are we doing a good enough job in finding the able and industrious, and, regardless of family finances, seeing to it that they are trained for their maximum value to their country?

One of the surprising things about the Russian educational development is the percentage of women that are being trained as scientists and physicians. I think here is one of the places where we must re-examine our practices and determine whether we are taking the full advantage of the ability that exists in the female part of our population for training in advanced fields. Personally I am sure we are not.

I am convinced that education generally, and higher education in particular, will have much to do with our success in the competition in which we are engaged on an international basis. And here at home where higher education plays a big role in the cultural and economic progress of each state, I am fearful that the people of some of the states in the Midwest are doing too little to expand and improve their colleges and universities. Our Missouri Valley states, of which Nebraska and Missouri are representative, are particularly vulnerable. While all of our universities and colleges have grown and improved over the past forty years, the rate of improvement and growth has not been as rapid as in many other regions, such as the old Northwest, the Southwest, the Pacific Northwest and the Southeastern states. Consequently in part at least our economic development has been retarded and, as a region, we are relatively less important nationally than we were forty years ago.

To meet the demands which will be made upon the colleges and universities it will be necessary to enlarge our educational expenditures in great measure. Nationally, all levels of education combined now get about one cent annually out of each dollar in what is called the gross national product. We spend four times as much for tobacco and alcohol as we spend for education.

In this foolhardy business of allocating too little of our wealth to one of the very things which made it possible for the wealth to be produced we are moving into a bottleneck which could be serious in respect to the strength and economy of the nation and the general welfare of the people. On the surface, at the moment, the greatest shortages appear to be in the scientific and technical areas, but I am convinced that the shortage is just as great in the fields of theology, teaching, psychology, the arts, economics, law, business, diplomatic service, and social welfare.

Alfred North Whitehead expressed it in 1916 in a way that I believe cannot be improved upon: "In the conditions of modern life the rule is absolute, the race which does not value trained intelligence is doomed. Not all your heroism, not all your social charm, not all your wit, not all your victories on land or at sea, can move back the finger of fate. Today we maintain ourselves. Tomorrow science will have moved forward yet one more step, and there will be no appeal from the judgment which will then be pronounced on the uneducated."

Just as education has played a dominant role in the development of our culture, so will education be the chief agent in preserving and improving it. In our philosophical justification, both for public and private higher education, we have never been willing to stop with technical training or the development of occupational skills. We have always based our justification upon the solid ground of good citizenship and moral growth, the ideals of perfection in a political and social sense that is a part of the American basic philosophy of the good life.

Higher education faces a real crisis in America today. We have come to the place in which we, as a people, are going to have to make some choices. More and more people want, and need, more and more education. In our modern, complex society it is essential that we develop and maintain a highly educated citizenry. Here is the first question—will we make the proper scope and quality of higher education available to those who can profit from it or will many be denied?

If we decide to make the opportunity available, then we come to the second question—what will be the most effective, and dollar-wise the most efficient, way to provide such opportunity? Some of the other questions will be as follows:

1. In what specific ways can proper financial support for higher education be provided?

2. How can a college education be made available to talented youth who are unable to meet the total costs themselves?

3. What curricula will best meet the needs of students and the needs of society?

4. How can the proper number of highly qualified teachers be obtained by the colleges and universities?

5. To what extent can mass media of instruction be employed effectively?

These are some of the questions which confront the nation today. We seek adequate solutions in Missouri, and I am sure that the people of Nebraska are joining in the search for the best answers. Nearly all colleges, private as well as public, will expand; the public institutions likely will expand more than will the private colleges. Some junior colleges will become four-year colleges. Some new junior and senior colleges will come into existence.

One hears and reads at times of people who are appalled at the magnitude of the program of providing for the growing demand for higher education. Some of these people counsel despair and propose to freeze the size of present universities and keep out students beyond approximately present numbers. This in education is the equivalent of the gentleman who, in 1840, resigned from the U. S. Patent Office because he was convinced all worthwhile patentable discoveries had been made.

Universities should not devote their resources to students who cannot do college work or who will not apply themselves. This type of person does not remain long in any reputable university now. But to raise admission requirements now for students, who, according to reasonable standards, can do creditable college work would be robbing the country of a vast supply of educated talent which is needed badly. . . . We badly need to save for professional careers a larger share of our best minds, but we also need to expand our supply of competent, if not brilliant, professional and semi-professional people in all businesses and occupations.

It would be to our advantage to induct more women into some of the professions which heretofore have attracted very few of them. I am thinking particularly of medicine, engineering, law, and dentistry. The number of women in college teaching could well be increased also. . . .

Good education is good business. By this I mean that good education pays big dividends for communities, for whole states, and nations. Some of the dividends are tangible while others are not so easy to see but are important none the less. If any sizeable number of your young people who are of high ability are not getting the advantages of higher education, the loss to society is bound to be tremendous. However, it is a loss which is spread over the community in such a way as to make its causes and its effects difficult to assess statistically.

While with rising costs and inflation everywhere, the amount of tax money used for education has increased substantially over the nation, what is often overlooked is that other sources of funds for education have increased much faster than public funds. In other words, income from tuition and from gifts from individuals and corporations have increased much faster over the past ten years than have public funds. Thus the percentage of support from public or tax funds has been going down.

Here are the most obvious sources upon which colleges and universities will have to depend for additional revenues:

1. Higher fees from students. Some families can afford high fees; but if applied to all, a real hardship and a denial of college opportunity to many youths will result.

2. More tax funds for the publicly supported institutions.

3. More funds from churches for the church-related colleges and universities.

4. More funds in the way of gifts from business, foundations, and organizations and individuals.

May I use at this point a quotation from a recent statement by Walter Lippmann:

> We must now learn that we are quite rich enough to educate ourselves as we need to be educated. There is an enormous margin of luxury in this country against which we can draw for our vital needs. We take that for granted when we think of the national defense. From the tragedies and the bitter experience of being involved in wars for which we were inadequately prepared, we have acquired the

will to defend ourselves even if we must do without something else that is less vitally important.

In education we have not yet acquired that kind of will. But we need to acquire it and we have no time to lose. We must acquire it in this decade. For if, in the crucial years which are coming, our people remain as unprepared as they are for their responsibilities and their mission, they may not be equal to the challenge, and if they do not succeed they may never have a second chance to try.

Now a final word to the graduates!

In obtaining a college education, which is paid for in significant degree by persons other than the students themselves, the students are morally obligated to assume additional responsibilities. In the first place you should remember that you are an advantaged group. If our society cannot expect a superior performance from you, then in some degree the effort put into higher education will have been wasted. Ordinarily the farther one carries his formal education the greater is his ability to be of worthwhile service to society, and the greater is his responsibility to render that service.

18

*The Support of Higher Education
in Missouri*

H IGHER education is facing its greatest period of expansion.
The nature of modern society has put a premium upon
highly educated talents. We have been thrown into an international competition as well as regional and local competitions within
the United States for highly educated personnel. It is not alone in
the field of science, agriculture, and engineering that these competitions are acute. They are just as evident in fields of medicine,
teaching, scholarship of all kinds, and management in every
field.

In some fields of higher education the Soviets have exceeded
us, with their system of paying high salaries to students to attend
schools in those areas where they feel national need requires it.

Delivered before the University of Missouri Alumni Association of St. Louis, Missouri, on December 2, 1959.

Competition is going on within the United States as every region attempts to improve its professions, its business and industry, by means of more and better higher education that will at least keep pace with its neighbors. There is a most interesting report from the Virginia State Chamber of Commerce of last August [1959] on this very problem and it recommends vigorously that in order to provide a better environment for industrial growth "the state's share in the support of public institutions of higher learning in Virginia should be increased to or above the levels in neighboring states."

The problem of growing numbers has been with us a long time. We doubled our enrollments in higher education in the United States in the past twenty years. It only became more acute with the rise of Soviet competition and the great expansion of our birth rate beginning after 1940. It seems clear that enrollments will have to double in the next ten years if we maintain our present position in the world.

The problem of financing higher education is one of the great problems before the American public today. The enormous expansion of higher education since World War II has spotlighted as never before the problem of paying the cost of this increasingly essential function. While the discussion involves both public and private institutions, the public institutions, of course, as all public bodies, are proper subject for discussion. Their policies and programs are open to public scrutiny and discussion at all times.

Higher education of the best quality is expensive, and the best quality is the only kind we are interested in offering at the University of Missouri. As one of the larger universities in the country, in terms of full-time enrollment, no list of the great universities that includes more than few is complete without our name. The programs, too, in the State Colleges and at Lincoln University are high quality programs and compare favorably in every respect with institutions of their type in other states. This is surprising to many people because of the small support that public higher education receives in Missouri compared with other states.

The reasons why high quality has been maintained are not hard to see. It is due to good management, at least in the past, and to the fact that unlike many states we support only one university and at that university we do not try to maintain all the professional schools and graduate programs that the more complete universities, such as Illinois and Wisconsin, maintain. This makes it possible to use the available funds in ways that are highly economical and to maintain high quality programs in all of those fields in which we educate students. One aspect of the controversy of financing higher education in the future is the question of *who* is going to pay the bill. In some quarters we have had a rash of suggestions that the parents should pay the whole cost or most of it. In this connection there are a few fundamental propositions that I think should be examined carefully by the citizens of this state.

The principles of public higher education were founded on the same philosophy as the public high school—to give everyone qualified the chance for education, regardless of his financial standing or that of his family. It was, and is, part of our democratic philosophy that education should be *available* to all because education is *valuable* to all. Anyone who attacks this theory at the college level also attacks it at the elementary and high school levels, because there is no difference in principle. There is no public high school in the United States that offers a differential cost to one parent as against another, and that is the same with every public and private college in the country. I might add, too, that the same practice is true in those few European universities which charge any kind of tuition or fee.

It is true that we have the practice of charging fees. Many states like Missouri forbid tuition as such to be charged at their state institutions, and the fees are permitted because of the student services that are supplied over and above the regular instructional services. As years have gone on, however, and different institutions have experienced financial difficulties, the fees have been expanded so as to become an important factor in the support of state institutions, just as the tuition in the private institutions. Today, at the University of Missouri, approximately half of our funds comes from state taxation. The other half comes from student fees, from federal government appropriations, usually for research or special projects, from gifts and grants from individuals, corporations, and foundations, and finally from the various student services and University enterprises which we operate on a self-sustaining basis.

Last summer [1959] after the General Assembly made its appropriation and it turned out substantially lower than most of our competing states in terms of its percentage increase, we announced an increase in our fees at the University of $30 a year in order to have the funds that are essential to maintain our high quality programs, recruiting new, well-prepared faculty and retaining our high quality staff members. This is the normal way in which state university and state college fees have been added in the past. They are still low enough, however, that nearly all high school graduates in the state can attend, given sufficient drive and willingness to work, and in the upper years at least, to borrow money if necessary in order to complete their education.

One must admit that there are some young people, however, of adequate and better than adequate ability, who live in areas distant from a public college and who do not have the family background that cultivates the desire to obtain a higher education and are not thus motivated to make a serious attempt. They might, if the college were next door, so they could continue to live at home and pay no, or very small, fees, continue their education, but since many are not so situated, we lose some potentially valuable educated people. Missouri has its problems, as well as every other state, of dealing with this type of young citizen.

At the University of Missouri for many years we have been

providing scholarships and grants to students in the top 20 per cent of their high school classes whose situation indicates they cannot expect much if any help from their families. Undoubtedly we have in our student body, as do all the state colleges, students from families that are well-to-do and, if we charged differential fees they could pay them. The number of families in this category we have never examined; in fact no one knows what it is, for the essential reason that opinions differ widely on how much a family can afford. But it is clear that as inflation has gone on, salaries of five, six and seven thousand dollars a year do not leave much margin, without great family sacrifice, to pay the charges of board and room, books and supplies, and transportation, in addition to fees or tuition charges. As our new families are coming up with several children relatively close together in age, any increase in college costs means almost invariably that some of the children must stay out of college.

Of course, this strikes immediately at one of the fundamental principles of equality in education. The public institutions were established to prevent this sort of thing happening, because a democratic philosophy is based above all else on equality of opportunity. When we establish fees that are high to families of students and the students themselves, who is bearing the real burden of the cost of education?

I cannot do better myself than did Professor John Dale Russell, Director of the Office of Institutional Research at New York University, when he recently wrote,

> . . . The tuition fee is actually a form of tax, a tax levied on parents for the most part, though the student may himself also have to bear some or all of it. The tax is levied on parents who have been so unfortunate as to bring into the world a son or daughter whose continued education beyond the high school should be encouraged. If one's children are all morons or if one has no children, he may enjoy the benefits of a society and a civilization that are made possible only because of the system of higher education, a system for

which other parents must bear the burden in the form of tuition fee payments. It seems very clear that, because of the general benefits of higher education, its support in publicly controlled institutions should be borne largely out of the public purse, rather than by tuition fees charged the parents and the students who attend the institutions.

Anyone who believes in equality of opportunity in a democratic society cannot help but support and feel sympathetic toward this view. There is no real equality of opportunity of course in our society if children of families who have low incomes cannot, without extraordinary exertion and unreasonable sacrifice, secure as good an education as children from families of great wealth. Let us turn it around for a moment and look at it from the other side.

The Ivy League of eastern private universities is a group of prestige institutions. They are excellent universities; they have academic and research programs that are indeed outstanding. They educate the children of many of the wealthy families and, through scholarship programs, a number of exceptional students from less wealthy families. As far as their undergraduate programs are concerned, they have a prestige that is social, rather than intellectual or educational, in comparison with state universities. Do any of these institutions charge the full cost of education to their students? Even those students who come from families of the very highest incomes in the country do not pay anything near the cost of their education. Who pays the rest of it?

Actually for the most part it is paid by the same taxpayer who supports the public institution. The money is raised from various funds and contributions that are tax deductible, in some cases as high as 90 per cent, which deduction increases the tax rate of every other taxpayer in the country. It is rather surprising to me that people proposing that parents in lower and middle income classes should pay the full college cost, or most of it, do not propose also that tax deductions be withdrawn from gifts to those institutions which do not charge full cost to students who could afford to pay. Of course such a proposal would be bad public policy, as is the proposal to raise public institution fees.

No university in the United States or anywhere else has differential rates, and no university thinks it is a practical possibility. The system in both public and private institutions of keeping tuition as low as possible considering other sources of income, and devoting some of their resources and a great many private gifts to assisting students who cannot pay the charges, is historically what seems to meet American needs. We do not have enough of this sort of money, of course, and, speaking for the University of Missouri, we could use large additions to our loan and scholarship funds and additional part-time jobs in order to meet the needs of our students. If we could satisfy all the demands, we would have a great many students who are now not getting the kind of education that society needs them to have.

It has been proposed in some quarters that we can charge full cost or nearly full cost and then have a scholarship program that would take care of those who could not pay full cost. The implication here is that such a system would be cheaper than one which operates on the low fee basis. This, in the public institution at least, is based upon a vast misunderstanding of the financial abilities of the kind of students we have and the kind of families from which they come.

President John Millett of the University of Miami, former Secretary of the Commission on Financing of Higher Education, has subjected this idea to analysis and, even ignoring the cost of the great bureaucracy that would have to be established so as to have financial data on the great majority of families who have children of college age, he estimates that the cost would be 150 per cent more than our present state taxation for public higher education for the students we now have. This is not to say that a well-designed state scholarship plan would not be of great value to the State of Missouri in enabling students from low income families to attend college, but if it only replaced fees, which would be increased, it would help no one; it would supply no more citizens to our professions or businesses than we receive now at much less cost.

It all goes back to the fundamental purposes of education. All our philosophy of public higher education and in the other public schools is based upon the idea that it is good for society to have an adequate supply of well-educated people. All of our young people need to finish the grade schools, and by present standards at least two-thirds to three-fourths should finish high school, and some one-third should attend college. And then we need a smaller number to have advanced professional training for the professions of medicine, veterinary medicine, and law, and graduate training where we get our scientists and scholars who do the research and the teaching that makes the difference culturally and scientifically and is now the basis of real world power.

If one assumes that the only purpose of higher education is to enable individuals to earn more money, there is a reasonable argument that they should be charged one way or another for the cost of that increase in ability to make money. But if we assume that it is desirable for society to have well-educated clergymen, college and school teachers, physicists, scientists—yes, businessmen, then a society is foolish to wait for people who can and will pay the bill for their education, and assume that by that process we will maintain ourselves as a society in the competitive world where the Soviets not only make their schools free but pay their students salaries higher than they could earn in any competing occupations, as long as they do good work.

It is easy to spotlight a thoughtless student whose family gives him more money than is good for him, and say he should pay the full cost of his education. But everyone who knows colleges knows that this type is a very small minority and next year he may well mature and start growing into a fine citizen.

Those who work in universities have cause to wonder what these advocates of full cost charges to students know about the actual cost of higher education. Every university man knows that if you charge medical students full cost there would soon be no M.D.'s because none could afford it. Likewise there would be no social workers, no teachers, and no graduate students at all, except perhaps those who carry a course or two while employed full time in order to earn that cost as well as a living. Actually our freshmen and sophomores pay a large share of a full cost now. It is when we get into the advanced work that costs multiply tremendously and only society in one way or another can pay for the education.

In our free society with its admirable system of public and private institutions, there are only three sources aside from churches from which the funds can come for states to finance higher education. One of these is direct taxes in appropriations, invidiously called "subsidies" in some quarters. Another is individual and corporation gifts and grants which are deductible from taxes in state and federal systems. The third is student fees. Now, whether we have the proper balance nationwide I do not know. I am willing to concede there is no perfect balance that must be adhered to.

All we can be sure about is that all of our institutions of higher education, public and private, church-related and non-church-related, must be supported, and supported better than they are now, as long as they can prove they are doing their work with reasonable efficiency. I do know, however, so far as Missouri is concerned that this situation is more simple than it is in most states. Because of these three sources of funds, appropriations, tax deductible gifts, and student fees, the only source from which Missouri meets the national norms or the average of other states is student fees. In our public and private institutions we charge as high fees as do universities and colleges in other states. We lag behind somewhat in gifts and grants and we lag behind in tax support in a degree that is shameful.

In 1957 our per capita support for higher education was $6.32 while the average of other states was $11.50. Missouri ranked forty-third among the old forty-eight states and forty-fifth out of fifty. I have great fear because of the better appropriations in nearly all states last year than in Missouri, that when the 1959 statistics are available we will be still further behind. With this situation in the United States, and being as laggard as we are in state taxes, it is quite amazing that anyone in Missouri would urge that we solve our problem by increasing our income from the *one* source where we now meet the national norms and by decreasing further that source of income that is already a blight upon the state's good name.

One of the side issues on this controversy that uninformed people sometimes believe is that it costs the taxpayers of our state large sums of money to educate students who come from other states, and that this should be forbidden here by legislation or by high charges to all such students. Special fees against out-of-state students developed in American universities because the location of some state colleges encouraged out-of-state students to attend them.

One of the state universities in the Big Eight Conference, for instance, had, a few years ago, a majority of its students from out of state, and that made a serious problem for that university and for that state. But certainly learning is not something that should be hedged about by protective tariffs. Even within the state, education and life on a university or college campus are improved in their intellectual and social qualities, if students are present from other states and other countries.

After some state universities developed out-of-state fees to protect themselves against large numbers of out-of-state students, and many of them, such as Missouri, set up higher entrance requirements as well, the practice of reciprocal fees developed. For many years we had forty-seven out-of-state fees at the University of Missouri. We charged a resident of Illinois exactly what the University of Illinois charged a resident of Missouri. It became a nuisance to have all of these different rates, so eventually all state universities have come to an approximation whereby we charge students from other states approximately the average of what they charge us, and have that set as our fee.

It happens that in our state we profit tremendously by the in-state and out-state migration of college students, because for every two students that come to Missouri to attend a public college or university, three go out of the state to attend a public institution. The reasons for this are clearly evident if you examine the geography of the state university and college locations. This is added to the fact that we do not at the University of Missouri supply all the professional schools or all the graduate work that more completely developed universities such as Illinois and Wisconsin provide.

Consequently, a student who wants to study subjects such as architecture, aeronautical engineering, dentistry, pharmacy, or graduate work on the doctoral level in any of twenty some different fields, must go to a state institution in another state if he cannot afford the tuition in private institutions here at home, if, indeed the program is offered in the state at all. If Missouri charges an Illinois resident an extraordinarily high fee, Illinois will be under pressure to charge Missouri residents the same amount. So if we set high fees, so will Illinois, so will Kansas, so will Iowa.

The admissibility of our students to these specialized programs in other states where costs per student are high, saves the Missouri taxpayers a very substantial amount. Just as soon as the out-of-state fees in our neighboring states get so high that our students cannot pay them, we in Missouri will be under tremendous pressure, not only from students and their parents, or from the professional organizations and the clients of their members to add these programs to our offerings.

We had an example of this in Veterinary Medicine when, because of the increase in students after the war, Iowa State University excluded Missouri students in order to take care of the students from Iowa. Immediately and without even a request from the University, the Missouri government appropriated funds for us to set up a program to take care of Missouri students and to start supplying the state with Doctors of Veterinary Medicine. This will apply in other fields just as surely as it did here if protective tariffs on out-of-state students are raised substantially.

The business community of St. Louis has a special interest in the free interchange of students between Illinois and Missouri that is more acute than in any other part of the state. The largest number of out-of-state students that come to the University of Missouri come from the St. Louis trade and industrial area just east of the Mississippi River. Our present out-of-state fees force many of these students to go to the University of Illinois instead of coming to the nearer university in Missouri, but a large number do come and the largest group of them graduate as engineers who are desperately needed by Missouri industry. Because of our location, St. Louis area industry on both sides of the river is able to recruit most of these graduates.

If we raise our out-of-state fees further we force these young people to go to Urbana to gain their engineering education. Any study of the placement of college graduates would indicate that nine-tenths of them would then end up in the Chicago industrial area instead of in St. Louis. I cannot think of any better way to insure the relative decline in the St. Louis industrial area compared with other centers. Any attempt to be self-sufficient educationally in the public institutions not only hurts the national culture and economy, but also leads to weak universities which waste resources on programs that would not be needed if students could cross state lines freely. The most statesmanlike approach to this situation is in New England where the state universities in six states have an agreement under which they do not charge out-of-state fees at all to students from the other states, providing the specialized programs the students study are not taught on their own campus. This is the best insurance in the long run that we can keep the costs in these highly specialized and expensive programs within reason.

This brings us back again to the great problem of how to maintain high quality education and how to finance it. All of us who study this problem realize that it is going to take all the funds we can raise through taxes, through private and corporate gifts, and through fees and tuition to meet our needs in the future. We are meeting them today rather poorly in Missouri, and if we did not have a system with almost no duplication in its one state university, and that one without a good many professional schools and graduate programs that others offer, we could not help but have a poor quality program.

The only source of higher education support in Missouri that meets the national norms is our fees and tuition. As a result Missouri is one of the most backward states in this region in higher education measured either by the percentage of our young people of college age in college or by the percentage of college graduates in the adult population. In fact only Arkansas, Kentucky, and Tennessee of the eight adjoining states are worse off than we. St. Louis itself is a particular problem, and of the thirty-three largest metropolitan areas, as a result of this neglect, only three have a smaller percentage of college graduates in their populations than does St. Louis. Twenty-nine metropolitan areas have better available annual supplies of trained personnel for local business and the professions.

Any significant increase in the fees for either public institutions or the private ones in Missouri, regardless of any other measure, would increase that differential still more. As far as Missouri is concerned a proposal in the direction of full cost fees at our institutions is a proposal to insure that Missouri becomes the most backward state in the Union and St. Louis the most backward city. There is nothing in our local situation that would warrant such a negative approach.

Only five of our fifty states levy a smaller per capita tax for higher education than does Missouri, and these are states with quite a different pattern of educational institutions. Of all states only Delaware levies a smaller part of its citizens' income for state purposes. Why can't Missouri support its educational institutions and other services as do other states?

In honor of Elmer Ellis—scholar, teacher, university administrator, friend—on the occasion of his sixtieth birthday, this volume is presented by the following colleagues and former graduate students in history at the University of Missouri:

LESLIE R. ANDERS
HATTIE ANDERSON
LEWIS ATHERTON
THOMAS S. BARCLAY
BERNARD L. BOYLAN
PATRICIA BRADFORD
LAWRENCE E. BREEZE
RICHARD S. BROWNLEE
SISTER M. CHELIDONIA, O.S.B.
HOMER CLEVENGER
G. W. COLEMAN
PAOLO E. COLETTA
DORA COWAN
HAROLD H. DUGGER
W. FRANCIS ENGLISH
GILBERT C. FITE
CHESTER G. FORNEY
LOUIS G. GEIGER
JANE GREGG
WILLIAM M. HAGER
JAMES G. HARRIS
H. A. HASWELL
WILLIAM WALKER HOWLETT
HOMER C. HUITT
CURTIS C. JENNINGS
LOUIS G. JOHNSON
WALTER K. KARPIAK
ARTHUR R. KIRKPATRICK
HOMER L. KNIGHT
DONALD KONOLD

FRANCES T. KYLLONEN
MARIAN DAWES LAGOMARSINO
GEORGE F. LEMMER
MARTHA LAYMAN LEONARD
JAMES L. LOWE
DAVID D. MARCH
PERRY McCANDLESS
KENNETH L. MOORE
ELSA NAGEL
JOHN W. OLIVER
WILLIAM E. PARRISH
NORMA LOIS PETERSON
WILLIAM PHILLIPS
JAMES N. PRIMM
MARY SUE REAGAN
MAYNARD G. REDFIELD
CLARENCE ROBERTS
WILLIAM A. SETTLE, JR.
HOMER E. SOCOLOFSKY
LEWIS W. SPITZ
CHESTER G. STARR
LUCINDA DE LEFTWICH TEMPLIN
RUTH W. TOWNE
ALICE H. TURLEY
CHARLES S. VIA
LAURA ELLEN WADSWORTH
MRS. B. A. WESTFALL
JOHN G. WESTOVER
LLOYD E. WORNER
THOMAS R. YANCEY